California in the New Millennium

California in the New Millennium

The Changing Social and Political Landscape

Mark Baldassare

UNIVERSITY OF CALIFORNIA PRESS
Berkeley · *Los Angeles* · *London*

A joint publication with the
Public Policy Institute of California

University of California Press
Berkeley and Los Angeles, California

University of California Press, Ltd.
London, England

Library of Congress Cataloging-in-Publication Data
Baldassare, Mark.
    California in the New Millennium: The
Changing Social and Political Landscape / Mark
Baldassare
        p. cm.
    "A joint publication with the Public Policy
Institute of California."
    ISBN 0-520-22512-0 (cloth)
    1. Public opinion—California. 2. California—
Politics and government—1951. 3. California—
Social conditions.   I. Public Policy Institute of
California.   II. Title.
    HN79.C23 P83   2000
    306.09794—dc21   99-055785

Printed in the United States of America

08 07 06 05 04 03 02 01 00 99
10 9 8 7 6 5 4 3 2 1

Californians on Political Distrust

Do you know why fewer people vote? They feel that everything is out of their control, that they have no say, so why bother?

Orange County Resident

I don't have any confidence in a politician. The only thing politicians think about from the day they get elected is getting reelected.

San Diego Resident

Californians on Racial and Ethnic Change

The demographics are changing to the point that there's not going to be any one group as a majority or a minority.

Sacramento Resident

No matter where you are there's that racial tension.

Fresno Resident

Californians on Regional Diversity

If they took the state of California and cut it in half maybe two states would be easier to govern than one.

Los Angeles Resident

The problems in California are so different they should go to San Luis Obispo and draw a line through to Fresno and separate the state.

San Francisco Resident

Contents

List of Tables

Foreword

Writing about California leads one to hyperbole. An example can be seen in a 1991 special issue of *Time* magazine, *California: The Endangered Dream:* "It is America's America, the symbol of raw hope and brave (even foolish) invention, where ancient traditions and inhibitions are abandoned at the border. Its peculiar culture squirts out—on film and menus and pages and television beams—the trends and tastes that sweep the rest of the country, and then the rest of the world. If California broke off and dissolved in salt water, America would lose its seasoning." And, as is often the case when writers turn their attention to the Golden State, the special issue assessed the moral character of the Californian: "What feels morally heavy Back East may dissolve into inconsequence in the delicious sunshine off Monterey." As colorful as such images of California are, drawn by residents and nonresidents alike, they tend to paint a rather distorted picture of California that is useful largely for attracting tourists, new residents, and arch humor. They do little to describe accurately a state that is in the midst of historic growth and change and whose population now plays an unprecedented role in directly shaping major public policy decisions through the ballot box.

In 1998, Mark Baldassare, a senior fellow at PPIC, began a statewide survey of 10,000 residents to accurately characterize their views on how California will cope with the challenges it faces in the twenty-first century. He focused his inquiry on three major forces under way today: a strong and increasing distrust of politicians and the political decision-making process, dramatic change in the racial and ethnic composition of the state's population, and the growing diversity of its regions—from the Bay Area and the Central Valley to Los Angeles, Orange County, and the Inland Empire. Baldassare's findings, the first based on such a sizable and systematic survey of the state's population, are reported in this volume.

Two of his findings are worth special note. First, consensus on major public policy issues will become increasingly difficult to attain in Sacramento. General distrust of the political process, growing ethnic diversity, and the emergence of regions with distinct populations and special interests all combine to create a mixture of conflict and uncertainty. Second, two of the regions expected to grow rapidly in the next century—the Central Valley and the Orange County–Inland Empire areas—are going to play a much greater role in determining policy agendas and securing decisions that reflect their interests. Baldassare profiles the Central Valley as a region with a more conservative population compared with the state's coastal areas. As the region continues to grow, greater attention will be focused on the Central Valley voter—a process that is already well under way. Orange and Riverside Counties are also projected to grow substantially well into the next century. Baldassare concludes that the jury is out on whether the growth in these regions will result in greater strength for conservative or more traditional liberal interests in the state. In either case, there is much at stake for representation both at the state capitol and by the California delegation in the U.S. Congress.

Resisting the temptations of hyperbole, Baldassare paints a realistic and rather sobering portrait of California in the next century. He sees neither a perfectly rosy future nor an apocalyptic disaster. Stepping outside the arena of today, the author turns to the public policy agenda that will lie at the heart of public debate for decades to come. He offers ten recommendations based on his analysis of the powerful undercurrents at work in California, one of which is the keystone to successfully meeting the diversity and change yet to come: voter registration and higher participation rates in elections. Distrust of the political process and disgust with government has kept huge numbers of voting-age residents from even registering. "About half of the eligible adults interviewed are not participating in presidential elections, and six in ten are not involved in the selection of their governor and U.S. senator in off-year state elections," he notes. The author recommends that the government become strongly involved in encouraging eligible adults to register and vote, and he concludes that "California could and should lead the nation in innovative efforts to increase voter registration and election turnout."

With the emergence of direct democracy in California through the initiative process, major decisions concerning the future of K-12 education, the development of an infrastructure capable of supporting rapid growth, and the measures for preserving the natural environment are likely to fall mostly on the shoulders of the electorate. Baldassare argues that with the emergence of diversity in both the overall population and the various regions in the state, it is more important than ever to ensure that the public is properly represented in the electoral process. Otherwise, the growing disparity between the "haves" and "have-nots" will only become worse. He concludes that encouraging enfranchisement is a far better role for the state than to stand by and watch even further disengagement of citizens from their government in the twenty-first century. There is no clearer or more important message that comes from these 10,000 interviews. Baldassare argues that it is a challenge well worth the public investment.

David W. Lyon
President and CEO
Public Policy Institute of California

Acknowledgments

There are many challenges to writing a book about California's changing social and political landscape. The state is geographically vast and incredibly diverse, with a population as large as many nations. The state's elections, governance structure, and initiative process are so complex that only a handful of political insiders and academic experts can fully explain them. Demographic and economic changes are occurring at breathtaking speed. California is subject to many myths about its current state and endless speculation about its future. The scope and complexity of the changes facing California make it hard to comprehend the rosiest and gloomiest predictions about the future of the Golden State. With these working conditions in mind, I am deeply indebted to many people and institutions who made it possible for me to write this book.

I was a senior fellow at the Public Policy Institute of California in San Francisco while writing this book. The genesis of the project was a dinner discussion I had with David Lyon, the president of PPIC, in the summer of 1997. I sketched out some general ideas about the changing political landscape. David pushed me to think more broadly about the social trends in California and to think more ambitiously about the survey data collection. I am very grateful to him for his unwavering belief and strong interest in this project. I was able to scope out the project plans in meetings with Joyce Peterson, Abby Cook, and Michael Teitz in the fall of 1997. The PPIC board of directors then approved my ambitious proposal to conduct focus groups and public opinion surveys during the 1998 elections as a way of learning about the state's changing social and political landscape. I am grateful for the financial support from PPIC and, in particular, the generosity of William Hewlett, the sole benefactor of the institute, whom I have never met.

Once the project began in January 1998, I learned a great deal from the many experts on the state's population, governance, and economy in residence at PPIC. I benefited from an early airing of my research plans at a seminar attended by the research fellows. I was helped along the way by Michael Dardia, Hans Johnson, Paul Lewis, Julian Betts, Belinda Reyes, Deborah Reed, Kim Rueben, Margaret O'Brien-Strain, Michael Shires, and Maureen Waller. Adjunct and visiting fellows at PPIC, including John Ellwood, Elisabeth Gerber, Thomas MaCurdy, Max Neiman, and Fred Silva, provided useful input at various stages. I discussed the survey themes and questions during the 1998 election cycle with Joyce Peterson, Abby Cook, Gary Bjork, and Michael Teitz. I was fortunate to have Ana Maria Arumi work with me as a survey consultant. At just the right time for this book project, Jon Cohen arrived from the University of California–Berkeley as my research assistant. Joyce Peterson and Michael Teitz read an early draft of this book and provided many useful suggestions, as did two anonymous reviewers from the University of California Press. Gary Bjork and Joyce Peterson edited the manuscript for both style and content. I am very appreciative of the careful reading and editing of the copy-edited manuscript by Arabella Cureton. Special thanks go to Naomi Schneider, my editor at the University of California Press. I drew inspiration from her enthusiasm for this book.

This book is based on a massive original data collection effort, which began in January 1998 with twelve focus groups involving diverse groups of residents in six regions. I thank Kay Lavish, a longtime colleague in public opinion research, for doing an outstanding job in organizing the focus groups, designing the group outline and respondent questionnaires, sorting through the issues of respondent recruitment, co-moderating the groups with me, listening to all of the tapes, and providing a summary report and key verbatim on the central issues of the changing social and political landscape. Discovery Research Group of Utah conducted the telephone interviews for all five survey waves, which included over 10,000 adult Californians. This organization collected the surveys in a timely and efficient manner, never flinched at my methodological requirements and deadlines, and always responded to my numerous requests for more detailed information in a quick and friendly manner.

I had an outstanding survey advisory committee that provided me with input on issues and general background information throughout the 1998 election cycle. The members were a diverse group of California experts from nonprofit organizations, the media, businesses, and universities: Nick Bollman, Bill Hauck, Sherry Bebitch Jeffe, Monica Lozano, Jerry Lubenow, Donna Lucas, Max Neiman, Carol Ramsey, Jerry Roberts, Dan Rosenheim, Cathy Taylor, Ray Watson, and Carol Whiteside. The committee members also provided me with much-needed access to the 1998 political arena, inviting me to insider lunches, parties, conferences, and meetings and making sure I had seats for the gubernatorial and senate debates. I am very grateful to Sherry Bebitch Jeffe for serving as a reviewer for the five survey reports that were published during the 1998 election cycle.

There are many scholars who are working on the topic of the changing political and social landscape of California. I was especially helped by reading books such as *The Color Bind*, by Lydia Chavez (1998); *The California Cauldron*, by William Clark (1998); *Constitutional Reform in California*, edited by Bruce Cain and Roger Noll (1995); *Governing California*, edited by Gerald Lubenow and Bruce Cain (1997); *The Coming White Minority*, by Dale Maharidge (1996); *Racial and Ethnic Politics in California*, edited by Michael Preston, Bruce Cain, and Sandra Bass (1998); *Paradise Lost*, by Peter Schrag (1998); and *The New California*, by Dan Walters (1992). I have also been influenced by the scholarly work of Jack Citrin, Michael Dear, Steve Erie, Bill Fulton, Sherry Bebitch Jeffe, Joel Kotkin, Harry Pachon, Susan Rasky, Gregory Rodriguez, David Sears, Ray Sonenshein, and the many other authors who are cited in this book.

Many journalists offered friendly advice and informal feedback. Some of my most memorable conversations were with Elizabeth Arnold, Mark Barabak, Dan Borenstein, Ron Brownstein, Amy Chance, Zach Coile, John Jacobs, Sarah Lubman, John Marelius, Carla Marinucci, Dion Nissenbaum, Warren Olney, Mark Paul, Todd Purdum, Raul Ramirez, Bill Schneider, Peter Schrag, Steve Scott, Scott Shafer, Mark Shields, George Skelton, Phil Trounstine, Dan Weintraub, Doug Willis, and David Wright. I have a new respect for those whose job is to explain California politics and elections to the public.

In the course of the 1998 California elections, I had the pleasure of conversing with many political insiders. Paul Maslin, the pollster for the Davis gubernatorial campaign, was always forthcoming with the numbers and helpful with interpretation. Dick Dresner, the pollster for the Lungren gubernatorial campaign, was always honest, open, and incisive in his comments to me. Steve McKinney, the pollster for the Fong senatorial campaign, provided me with timely updates and explanations of his survey findings throughout the election cycle. I also benefited from discussions, presentations, and the frequently published reports during the election cycle by Mark DiCamillo of the Field Poll and Susan Pincus of the Los Angeles Times Poll. During and after the election, I appreciated the conversations with people who have a working knowledge of political campaigns in California, including Gary Hunt, Leslie Goodman, Susan Kennedy, Julie Buckner Levy, Dave Puglia, Sal Russo, Dan Schnur, Gary South, Larry Thomas, and Ron Unz. I especially thank the *Sacramento Bee* editorial board for inviting me to participate in a lively election postmortem with political consultants from the campaigns.

I also wish to thank Bruce Cain, Jerry Lubenow, and the staff at the Institute of Governmental Studies library at the University of California–Berkeley. They provided me with visiting scholar status and a steady stream of relevant books, journal articles, and state government reports. Their postelection conferences were highly informative.

I was on an unpaid leave of absence from the University of California–Irvine while working on the book. I appreciate the encouragement from colleagues, including Scott Bollens, Ralph Cicerone, Rich Elbaum, Helen Ingram, Bill Lillyman, and Jack Peltason.

I would like to thank Cheryl Katz for her help at every stage. She pitched in with the data collection and statistical analysis whenever I was without a research assistant. Cheryl also helped me with library searches for relevant books, journal articles, surveys, and newspaper articles. She offered suggestions on the focus group issues and survey questions. She listened as I thought through the book, and she provided honest feedback and good advice on the manuscript. Daniel and Benjamin, the California-born members of our household, who were 5 and 10 years old at the time, showed interest in the 1998 elections as my work progressed and kept me up to date on the televised political commercials. It is for their generation that I dedicate this work. I hope the book will help to chart a better future through all of this tumultuous social and political change.

Mark Baldassare
San Francisco CA
July 1999

CHAPTER 1

Introduction

*The Changing Social
and Political Landscape*

California is a work in progress. The state has experienced many periods of rapid growth and change over the past 150 years. There will be no pause for reflection at the millennium. Forces and trends are converging that will, by the middle of the twenty-first century, transform California into a very different state from the one we know today. How California will cope with the challenges it faces is far from clear. The purpose of this book is to explore this question in light of three major phenomena: Californians' strong and increasing political distrust, radical change in the racial and ethnic mix of the state's population, and the growing diversity of its regions.

HOW THE STATE IS CHANGING

Many troubling questions arose about the state's future in the 1990s. The Los Angeles riots shook the foundations of racial harmony in this multicultural state. Asians, blacks, Latinos, and whites were drawn into a bloody conflict.[1] Voter approval of initiatives aimed at immigrants and racial groups raised questions about how whites would react to living in a state where they were no longer the majority. State and local governments had to react to a series of natural disasters, including fires, droughts, floods, and earthquakes. A severe recession brought about huge state budget deficits, resulting in local government fiscal crises such as the Orange County bankruptcy. These difficulties have taken a toll on the collective mood. Today, many believe that the government is

---

1. For the sake of brevity, the designation "whites" will be used in place of "non-Hispanic whites" thoughout this book.

no longer capable of dealing with the size and complexity of the state's population and problems.

The events of the recent past raise fundamental questions about the future. Will California be a highly populated state where people with different racial and ethnic backgrounds can find happiness, decent jobs, and housing, and can live together in peace? Or will California take on the nightmarish qualities of the movie *Bladerunner*, evolving into a state plagued by racial and ethnic conflict, poverty, lawlessness, congestion and overcrowding, and environmental pollution? Will growing income inequality create a state in which the highly affluent lead comfortable and healthy lives while most of the populace struggles with poverty and debased community conditions?

The major constant in all of the talk about California's future is rapid population growth, much of it the result of a phenomenal surge in immigration. If the state's past population trends, shown in Table 1-1, are any indication of future trends, the predictions of massive growth will be realized. Much of the state's previous population growth was fueled by a combination of migration from within the United States and the heightened fertility rates of the Baby Boom era. The demographic equation changed sharply in the 1980s, as immigration from abroad and the high birth rates of the newcomers led to another surge in growth, resulting in a total population of nearly 30 million people.

All of the pre-2000 census counts and estimates indicate that growth has continued at a fast pace in California, except for a brief period during the recession of the early 1990s. The state's population was about 33.5 million at the time of the 1998 elections and is estimated to reach nearly 35 million by 2000. This means that the state's population will have more than tripled in 50 years, and this rapid growth is expected to continue through the beginning of the new millennium. The population is expected to reach 40 million by 2010 and 50 million by 2028 (California Department of Finance, 1998a). It should be noted that these are modest predictions compared with some others (Bouvier, 1991; Center for the Continuing Study of the California Economy, 1999).

This growth will significantly change the demographic diversity of the state. The white population will grow from 17.4 million in 2000 to 18 million in 2040, and the black population will grow from 2.4 million to 3.2 million over this period. These are modest gains compared with the growth of the Asian population, from 4 million to 9.1 million, and the Latino population, from 10.7 million to 28.1 million. The growth in the Latino and Asian populations reflects a rate of immigration to California

TABLE 1-1   CALIFORNIA POPULATION,
PAST AND PROJECTED
(*in millions*)

1950	10.6	2000	34.7
1960	15.7	2010	40.0
1970	20.0	2020	45.4
1980	23.7	2030	51.9
1990	29.9	2040	58.7

SOURCE: Bouvier (1991); California Department
of Finance (1998a).

since 1980 that has been nothing short of phenomenal. Immigration and births to immigrant women account for most of the population increase. The state gained about 2.8 million residents through immigration between 1980 and 1994. Moreover, this figure does not include illegal immigrants during this period, estimated to be between 1.4 million and 2 million people (Johnson, 1996). Most of the legal and illegal immigrants arrived from Mexico and Asian countries. By 1994, nearly 24 percent of Californians were foreign born (California Department of Finance, 1997), and about 42 percent of the school-age population of California consisted of immigrants or the children of immigrants (McConnell, 1999).

The effects of immigration will be felt for several decades through uneven fertility rates.[2] In 1980, more than two-thirds of the state's population was white, 19 percent was Latino, 7 percent black, and 7 percent Asian. By 1990, the white population had fallen to 57 percent of the total population while the Latino population had grown to 26 percent and the Asian population to 10 percent (see Table 1-2). State demographers now estimate that sometime in the year 2000 whites will no longer be the majority population in the state, as Latinos increase to 31 percent and Asians to 12 percent. Latinos will outnumber whites sometime in the early 2020s and could well become the outright majority in the 2040s (California Department of Finance, 1998a).

The population growth in the twenty-first century will also significantly change the regional balance in the state. Today's population is not evenly distributed across geographic regions. Most residents live in a

2. I was helped by discussions with Hans Johnson, who provided me with some of the statistics he has created on racial and ethnic change in recent decades from data collected by the California Department of Finance.

TABLE I-2   RACIAL AND ETHNIC CHANGE IN CALIFORNIA

	Percent of State Population			
	Latino	*Asian*	*Black*	*White*
1980	19	7	7	67
1990	26	10	7	57
2000	31	12	7	50
2010	35	13	7	45
2020	39	14	7	40
2030	44	15	6	35
2040	48	16	5	31

SOURCE: California Department of Finance (1998a).
NOTE: Other races amount to less than 1 percent.

TABLE I-3   REGIONAL POPULATION
SHIFTS IN CALIFORNIA

	Percent of State Population			
	Los Angeles County	*SF Bay Area*	*Central Valley Region*	*Inland Empire/ Orange County*
1980	32	22	15	15
1990	30	20	16	16
2000	28	20	17	17
2010	26	19	17	19
2020	25	18	18	20
2030	24	17	19	21
2040	23	16	20	22

SOURCE: California Department of Finance (1998a).
NOTE: Other regions are not included in these percentages.

handful of southern counties, and nearly three in ten residents live in Los Angeles County alone. As shown in Table 1-3, almost half of state residents live in Los Angeles County, Orange County, and the Inland Empire (i.e., Riverside and San Bernardino Counties). In all, six in ten residents live in the greater Southern California area, including Los Angeles, Orange, Riverside, San Bernardino, Imperial, San Diego, and Ventura Counties, which can be seen in Map 1-1. The next most populous region in the state is the San Francisco Bay area, home to 20 percent of the state's population. This includes the nine counties of Alameda, Contra Costa, Marin, Napa, San Francisco, San Mateo, Santa Clara, Solano, and Sonoma. One in six residents lives in the Central Valley region, which consists of eighteen inland counties stretching from the cities of Bakersfield to Redding, including Butte, Colusa, Fresno, Glenn, Kern,

Map 1-1.   California Counties

SOURCE: Department of Commerce, Economics and Statistics Administration, Bureau of the Census.

Kings, Madera, Merced, Placer, Sacramento, San Joaquin, Shasta, Stanislaus, Sutter, Tehama, Tulare, Yolo, and Yuba. Less than 10 percent of the population lives in the rest of the state, including the central coast and Northern California. It is important to note that the four major regions of the state—Los Angeles, the San Francisco Bay area, Orange County and the Inland Empire, and the Central Valley—are having their own unique experiences with growth and change.

TABLE 1-4   CALIFORNIA'S YOUNG
AND OLD POPULATIONS
(*in millions*)

	Under 15	60 and Older
1980	5.2	3.4
1990	6.7	4.2
2000	8.4	4.9
2010	9.0	6.5
2020	10.6	9.0
2030	12.4	11.4
2040	14.1	12.5

SOURCE: California Department of Finance (1998a).

All of the major regions will experience growth, but today's dominant coastal regions of Los Angeles County and the San Francisco Bay area will lag behind the Central Valley, and the Inland Empire and Orange County in overall population gains. In a few decades, the population of the latter will be greater than the population of the former.

The age structure of the state's population will also change. The number of older Californians will increase dramatically as the Baby Boom generation ages (see Adams, 1992). At the same time, a large number of children will be born to the immigrant population. Although children in the state will outnumber people 60 and over, the older population will grow at a faster pace, as shown in Table 1-4. Between 2000 and 2040, the number of children under 15 will increase by 68 percent and the number of people 60 and over will increase by 154 percent. Thus, there will be a growing proportion of "dependent" residents and a shrinking percentage of working-age Californians.

CAN CALIFORNIA COPE WITH THIS GROWTH AND CHANGE?

The changes in store for California are truly phenomenal. Adding 24 million people to even a large state in a 40-year period is problematic. As if the growth were not enough, there are the complexities of the changing ethnic and racial mix, huge development in the Central Valley and the suburban regions of Los Angeles, and large numbers of young and old Californians. What is the likelihood of the state successfully coping with all of this growth and change? To answer this question, we look to the evidence on jobs, housing, infrastructure, and government.

One of the most important considerations is whether or not the economy will grow as the population does. If the economy shrinks or becomes stagnant, there will be high unemployment, increasing the cost of government services at a time when the state government's revenues will be shrinking. If the economy grows apace with the working-age population, there is a greater possibility that the state can cope with the population growth. The predictions for the next few decades are fairly bullish, yet there are concerns associated with even the rosiest predictions. Job growth is expected to fall short of population growth (Center for the Continuing Study of the California Economy, 1999). Manufacturing jobs are expected to become more scarce, and increasing numbers of people are expected to engage in service work (Kimball and Richardson, 1997). These job trends may result in a better standard of living for average residents, but growing income inequality between the rich and the poor is a troublesome possibility (see Clark, 1998; Reed, 1999). There are plenty of signs of upward and downward pressure on job expansion, and, as always, the state's economic fortunes are hostage to global events and business cycles.

California has had its share of ups and downs. In the past two decades, the California economy has been on a roller coaster ride of very good times, followed by very bad times, and then very good times again. The 1980s California employment numbers were stellar. Between 1983 and 1990, 3 million jobs were created at a growth rate of 29 percent. The state's economy then went into a tailspin: more than 400,000 jobs were lost between 1990 and 1993, and the unemployment rate jumped from 5.8 percent to 9.4 percent (Employment Development Department, 1996). In the mid-1990s, the median household income was falling at a sharper rate in California than in the nation, and there were troubling signs of a widening income gap between the wealthy and the poor (Reed, Haber, and Mameesh, 1996).[3]

When California voters went to the polls in 1994, it was one of the darkest of economic times in the state's history. The end of the Cold War had left a hole in the job base of the defense industry that other industries seemed unable to fill. The savings and loan crisis had resulted in a loss of jobs in the critical real estate and construction industries. Home

3. I was helped by discussions with Michael Dardia, who provided me with some of the statistics he has created on monthly employment growth and unemployment rates in the 1990s from data collected by the Employment Development Department.

prices had fallen dramatically from their lofty levels, and consumer confidence was low. But the economy had turned around by the time of the 1998 election, and bullish opinions about the state and its economy had returned. Civilian employment grew from 14,175,200 in October 1994 to 15,341,600 in October 1998, and unemployment declined from 8.1 percent to 5.9 percent (Employment Development Department, 1998).

Yet the state's overall numbers hide significant variations among the major regions of the state in both good times and bad. Los Angeles County was much harder hit than the rest of the state in the last recession and has taken much longer to recover the jobs that were lost. Orange County and the San Francisco Bay area had a softer landing, and each has had robust job growth for most of the 1990s. The Inland Empire never really experienced much of an economic recession and has had solid job growth since the middle of the 1990s. The Central Valley, with its reliance on agriculture, is in its own orbit when it comes to boom and bust cycles. In sum, this regional variation warns us to be cautious about reading too much into statewide economic statistics, because economic conditions in one part of the state may differ from those in other parts of the state (Dardia and Luk, 1999).

The housing stock will also be strained as a result of the expected population growth. To date, there is no plan in place to address this issue. Housing supply and cost are already placing serious constraints on homeowners and renters in many areas of the state. The current predictions suggest that it will become much worse. During some of the peak years of California growth, about 200,000 private residential building permits were issued each year. Some experts estimate that California will need to produce about 500,000 new homes per year, even taking into account the larger household size and slower rate of household formation that are common in immigrant populations. Housing may never grow at that rate in California, especially given the added legal, community, and financial complexities of residential building in the state today. Moreover, there are serious doubts that housing can be offered to the growing population at a price that will be affordable for most residents (see Lieser, 1999).

Infrastructure is another problem. There is nearly uniform agreement that California does not have the public infrastructure in place to accommodate the growth projected for the state. This includes roads, schools, sewers, water, bridges, and government buildings. Nor is the state government investing the funds necessary to meet future growth. As shown in Table 1-5, California ranks near the bottom among the fifty

TABLE 1-5   CALIFORNIA'S INFRASTRUCTURE

California's Place among the Fifty States in Spending on Infrastructure

Highways	48
Higher education	37
Public schools	31
Prisons and corrections	8

Capital Needs, 1997–2007 (in billions)

Transportation	29.5
Public schools	28.4
Higher education	13.6
Corrections and prisons	9.2
Resources and EPA	7.5
Other	2.3
Total	90.5

SOURCE: California Business Roundtable (1998, pp. 8, 9).
NOTE: Transportation does not include local public facilities or regional projects such as airports and ports.

states in per-capita spending for highways, and it spends less on a per-capita basis than most other states on public schools and public colleges and universities (Bowman et al., 1994; California Business Roundtable, 1998; Ellwood, 1994a, 1994b). It is also possible that the lack of state involvement in regional planning may foster suburban sprawl and inefficient land uses that will further increase the costs of providing infrastructure for the state's growing population (American Farmland Trust, 1995; California State Treasurer, 1999; Center for the Continuing Study of the California Economy, 1998). Moreover, as the state grows, the need for infrastructure funding is far outstripping the revenues available in state coffers.

One final consideration in gauging how well California will do in meeting the future is the government itself. To begin with, the state's budget process poses some major difficulties. Many experts who follow state and local government finance in California worry that there is insufficient flexibility on either the revenue-raising or the spending side to cope with growth and change. Much of local government spending today is required by state and federal mandates to go toward specified services and programs, and the voters have passed initiatives that place real constraints on the abilities of state and local elected leaders to raise taxes for new programs and future-oriented projects.

There are also many reasons to be concerned about how the state's elected officials will handle the pressures of population growth and its concomitant problems. The governor and the state legislature do not have a recent history of working together to solve problems. Even if the executive and legislative branches can get beyond partisan bickering, the legislature itself is deeply split along north/south regional lines— even within the same party. The kind of long-range planning needed to cope with population growth and change is difficult to achieve in any legislative environment in which politicians are geared toward making popular decisions that they hope will get them reelected in a 2-to-4-year time frame. Term limits, of course, in California provide additional in- centives for short-term thinking.

Other worrisome elements in the political equation are general po- litical disengagement and the mismatch between the demographics of the voting population and the demographics of the state's population. In California, seven in ten eligible adults are registered to vote.[4] Table 1-6 shows that about 6 million residents who could participate in elec- tions are not registered to vote. Further, despite the state's rapid growth since 1980, the voting population has increased little, if at all. For ex- ample, nearly 5 million more adults were eligible to vote in the 1998 gubernatorial election than in the 1982 gubernatorial election. Yet par- ticipation in the November gubernatorial election grew only from 8.1 to 8.6 million (California Secretary of State, 1998b). Moreover, those who do vote are not representative of the state's population as a whole. In the 1998 California elections, about 75 percent of the voters were white (Voter News Service, 1998), but whites accounted for only 52 percent of the population. Voting statistics thus lag reality, reflecting an ethnic and racial profile reminiscent of California in the 1970s.

It also bodes ill for California's ability to cope with growth and change that in grading all of the states on government performance, *Governing* magazine gave California one of the lower scores, a C–. Table 1-7 illus- trates the problem in the relative ranking of California and the other major states. Among the stinging criticisms are that "California doesn't have a strategic plan and there are no plans for one. . . . The use of per-

---

4. Despite considerable efforts to remove "deadwood" from the voter lists, some sug- gest that there are still many ineligible voters. If that is the case, then there is an even larger proportion of eligible adults who are not registered to vote.

TABLE 1-6   CALIFORNIANS AND VOTING
November 1998 Election

Total votes cast	8,621,121	41%
Registered and not voting	6,348,064	31
Eligible and not registered to vote	5,837,277	28
California adults eligible to vote	20,806,462	100%

SOURCE: California Secretary of State (1998b).

TABLE 1-7   AVERAGE GRADES ON
GOVERNMENT PERFORMANCE FOR THE
MOST POPULOUS STATES

Virginia	A–
Michigan	B+
North Carolina	B
Ohio	B
Pennsylvania	B
Texas	B
Massachusetts	B–
New Jersey	B–
Illinois	B–
Georgia	C+
Florida	C+
New York	C–
California	C–

SOURCE: *Governing* (1999).
NOTE: The list includes thirteen states with 6 million or
more population.

formance measurement is minimal. . . . The budget process itself is pro-
tracted, contentious and cumbersome, complicating the lives of many
state government managers" (*Governing,* 1999, p. 33).

THE MAJOR THEMES OF THE BOOK

The grade and the prognosis just noted might have been even worse if
the staff at *Governing* had considered the three issues addressed in this
book: Californians' pervasive political disengagement and distrust of
government, the changing ethnic and racial mix of the state's population, and the state's regional diversity. Californians desperately need to
build a consensus about meeting these challenges, to engage in the political processes required to make their solutions realities, and to em-
power their political institutions and government representatives to
respond. The breadth and depth of these problems will make it much

more difficult for California to find the will or the way to meet its millennial challenges.

Other major social and economic trends undoubtedly will complicate the response. The aging of the large Baby Boom generation, combined with the surge in school-age youth born to recent immigrants, is surely important. State politics is affected by a "gender gap" involving differences in policy and candidate preferences between men and women (Jeffe, 1998a). Increasing economic inequality between the rich and poor in the state could create a society divided between the haves and have-nots. As the state shifts out of federal defense contracts and into an information-age job market, structural changes in the economy are creating new positions for college-educated residents and offering dwindling opportunities for blue-collar work. These and other social, political, and economic crosscurrents increase the difficulty of addressing the issues today that will shape the future of the state. However, the analysis in this book focuses primarily on political distrust, ethnic and racial change, and regional diversity because they have had, to date, the most profound effects on the changing political and social landscape of California. Exactly what characterizes these three phenomena?

POLITICAL DISTRUST

The most pervasive and important statewide trend examined in this book is political distrust: the public's expressed low confidence in government and elected officials. The lack of political trust is generally related to the perception that the government is unable to solve problems, to spend money in an effective and efficient manner, or to represent the interests and policy preferences of average voters. Californians are quick to blame the government bureaucracy and elected officials for doing a poor job of handling key public issues, wasting the taxpayers' money, and ignoring their needs in favor of special interest groups.

The roots of political distrust—if we look at the public opinion surveys for evidence of its origin—can be traced to the Vietnam War controversy, the Watergate presidential scandal, and the citizens' revolt against higher taxes in many states. Most would probably agree that the era of political distrust in California was decisively underscored when Howard Jarvis placed Proposition 13 on the state ballot in June 1978, and when voters passed it by a wide margin despite the dire warnings of their state and local elected officials. Most observers would also agree that Proposition 13 remains a powerful and unpredictable force in California politics to this day.

What are the implications of political distrust for elections and public policy in California? This distrust has been strongly expressed in citizens' initiatives that have fundamentally shifted the way the state conducts its elections and develops its public policies. So deep are the feelings of political distrust that voters have made it extremely difficult for local governments to increase existing taxes or initiate new ones. Voters have also *required* the state's elected officials to spend a certain amount on education each year—just in case these officials might not pay attention to the budget items that matter most to the public. The voters have so little respect for how their governor, state legislators, and other major elected state officials have governed California that they have punished them by restricting the number of terms they can serve in office. Voters have tired of political parties exerting too much control in the selection of candidates for statewide offices, so they have created an open-primary process allowing them to vote for any candidate they choose for each office, regardless of the candidate's party. The effects of political distrust are so far-reaching and have been evident over such a long period of time that they can only lead us to ask one question: What will the voters do next?

RACIAL AND ETHNIC CHANGE

California has always had racial and ethnic diversity, but the balance of that diversity is changing radically. The state has experienced record levels of immigration from other countries for more than two decades. When immigrants moved to the eastern United States a century ago, they were mostly whites from Europe. Today's immigrants to California are largely from Asian countries, such as China, Taiwan, Korea, Vietnam, and the Philippines, Central and South American nations, and especially Mexico. This immigration has transformed California from a state where the vast majority were white to a multiracial society consisting of sizable proportions of whites, blacks, Asians, and Latinos. No other state in the nation has the level of demographic diversity seen in California today. This is all the more dramatic given that California is by far the most populous state in the nation. Also remarkable is the fact that this social change has occurred rapidly, most of it within a 20-year period. This demographic diversity is particularly significant because the trends we see today are widely expected to continue throughout the early decades of the twenty-first century.

Demographic diversity has been and will continue to be an influential element in California elections and public policy in two principal ways. First, white voters have held ambivalent and at times negative attitudes toward immigration and racial and ethnic change. This has led to the surfacing of "wedge issues" in state politics and to the passage of citizens' initiatives intended to address the concerns of white voters—for example, Proposition 187, restricting public services to illegal immigrants; Proposition 209, ending affirmative action in state and local government; and Proposition 227, limiting bilingual education programs in public schools. The second factor is the growing size of the Asian and, especially, the Latino vote. As the new California immigrants have become citizens, they have emerged as the fastest-growing groups of new voters. It is likely that their participation in elections has been hastened because they have felt threatened by political reaction to their growing presence, as demonstrated in the propositions just noted. Since the 1998 California elections, it has become increasingly clear that Republicans, Democrats, and initiative proponents are reaching out to the Latino and Asian voters because of their increasing political clout. Thus, demographic diversity is changing elections and policy discussions, as California faces the sometimes conflicting demands of white voters and Latino and Asian newcomers to the political process.

REGIONAL DIVERSITY

Regional diversity is characterized by the distinctiveness and separateness of the major population centers in the state. California is so large in geography and population that it should be considered a collection of unconnected metropolitan regions. Historically, there has been a sharp political division between Northern California and Southern California, most notably in terms of the age-old conflict over who can lay claim to the water supply. Northern California was the dominant influence in the state during the Gold Rush in the mid-1800s. Southern California became the center of attention with the discovery of oil and the establishment of the motion picture industry in the early 1900s. Today, about 30 percent of the state's residents live in Los Angeles County, making it by far the most heavily populated county in the state and nation. Twenty percent live in the San Francisco Bay area, which includes the cities of San Francisco, Oakland, and San Jose and nearly 100 suburban locales in the nine-county area. These two regions are the traditional political and economic powerhouses of the state, and they are destined to continue to grow and change well into the future.

Meanwhile, there are two up-and-coming regions whose growing populations are adding diversity to the state's political and social landscape. The Central Valley is home to about 16 percent of Californians and is the fastest-growing region in the state. This vast area includes the state capital of Sacramento, with the cities of Fresno, Merced, Modesto, and Bakersfield to the south and the cities of Red Bluff and Redding to the north. The other rapidly growing and changing region consists of the "mega-suburbs" of Orange County and the Inland Empire of Riverside and San Bernardino Counties, which lie to the south and east of Los Angeles. This region accounts for another 16 percent of the state's residents.

The four major regions of California that we focus on in this book—Los Angeles, the San Francisco Bay area, the Central Valley, and Orange County and the Inland Empire—contain most of the state's population, economic base, and voters. The only other major population center of the state is San Diego County. Although it is approaching 3 million residents, it is not considered in this book because it is not as populous as the other four regions. Therefore, it did not offer the sample sizes needed for analysis of the survey data. And although this metropolitan area lies adjacent to Orange County and the Inland Empire region, it could not be combined with that region because it is spatially distinct and organized differently in political terms from a mega-suburb.

There are major implications of regional diversity for elections and public policy in California. It is more difficult for the state to reach consensus on policy directions, and sharp divisions are evident in election choices. Growth has made regional diversity even more salient; each of the major regions has grown so much in recent decades that it has become large enough to be its own state.

The barriers posed by regional diversity are difficult to overcome. Each of the major regions has its own television stations, radio stations, newspapers, colleges and universities, sports teams, and city centers. Each has a rather distinctive and independent economy. Whereas one region may focus more on making computers, another may be more interested in growing fruits and vegetables, another in manufacturing clothing, and yet another in foreign trade and tourism. The regions have unique patterns of growth and change. Although immigration has affected the entire state, the Los Angeles region has been more profoundly affected than any other region. The regions are also separate political worlds. The San Francisco Bay area is overwhelmingly

Democratic and tends to vote for more liberal causes compared with the more politically diverse Los Angeles region. The Central Valley and Orange County and the Inland Empire have more Republican leanings and have been friendlier to conservative causes that have been presented in initiatives.

Most important, the policy challenges facing the respective regions often have little in common. Thus, the state lacks a common vision of its problems and goals. The Central Valley worries about vanishing farmlands and the sudden emergence of ethnic gangs. Orange County and the Inland Empire have concerns about violent crime and racial and ethnic change. The San Francisco Bay area struggles with traffic gridlock and sky-high housing costs. The Los Angeles region faces enormous public health care costs for its large and poor immigrant population. Regional diversity has created a myopia: public policy issues facing the entire state, such as the water supply and aging infrastructure, are often invisible to voters. The lack of political consensus by elected officials representing the major regions also impedes the debate about how the state should plan for the rapid growth it is likely to experience in the future.

THE EXPERIENCES OF CALIFORNIA
ARE RELEVANT FOR THE NATION

Why should people in the rest of the nation care about political distrust, demographic change, and regional diversity in California? Some may argue that what happens in California has little to do with Main Street America. The state is perceived by many to be a home of quirky political movements and unconventional social trends. It is a state that has experienced massive waves of immigration from Asia and Mexico. No other region of the country has experienced the demographic change that California has in the past two decades. California has not one but many diverse and heavily populated regions. Only a handful of states have witnessed so much growth and change in so many regions. Since the late 1970s, California voters have severely limited the taxing abilities of their local governments, established term limits for elected officials at the state level, and given voters the option of crossing party lines in state and presidential primaries. California has experimented with state and local governance and elections to an extent not found anywhere else. Finally, California politics are deeply influenced by citizens' initiatives. Such tools of governance are not found in every state and rarely have had the profound policy consequences that they have had in California. And yet, in spite of all of this, there are many compelling reasons for those in other states to closely watch California.

One reason to pay special attention to social and political trends in California is its colossal size. The Golden State's population recently reached 33.5 million. All of the current demographic projections suggest that it is headed toward 50 million within a few decades. It is by far the largest state in the nation, and with rapid growth ahead it will remain so for the foreseeable future. This means that major events in California are felt throughout the nation. For instance, when the California economy fell into a deep recession in the early 1990s, the rest of the nation felt the slowdown in consumer spending. The nation as a whole did not arrive at full recovery until California emerged from its recession. State trends also affect national politics and public policy. California's fifty-two-person delegation to the U.S. Congress dwarfs those of all other states. The redrawing of congressional boundaries by state officials could shift the balance of power in Washington. California's fifty-four electoral college votes make the state a central player in determining the outcome of presidential elections. The state's voters have been credited with Ronald Reagan's and Bill Clinton's successes and have played a decisive role in the failure of the presidential bids of George Bush and Bob Dole. Fully aware of this, the presidential candidates in the 2000 election have courted the state's voters. Both the Republicans and Democrats are hard-pressed to find a strategy for winning a national election without carrying the Golden State.

Another reason for following the latest trends in California is that this state has become a political microcosm for the nation. California voters are overwhelmingly middle-class residents of fairly modest means. Although they may have higher-than-average incomes, much of this extra income is consumed by higher housing costs. Many voters live in the suburbs, own their homes, and drive their cars to work. They worry about paying the bills and making ends meet each month and about which politicians they can trust with the critical task of making the good economic times last. They are concerned about their quality of life, public schools, and the crimes they see on television. Californians are mainstream Americans. This explains why winning the national election for president has become so highly correlated with winning in California. The nation and the state have voters with similar political interests and demographic profiles.

We also have to consider California the social trendsetter for the nation, even though the vast majority of its residents are in the middle class. The size and diversity of California provides the "critical mass" of people for starting many new social movements in areas such as the arts, fashion, music, automobiles, food, health, psychotherapy, outdoor recreation, and politics. In addition, the powerful television and movie images of California reach into every household and have provided a measuring stick for American consumers to evaluate their success. Today, add to the media images the increasing influence of computers and Internet use that originated in California's Silicon Valley and have swept across America. For these reasons, social trends that are born in California are likely to influence how Americans living elsewhere will think about their own lives.

We see in the three themes addressed in this book a mirror image between the state and the nation. Much of the political malaise evident in California today is no different from that which is experienced in the rest of the nation. In both the state and the national realm, many have checked out of the voting process and many of those who *are* voting feel deeply distrustful of politics. People throughout the nation are disgusted with how many candidates conduct their campaigns and, specifically, all of the money spent on television commercials. Many Americans think that politicians listen to powerful special interests, rather than to average citizens, once they are elected. The public does not have a lot of confidence in how government leaders go about trying to solve the problems that are of most concern to them. Voters in California and elsewhere in America have lost faith in the abilities of their state and national officeholders to spend the taxpayers' money in an effective and efficient manner. A large number assume that their politicians are dishonest. They have become so jaded that presidential scandals about sex, lies, and perjury don't even faze them. The close similarities between California and the nation in terms of political apathy and distrust—clearly evident in the public opinion surveys discussed in Chapter 2—offer another compelling reason to study California in some depth for the clues it may offer to ongoing national trends.

A look at the regional and demographic diversity in California today provides a glimpse at things to come for the rest of the nation. For instance, there is a preponderance of very large and growing suburban regions not only outside of cities such as Los Angeles, San Diego, and San Francisco but also in many of the U.S. metropolitan regions in the East, South, Midwest, and West (Garreau, 1991). Also, the transformation from agriculture and farmland regions to sprawling urban areas not only is occurring in the Central Valley and Inland Empire of California but also is in full swing in the previously underpopulated states in the mountain region, such as Idaho, Montana, Nevada, Utah, and Wyoming. Other states, and indeed the nation as a whole, struggle with policy disagreements emerging from regional diversity.

Also, California is not the only state where the Latino and Asian populations have grown rapidly. Many places in the nation have been struggling with racial and ethnic change and tolerance for diversity. Projections call for the nation to become a much more multiethnic society by the middle of the next century.

California is the place the nation can look to for signs of how political distrust, regional diversity, and demographic change are likely to affect the country's social fabric. These social and political trends are magnified in California, having started sooner and had more impact to date, and they are likely to continue in a dramatic fashion. California is also large and powerful enough as a trendsetter in its own right to affect the whole nation. For many reasons, then, the rest of the nation would be well served to study how California is coping with these issues.

THE APPROACH: STUDYING
THE 1998 CALIFORNIA ELECTION

One way to understand how the ongoing political and social changes in California today are affecting elections and public policy—and the approach taken in the study that produced this book—is to follow closely an actual statewide election. In a nonelection year, asking people how they feel about politics and government can seem rather abstract and esoteric. In contrast, when there is a statewide election, people have to make real choices. My approach was to develop an in-depth profile of the social and political forces at work during the 1998 California elections.

The 1998 elections offered an excellent opportunity to study California politics. This was an "off-year" statewide election, which meant that there would be none of the distractions of a national presidential election. There was a competitive governor's race at the top of the ticket. With the current governor, Pete Wilson, out of the running because of term limits, this was sure to be a hotly contested race. There was also a U.S. Senate race. The current officeholder, Democrat Barbara Boxer, was projected to have a tough reelection bid because of her liberal voting record. Many of the constitutional offices of the state, such as lieutenant governor, treasurer, and attorney general, would be vacated because the officeholders were "termed out" or seeking higher office.

The June primary also held the intriguing promise of being the first ever "blanket," or open, primary. Ushered in by the voter initiative that passed in 1996, an open primary would allow all voters to choose from a slate of candidates from all parties: Democrats, Republicans, other-party members, and independents could vote for either Republican or Democratic candidates for each office. No one knew how the open primary would work out, and the major parties worried about everything from "sabotage" to enormous expenditures in trying to reach all voters in the primary.

There were also a host of controversial citizens' initiatives headed for the June primary ballot and the November general election. One sought to limit the time non-English-speaking students could spend in bilingual education programs in the public schools. Another attempted to restrict the way that union dues can be used to contribute to political contributions. Another aimed at undoing the state legislature's laws on electric deregulation. Another sought to extend gambling on Indian reservations. Another sought to impose a hefty tax on cigarettes. And several were geared toward improving the state's troubled school system.

Altogether, the state ballot included eight state constitutional offices, a U.S. Senate seat, and a total of twenty-one state propositions in June and November. To include questions on all of these would have swamped the surveys. Instead, we focused intensively on two statewide races, two initiatives on the June ballot, and two initiatives on the November ballot. We wanted to select the state races that were likely to attract the most public attention and the state propositions that reflected some of the different kinds of public policy choices that people are asked to make at the ballot box. As a result, the surveys included the top-of-the-ticket governor's race and the U.S. Senate race to watch in the June primary and again in the November election; Proposition 226 on union contributions and Proposition 227 on bilingual education in the June primary; and Proposition 1a for the $9.2 billion school bond and Proposition 8 for school reform in the November election. We wanted to follow the latter three measures because voters said before and throughout the election that education was the one issue that concerned them the most.

This election year had its share of surprises. From the start, the presidential sex scandal and congressional impeachment came in as background noise. At times, they seemed to drown out media coverage and distract public attention from the California elections. Although the events in Washington could have skewed the political views of the California electorate, the scandal offered an excellent opportunity to test public apathy in government and the depths of distrust in political leaders and our governance system. The California economy was booming, and residents were in a jubilant mood about the direction of the state. Jobs were being created, incomes were rising, and unemployment rates were sinking. Crime rates were on a sharp decline, leaving politicians without much to say about their perennial campaign issue. The state government was fretting over what to do with a budget surplus. The public mood was in stark contrast to that of four years earlier, when voter surveys found that people held a pessimistic vision of California's future and negative feelings about the current effects of immigration. The findings thus need to be viewed in terms of how Californians respond in good times.

The voters were confronted with stark contrasts in the governor and U.S. Senate candidates on the June primary ballot. In the governor's race, Republican Attorney General Dan Lungren did not have a serious challenger, while the Democratic choices included billionaire businessman Al Checchi, Lt. Governor Gray Davis, and U.S. Congresswoman Jane Harman. In the U.S. Senate race, Democratic U.S. Senator Barbara Boxer was uncontested, while the Republican choices included millionaire businessman Daryl Issa and State Treasurer Matt Fong. Record amounts of money were spent on the primary campaigns, reflecting at least in part the use of personal wealth to fund the television commercials aired by Al Checchi and Daryl Issa. The winners of the primary were from the political establishment—Dan Lungren and Gray Davis for the governor's race, and Barbara Boxer and Matt Fong for the U.S. Senate race. The fall campaigns were perhaps highlighted by the unprecedented four debates for the governor's race and two debates for the U.S. Senate race. Unfortunately, not one of the debates enjoyed statewide live television coverage by the major noncable stations. With minuscule coverage on television news broadcasts, both of these statewide elections again revolved around 30-second television commercials shown in the major media markets. In the end, Gray Davis was elected governor by a 20-point margin, and Barbara Boxer was elected U.S. senator by a 10-point margin.

This was not a quiet year for initiatives. Once again, initiative campaigns were funded with tens of millions of dollars from special interests, including but not limited to out-of-state businesses, gambling interests, political groups, tobacco companies, labor unions, and teachers' unions. Of the four initiatives that I closely followed, the largest infusion of money and the most television commercials were devoted to Proposition

226 on union contributions and Proposition 8 on school reform. Proposition 226 pitted business against labor groups in an expensive campaign. Proposition 8 got the attention of the state's teachers' unions, and they spent heavily to defeat it. However, Proposition 227 on bilingual education attracted the most controversy and most media attention, since it had a direct impact on the education of the growing Latino population. Proposition 1a had no major detractors, so the state's largest school bond measure in history received little attention. In the June primary, Proposition 226 for restricting union contributions failed, 46 to 54 percent, while Proposition 227 for changes in bilingual education passed, 61 to 39 percent. In the November election, Proposition 1a for school bonds passed, 63 to 37 percent, while Proposition 8 for school reform lost, 37 to 63 percent.

THE METHODS: SURVEYS AND FOCUS GROUPS

It is important to note that predicting the winners and losers was not my intention in studying the 1998 elections. I wanted to understand why the voters were making the choices they made at the ballot box. I was interested in how the underlying social, economic, and political trends were influencing elections and public policy discussions in the state. Most important, I wanted to know about the influence of the three factors I see as significantly changing the social and political landscape of California: demographic diversity, regional diversity, and political distrust. For this reason, I gathered data from focus groups consisting of diverse groups of people in different regions of the state and conducted five large statewide public opinion surveys during and immediately following the 1998 election. This book offers an analysis of those original sources, supplemented with voting records and other published data.

The first stage of data collection consisted of a series of focus groups assembled in six regions of the state in January and February 1998. We conducted twelve focus group sessions with a total of 142 respondents. The participants were specifically chosen to reflect the regional, racial and ethnic, and political diversity of California. The groups also included a mix of men and women, a mix of voters and nonvoters, and participants of different ages. The main purpose in conducting the focus groups was to better understand the public's concerns and preferences regarding the political, social, and economic trends under way in the state. We also probed their thoughts about the upcoming state elections and initiatives. I have used the focus group information in two ways. First, hearing people describe the issues in their own terms helped me in writing the survey questions. Second, I gathered quotes from a wide variety of focus group participants on key issues, believing that it would be informative for the readers of this book if I could capture in people's own words their views on the state's changing social and political landscape.[5]

The main source of information for this book is a series of comprehensive public opinion surveys of California adult residents conducted in 1998.[6] These surveys provide a more in-depth picture of the political process than does studying the results of voting in elections. Moreover, the surveys allow us to contrast the responses of those who are voting and those who are not, as well as those who are registered to vote and those who are not. In all, 10,037 California adult residents were interviewed in five separate random telephone surveys conducted throughout 1998, with each survey including representative samples of at least 2,000 adult residents and a minimum of 400 Latinos. The surveys each had questions, which generally varied from survey to survey, on five topics: the elections; California policy preferences; and political, social, and economic opinions. The interviews were translated into Spanish and conducted in English or Spanish as needed.

Two of the statewide surveys were conducted in early April and early May in advance of the June 2 primary. Another two were conducted in early September and early October, prior to the November 3 general election. The fifth survey was conducted in early December, a month after the election. Some of the questions were repeated across surveys, offering both "tracking questions" during the 1998 election cycle and an opportunity to combine responses for large samples of demographic and regional groups (e.g., Latinos, Central Valley residents, and independent voters). I also repeated a number of questions that were recently asked in national surveys, so that I could compare the state and the nation. I also repeated questions from statewide surveys that I conducted during the 1994 elections, so that I could see how policy preferences and political, social, and economic attitudes had changed.

5. See also Appendix A, which provides a summary of the purpose, methodology, and results of the focus groups.

6. See also Appendices B, C, D, E, and F, which provide a summary of the methodology, questions, and percentage responses for each of the five survey waves. It should be noted that the methodology was the same across surveys.

SUMMARY OF CHAPTERS

This book is divided into six chapters. This chapter has provided an overview of the major challenges facing California today. The rapid growth and change of recent times will be followed by a potentially more dramatic transformation of the state in the next few decades. Several factors impede the state's ability to rise to this momentous challenge. These impediments represent the three major themes of this book, which are political distrust, racial and ethnic change, and regional diversity.

Chapter 2 takes a detailed look at California's overall political climate in recent years, paying particular attention to the causes of political distrust. I discuss how the lack of confidence in government exists within a broader framework of political apathy, civic disengagement, and declining voter involvement. I also identify the dimensions of political distrust and investigate whether this view is uniform across the population.

Chapter 3 returns to the theme of political distrust, considering two of the most important consequences of the voters' revolt against conventional politics. I examine the growing trend of disengagement from political parties and seek to understand how the "decline to state"—or independent—voters differ in their political attitudes and ballot choices from major-party voters. I also examine attitudes toward citizens' initiatives and efforts to reform the voting process, exploring the public's views of direct democracy relative to representative government.

Chapter 4 examines the state's racial and ethnic changes and includes an extensive analysis of the Latino population. California is on the verge of becoming a majority-minority state, that is, a state in which no racial or ethnic group represents over 50 percent of the total population. I discuss white attitudes toward race and immigration and then examine the voter participation rates and political attitudes of the Latino population. We were especially interested in learning how the increasing participation of Latinos in voting is likely to change the outcomes of the state's elections and policy debates.

Chapter 5 takes up the issue of regional diversity. I compare the evolving Central Valley and mega-suburbs of Orange County and the Inland Empire with the more established coastal metropolises of Los Angeles County and the San Francisco Bay area. The Central Valley and mega-suburbs are unique in their recent growth experiences and right-of-center politics, whereas the coastal metropolises have experienced racial and ethnic change from immigration and are more Democratic and liberal in their politics. We explore how these and other differences in regional outlook are affecting state elections and the ability to reach policy consensus.

Chapter 6 offers some perspectives on future directions for the Golden State. I first look at the perceptions of Californians in light of the future trends of population growth and demographic change. I discuss the likely social and political effects of these predicted changes. I then offer policy recommendations for overcoming the impediments of political distrust, racial and ethnic change, and regional diversity so that the state can successfully confront the challenges that lie ahead.

CHAPTER 2

A Climate of Political Distrust

California is at a critical juncture. The problems it faces require not only building consensus about how to respond, but also empowering the state's political institutions and government representatives to carry the ball. Yet Californians are so politically disengaged and profoundly distrustful of those very institutions and representatives that government may be hamstrung in its efforts to respond. The more significant the problem, the more public trust is required for government to act effectively. With anything short of a miracle, that trust is unlikely to be forthcoming.

From the focus groups and survey responses, it is clear that Californians don't care much and are cynical about politics. They are not keen on voting. They see their governments as bloated bureaucracies and believe that their elected officials are in the pockets of special interest groups. They don't believe what candidates are telling them in television commercials. They think that what they read in the newspapers about politics and government is probably slanted or biased. A resident of the state capital, Sacramento, summed up many people's feelings by saying, "The name 'politician' is synonymous with 'crook.'"

This chapter explores the dimensions of this political disengagement and distrust. Topics include voter turnout, interest in politics, political information seeking, attitudes toward the federal and state government, attitudes toward governmental intervention in people's lives, and how disengagement and distrust affected 1998 voting decisions. California is also compared with the United States in an effort to determine if the state is unique or representative of national trends.

TABLE 2-1   VOTING IN STATEWIDE
GENERAL ELECTIONS

	Presidential	Gubernatorial
1998	41%	
1996		52%
1994	47	
1992		54
1990	41	
1988		53
1986	43	
1984		59
1982	51	
1980		57
1978	48	
1976		57
1974	47	
1972		65
1970	55	

SOURCE: California Secretary of State (1998b).

EVIDENCE OF POLITICAL DISENGAGEMENT

DECLINE IN REGISTRATION AND VOTING

Californians' political disengagement is evident in low voter turnout. As Table 2-1 indicates, the percentage of eligible voters coming to the polls has declined. Two-thirds of eligible adults, that is, voting-age adults who are native or naturalized U.S. citizens, voted in the 1972 presidential election. Only about half of the eligible adults participated in the most recent presidential election, in 1996. In gubernatorial elections, the turnout rates are consistently about 10 points below the presidential election years, and the decline over time has also been significant. In the 1970 election, 55 percent of the eligible adults voted; in 1998, only 41 percent did. National statistics are not collected in the same way; however, during the 1972 to 1996 time period voter turnout rates for the United States also declined, though less sharply (see Polsby and Wildavsky, 1996; National Election Studies, 1998).

Paradoxically, the percentage of voting Californians has gone down as the population has risen. California grew from about 23.7 million people in 1980 to about 33.5 million in 1998, increasing the number of eligible voters by 5.4 million adults—from 15.4 million to 20.8 million. However, because participation rates declined by 10 points over that

TABLE 2-2   VOTING IN
STATEWIDE PRIMARIES

	Presidential	Gubernatorial
1998		30%
1996	31%	
1994		26
1992	34	
1990		28
1988	32	
1986		28
1984	34	
1982		37
1980	44	
1978		47
1976	45	
1974		38
1972	49	
1970		41

SOURCE: California Secretary of State (1998b).

period, the number participating in elections did not keep pace. There were 8.1 million voters in the 1982 gubernatorial election and 8.6 million in the 1998 gubernatorial election, an increase of only 500,000 voters (California Secretary of State, 1998b).

California primaries also show dramatic declines in turnout. In the presidential primaries, 49 percent of eligible adults voted in 1972 but only 31 percent in 1996 (see Table 2-2). In fact, participation rates have varied within a narrow range since the 1984 primary, averaging about 33 percent. The state government's efforts to encourage voter involvement in selecting a presidential candidate in 1996 by moving up the date of the primary apparently did not stimulate voting. In the gubernatorial primaries, 41 percent of eligible voters participated in 1970, but only 30 percent did in 1998. That 30 percent turnout was actually the highest since 1982. This may reflect the fact that the 1998 primary was the state's first open primary, which attracted more independent voters to the polls. Still, this slight improvement represents a very low rate of participation in statewide elections.

The actual number of votes cast in primaries has not increased much during the rapid-growth years of the 1980s and 1990s. There were 5.8 million votes cast in the 1982 gubernatorial primary and 6.2 million cast in the 1998 gubernatorial primary, an increase of only 400,000 ballots. There were 6.8 million votes cast in the 1980 presidential primary and

6.1 million in the 1996 presidential primary, so there was actually a decline of 700,000 ballots (California Secretary of State, 1998a).

Not only is voter turnout low, but those who do vote are not representative of the California adult population. According to the exit polls, voters are more likely than California adults as a whole to be white, highly educated, affluent, and older. In the 1998 general election, about 75 percent of the voters were white, 80 percent had some college or had college degrees, over 55 percent had annual incomes over $50,000, and almost 85 percent were over 30. The voter ranks on election day are relatively thin in terms of the representation of nonwhites, those wit a high school education or less, lower-income households, and adults under 30 years of age (Voter News Service, 1998). The demographic profile of voters tends to reflect the characteristics of Republican voters more than those of Democratic and independent voters, which helps explain why Democrats can lose statewide races despite having a 10-point advantage over the Republicans in voter registration.

Why do people who can vote choose to stay away from the polls? In the survey, the four answers most commonly given were "don't know enough about the choices" (36%), "don't have enough time to vote" (24%), "voting doesn't change things" (16%), and "just not interested in politics" (9%). At the focus group held in Irvine, one respondent summed up the feelings of those who say that voting doesn't change things: "Do you know why fewer people vote? They feel that everything is out of their control, that they have no say, so why bother?"

Aside from the registered voters who stay away from the polls, about 30 percent of California adults who are eligible to vote have not registered. National figures indicate that about one-third say they are not registered, but those statistics are inflated because they include ineligible adults who are noncitizens (U.S. Census, 1998). The California numbers are striking because there are more nonregistered eligible adults than Republicans or independents (see Table 2-3). Among the Californians who are registered, Democrats outnumber Republicans by about an 11-point margin, similar to national trends in self-reported party affiliation (National Election Studies, 1998).

Because public opinion researchers have focused on the characteristics of voters, as measured in exit polls, little is known about those who are not registered to vote. We refer to them as "the unregistered" for the sake of brevity. Analysis of our survey data on the unregistered provides some insight into the reasons for both low voter registration and

TABLE 2-3   VOTER REGISTRATION

	Number	Percent of Voters	Percent of Eligible Adults
Democrats	6,989,006	47	33
Republicans	5,314,912	36	26
Other voters	2,665,267	17	13
Not registered	5,837,277		28
Eligible adults	20,806,462		

SOURCE: California Secretary of State (1998b).
NOTE: "Other voters" include independents and other parties.

TABLE 2-4   DEMOGRAPHIC PROFILES OF ALL VOTERS AND THE UNREGISTERED

	All Voters	The Unregistered
White	68%	39%
Latino	19	45
Black	6	4
Asian, other	7	12
18 to 34	27	59
35 to 54	43	32
55 and older	30	9
Income under $40,000	42	65
Income $40,000 or more	58	35
Homeowner	69	37
Renter	31	63

SOURCE: PPIC Statewide Survey, 1998, all adults.
NOTE: "All voters" includes those who said they are registered to vote, whether or not they participated in any particular election. "The unregistered" refers to those who said they are not registered to vote.

low participation rates in California.[1] Seventy-five percent are native or naturalized U.S. citizens, so most of those who are not registered are currently eligible to vote. What is most striking about the unregistered is their Latino background, relative youth, lower incomes, and renter status (see Table 2-4). In addition to the information shown in the table, other demographic differences were evident. Sixty percent of the unregistered are men, whereas voters are evenly split between men and women. Fifty percent are high school graduates or less, compared with

1. This analysis is based on the combined sample of 1,831 California adults across all five surveys who said they were not registered to vote. The differences between independent voters and majority-party voters with respect to political attitudes are discussed in Chapter 3, and racial and ethnic differences are reported in Chapter 4.

only 25 percent of voters. The surveys revealed that most of the unregistered have very little interest in politics. About 60 percent said they had "only a little" or no interest in politics. Almost as many said that they received most of their political news from television. Seventy-five percent were "not at all" or "not too closely" following news stories about the California elections. There are, indeed, large numbers of Californians who are not registered to vote and who are quite oblivious to the election process. Moreover, many of the unregistered seem uninterested in joining the election-day voting ranks. Thus, it seems unlikely that the declining turnout rate will reverse itself any time soon.

LACK OF INTEREST IN POLITICS

The unregistered are not unique in their lack of interest in politics. Many Californians are out of touch with the policy decisions being made each day in the halls of government. Many are indifferent to what the candidates for offices such as president, governor, U.S senator, congressperson, and state legislator say during elections. In general, and predictably, there's a strong correlation between lack of interest and not voting. However, lack of attention to elections and the day-to-day business of government is common among voters as well. Moreover, when citizens do pay attention, the quality of that attention, as indicated by the sources of their information, is not high.[2]

Most Californians do not express much interest in politics. As Table 2-5 shows, during the 1998 election cycle, fewer than 20 percent said they had a great deal of interest in politics, and more than one-third had little or no interest. What the table does not show are the findings of each survey on this subject, as reported in the appendices. In short, as the election drew closer, it didn't seem to generate much additional interest. Between the May and October surveys, the number of Californians saying they had a great deal of interest in politics increased by 6 points, and the number saying they had little or no interest in politics declined by 9 points. Still, only about 20 percent had a great deal of interest, and about 30 percent had little or no interest at a high point in the election cycle. The Pew Research Center (1996a), during the 1996

2. Multiple regressions controlling for age, gender, income, region, and race and ethnicity indicate that nonvoters were significantly different from voters. Those who are not registered to vote had lower political interest, as indicated by the following B's and significance levels (in parentheses) in the final equations with all variables: follow public affairs = −.44 (.001), interest in politics = −.42 (.001), television as main news source = .11 (.001).

TABLE 2-5   POLITICAL INTEREST

	California	U.S.
"How much interest would you say you have in politics?"		
A great deal	18%	25%
Fair amount	48	50
Little or none	34	25
"Would you say you follow what's going on in government . . . ?"		
Most of the time	36%	36%
Some of the time	39	34
Only now and then	18	21
Hardly ever, never	7	9

SOURCE: PPIC Statewide Survey, 1998, all adults; Pew Research Center, 1996a, 1998b.

national elections, found one-quarter of Americans reporting a great deal of interest in politics and one-quarter reporting little or none.

Political interest does vary significantly by voter registration, as one would expect. About 20 percent of registered voters say they have a great deal of interest in politics, and 30 percent have little or no interest. In contrast, 10 percent of the unregistered express a great deal of interest in politics, and 60 percent have little or no interest. Democrats and Republicans are alike in level of political interest, with fewer than 25 percent of voters in either political group expressing high interest.

Levels of interest vary across demographic groups, most dramatically by age. Only 10 percent of those under 30 years old are greatly interested, and half have little or no interest. In contrast, 30 percent of those 65 years or older are greatly interested, and 20 percent have little interest. Education and income are also important factors. In general, the more education and the higher the income, the more political interest. Race and ethnicity also play an important role in explaining interest in politics, with Latinos and Asians having less interest than blacks and whites. Of course, all of the demographic factors that are correlated with interest in politics—such as age, income, and education—are also strongly associated with registering to vote and voting in elections. Similar demographic trends in political interest have been noted in national studies.

Californians' attention to government may be higher than their expressed interest in politics. About one-third pay attention to what's going on in government and public affairs most of the time. This is comparatively higher than the one in five who said that they had a great deal of interest in politics, but this could be because people define "a great deal" more narrowly than they do "most of the time." In any case, the overall trend in this response points to a largely disinterested public. In the national survey by the Pew Research Center (1998b), a similar 36 percent of Americans said they followed government and public affairs most of the time.

Again, the consistency throughout the election cycle is remarkable. The number of people saying that they frequently followed government and political news varied within a narrow 5-point range in four of the surveys. Unfortunately, this question was not included in the October 1998 survey because of space constraints. However, it is unlikely that the number who followed government news would have increased by more than a few points, given the similarities in the trends over time for political interest.

Like interest in politics, attention to government is correlated with registration to vote. Registered voters are twice as likely as those who are not registered to say they follow government and public affairs with regularity. Republicans (45%) are not much different from Democrats (39%) in following government and public affairs most of the time. Still, fewer than half of the state's voters can be said to be closely attuned to the world of government and public affairs. Public attention to government issues varies significantly across demographic groups, and the patterns are very similar to those found for interest in politics.

The public's lack of interest in politics and lack of attention to government and public affairs news has taken its toll on knowledge of even the most basic facts. The political inattentiveness we have seen may explain why only about half of California adults could name the newly elected governor a month after the election. The December survey asked an open-ended question: "California voters elected a new governor on November 3. Could you give me the name of the new governor of the state of California?" Fifty-three percent named Gray Davis, 5 percent gave other names, and 42 percent said they were not sure about the name of the new governor.

Predictably, the public's ability to name their governor varied by political participation. Only 31 percent of the unregistered knew that the new governor's name was Gray Davis. Sixty percent of registered voters gave the correct name, and 68 percent of those who said they frequently vote in elections were able to name the winner. However, the results reflect a lack of recall even among those who are more politically involved.

The ability to name the new governor also correlates strongly with age, education, and income. Only 32 percent of those under 30 years old knew his name, compared with 68 percent of those 45 and older. Only 36 percent of those with a high school education or less identified him by name, compared with 69 percent of those who graduated from college. Those living in households earning under $40,000 a year were less likely to recall his name than those earning $40,000 or more (42% vs. 62%). The results of this simple test indicate the great extent of the disconnect today between California elections and politics and the everyday lives and memorable experiences of average California residents.

CIVIC DISENGAGEMENT

Are there broader, societal factors that could be associated with the low level of voting and the disinterest in politics that we see in California today? The hypothesis recently posed by Robert Putnam (1995) in his influential work on "bowling alone" suggests that Americans have become less socially connected. In doing so, they have drifted away from group and institutional involvement in favor of individuality. Some have linked the decline in civic involvement to low participation in the political process and the lack of trust and confidence in government. In a national survey conducted on this topic for the American Association of Retired Persons (AARP), the researchers concluded that "the vital links between social connectedness, civic engagement, and political participation are verified by these study results" (Guterbock and Fries, 1997, p. 115).[3] I repeated four of the questions from this 1996 national survey to see if Californians also showed signs of civic disengagement. I asked about rates of volunteering, work on state and national issues, work on local and neighborhood issues, and work on political campaigns and elections. In fact, Californians do fit the profile of civic disengagement along with low political interest.

First, they are not very involved in political activities. Their lack of involvement is startling, even given their low level of political interest and turnout rates. As Table 2-6 indicates, 83 percent say they are not involved in political parties, elections, and campaigns; as can be seen, the rates of participation for California are even lower than for the nation.

Very few Californians are active in work on public issues or problems at the state or national level, and these findings are very similar to the national trends. Most Californians do not work on local issues or

---

3. See also the report by the National Commission on Civic Renewal (1998), which includes the findings and discussion of an index of national civic health.

TABLE 2-6   CIVIC INVOLVEMENT

	California	U.S.
Political Activities		
Very involved	2%	5%
Somewhat involved	15	23
Not involved	83	72
State or National Issues		
Very involved	3%	3%
Somewhat involved	18	14
Not involved	79	83
Local or Neighborhood Issues		
Very involved	7%	9%
Somewhat involved	34	32
Not involved	59	59

SOURCE: PPIC Statewide Survey, October 1998, all adults; American Association of Retired Persons, 1996.

neighborhood problems where they live either. Again, the trends are almost identical to those of the nation. However, another survey question did reveal that many Californians engage in volunteer and charity work for which they are not paid. Twenty-one percent were very involved and 40 percent were somewhat involved in charity work. Comparable national figures were not available.

Voter registration and civic involvement are indeed somewhat related, as the authors of the national study indicated. About half of registered voters are working on local and neighborhood problems, compared with one-quarter of those who are not registered to vote. Two-thirds of registered voters are involved in volunteer or charity work, compared with fewer than half of the unregistered. However, party affiliation and voter registration have no effect on the level of the public's involvement with state and national issues. Twenty percent of Democrats and Republicans say they have worked for political parties or elections, compared with about 10 percent of the unregistered.

There are no major differences across demographic groups in the level of involvement with political parties, candidates, and election campaigns. Across all age, household income, education, and race and ethnic groups, 80 percent say they are not involved in any political activities. The public's disengagement from the political process, beyond simply registering to vote or voting in elections, is uniform across the population. Similarly, there are no demographic differences in terms of working on public issues or problems at the state or national level. About 80 percent in each age, household income, educational, and racial and ethnic group report no involvement in these civic activities.

There are, however, a number of demographic factors associated with local involvement and volunteer work. Less-educated and lower-income Californians are less likely to say they are working on local issues or volunteering for charities. Those between the ages of 30 and 54 are more likely to work on local issues and to volunteer for charities than younger or older residents. Whites and blacks are more likely to engage in volunteer work than Latinos and Asians. However, there are no racial or ethnic differences when it comes to people's work on local and neighborhood problems.

In sum, there is ample evidence that civic disengagement exists alongside the trends of political inattentiveness and low election turnout. The public has tuned out of state and national issues and become indifferent about elections.

RELIGION AND POLITICAL INVOLVEMENT

The surveys also explored the possibility of a link between low religious activity, civic disengagement, and lack of political involvement. In their national study, Guterbock and Fries (1997, p. 27) report that those who frequently attend religious services are more involved in activities outside of the home. To test that correlation for California, I included two questions from a national survey by the Pew Research Center (1996b), one asking about the importance of religion and the other about the frequency of attending religious services. In fact, Californians are less religious than the rest of the nation on both dimensions by a 10-point margin. However, in California there does not seem to be a strong link between placing a high importance on religion and being politically involved. About half of the Democrats and Republicans say that religion is very important in their lives, but so do half of those who are not registered to vote. The trends are equally ambiguous for attendance of religious services. Forty percent of Republicans and one-third of Democrats say they go to religious services at least once a week, similar to the 30 percent of those who are not registered to vote.

Many of the demographic factors associated with strong religious ties are also related to low political participation. For instance, less-educated and less-affluent residents are more likely to say that religion is very important to them. This association may explain why we could not find good evidence for the influence of religious attachment on political involvement.

There are, however, ways in which Californians' lower involvement with religion does affect politics and elections. First, not many Californians are subject to political instructions from religious leaders. Only 11 percent say that the clergy at their place of worship or some other religious group urged them to vote in a particular way during the recent elections. Blacks and Latinos are more likely than whites, and younger voters more likely than older voters, to say that religious leaders gave them voting instructions.

Further, Californians are fairly intolerant of mixing religion and politics. Nearly 60 percent disapproved of political candidates talking about religious values when campaigning for office, although 40 percent approved. However, Republicans (50%) are more likely than Democrats (34%) and conservatives (52%) are much more likely than liberals (28%) to like it when candidates talk about religion. The percentage approving religious discussions in political campaigns also increases with age, a demographic trend that points to its greater favor among Republicans.

Nevertheless, disapproval of religion in political campaigns outweighs approval in all education, income, and racial categories. Overall, the trends indicate the limits and dangers of mixing politics and religion in California. An appeal from a religious group or a religious message from a candidate may have an effect on narrow bands of voters, but it is likely to go unheard by or to alienate most of the electorate.

WHERE CALIFORNIANS GET THEIR POLITICAL NEWS

Californians' lack of interest in politics and elections is consistent with their sources of information on the subject. They take the path of least resistance, a passive approach requiring the least amount of their time and effort. In today's world, this means that television is king in California politics.

There is little doubt that Californians are generally hooked on television as the source of all news. Our survey repeated two questions from the 1996 AARP national survey, asking people how often they watched local news on television and how often they read a local newspaper (see Table 2-7). Fifty-nine percent watched local television news every day and 24 percent a few times a week. Forty-five percent read

TABLE 2-7 NEWS SOURCES

	California	U.S.
Watching Television News		
Every day	59%	62%
A few times a week	24	21
Once a week	8	5
Less than once a week	4	6
Never	5	6
Reading the Newspaper		
Every day	45%	51%
A few times a week	21	19
Once a week	13	16
Less than once a week	8	7
Never	13	7

SOURCE: PPIC Statewide Survey, October 1998, all adults; American Association of Retired Persons, 1996.

the local newspaper every day and 21 percent a few times a week. In other words, television has a 14-point lead as the source of news that people turn to every day and a 17-point lead as the news source they turn to at least a few times a week. In the national survey, 62 percent said they watched television news every day and 51 percent said they read a local newspaper on a daily basis, giving television an 11-point lead over newspapers.

People who are more engaged in the political process also tend to be more tuned into the news and give television a slimmer lead over newspapers than people who are less involved. Sixty-three percent of Republicans and Democrats watch local television news every day and 52 percent read a newspaper daily, resulting in an 11-point advantage for television. By contrast, fewer than half of the unregistered watch local television news every day, and only one-quarter read a local newspaper on a daily basis, amounting to more than a 20-point edge for television.[4]

Given their preferences for news sources in general, it isn't surprising that Californians rank television as their top source of information about what's going on in politics today (see Table 2-8). In the surveys, 41 percent said television was where they got most of their information

4. Fewer than half of those who are not registered to vote watch local television news every day (46%). Only 25 percent in this group read a local newspaper every day, and one-third read a newspaper either less than once a week (12%) or never (22%).

TABLE 2-8   POLITICAL
INFORMATION SOURCES

*"Where do you get most of your information
about what's going on in politics today?"*

Television	41%
Newspapers	34
Radio	10
Talking to people	7
Magazines	3
Internet, online services	3
Other	2

SOURCE: PPIC Statewide Survey, April and May
1998, all adults.

about politics, and 34 percent named newspapers. Other sources trailed
considerably, including the Internet, despite its growing use in politics.

Among those registered to vote, television leads newspapers as the
major source of political information by a slim margin (38% to 36%).
Among the unregistered, more than half name television as their major
source of political information (53%), while fewer than one in four
name newspapers (23%).

There are major demographic differences in the reliance on television
news versus newspapers. As expected, income and education are significant. This is because these two demographic factors are predictors
of subscribing to a newspaper. However, some of the trends also suggest that television may play an even more dominant role in the future
as a result of demographic changes under way. For instance, television
is named more often than newspapers by all age groups as their main
information source, although the advantage for television is largest in
the under-30 age group (46% to 26%) and narrower among older
adults (39% to 36%). As for ethnic and racial groups, whites choose
television over newspapers by a narrow margin, but Latinos, blacks,
and Asians choose television by a very wide margin. As the Latino and
Asian populations increase, television may become more important as
a tool for disseminating political information, while newspapers may
decline in significance unless these groups begin to match whites in their
educational attainment and income levels.

Television might be named more often as the source of political news
if it were not for the reality of local television news coverage. The television stations are ratings driven, and their market research tells them that
Californians are not that interested in politics. Viewers would rather
watch the weather report, catch up on the sports news, and see breaking

news stories about their broader region. The television stations have responded by cutting down on news from the state capitol and state elections and by giving people more news on sensational topics such as crime.

During the 1998 California elections, two researchers monitored 8,664 hours of local television news in the major media markets of Los Angeles, Bakersfield, San Diego, Sacramento, and San Francisco. They found 26 hours and 57 minutes dedicated to the governor's race, or one-third of 1 percent of the local newscast time. Some have criticized the methodology of this content analysis, but few would dispute the authors' general conclusions about television news coverage of state elections. "Free media basically doesn't exist," said Marty Kaplan, one of the authors. "Television news seems to be so entertainment driven that people don't want to take the risk of alienating viewers by putting something on that might be considered dry" (Purdum, 1999a).

How can it be that people get their political and election information mostly from television when television doesn't spend much time covering this kind of news? One answer is that people apparently don't seek much of that information. All of the preelection surveys asked people how closely they were following the news stories about the upcoming California elections. Altogether, 40 percent said they followed the election news very or somewhat closely (8 percent and 32 percent, respectively) and 60 percent said they did not follow it closely. Attention to election news was not impressive even among "likely voters" in the 1998 election. Throughout the entire election cycle, 11 percent of likely voters followed the election news very closely, 47 percent somewhat closely, and 42 percent not closely.

THE SWAY OF TELEVISION COMMERCIALS

So what happens to the political information void created by television news? It is filled, predictably, by paid television commercials for the statewide elections. Californians have become conditioned to gathering their election-year information from commercials.

The June primary for governor set spending records: a total of almost $70 million, most of it going to television commercials. Billionaire Al Checchi spent $39 million, millionaire Jane Harman spent $16 million, Gray Davis spent $8 million, and Dan Lungren spent over $6 million (Gissinger, 1998). Including the November election, the candidates spent $119.8 million, eclipsing the previous record of $60.6 million set in the 1994 governor's race (Lucas, 1999).

TABLE 2-9   TELEVISED POLITICAL COMMERCIALS

	Percent Who Recall Seeing Ads in the Past Month	
	---	---
	Governor	*U.S. Senate*
April	79	17
May	77	21
September	38	—
October	64	53

SOURCE: PPIC Statewide Survey, 1998, all adults.

Most of this money went for television commercials. For instance, Davis and Lungren reportedly spent $13 million on television during just two and a half weeks in October. Political consultants estimate that it could cost up to $1.6 million to saturate the state with just one 30-second commercial. "The real shame of it is that most of that money is spent on advertising meant to confuse voters, manipulate voters, instill fear in voters," said Kim Alexander of the nonpartisan California Voter Foundation (McCormick, 1998). California voters had already passed campaign finance reforms through the initiative process, but the public's desire to curtail election-year spending had been overturned by the courts.

It was evident from the focus groups that when you ask Californians about the elections, they talk about the television commercials. One San Francisco respondent said of his choice in the governor's race, "Checchi, because the television commercial stuck in my head." There were also ads with Jane Harman standing in front of her old high school. Gray Davis countered them both with ads talking about "experience that money can't buy." In fact, because of the millions of dollars spent by the candidates on television advertising, their commercials dwarfed all other sources of political information. Nearly eight in ten Californians said they recalled advertisements from the candidates for governor in the two surveys before the June primary. One-third had seen commercials by Lungren or Davis when we conducted the September survey, and the number climbed to six in ten in the October survey. About half had seen commercials by the two candidates for the U.S. Senate before the November general election (see Table 2-9).

The recall of political advertising is a testament to the power of television in reaching a broad audience with a political message. But the fact is that the record-setting money spent on television commercials has done very little or nothing to encourage people to register to vote or to participate in elections. The political commercials are instead serving the purpose of informing a large portion of the electorate who do not want to take the time or devote the energy to sort through information in other sources, such as newspapers, the Internet, and voter guides.

DISTRUST IN GOVERNMENT

Along with their lack of interest in elections and government, Californians generally distrust government, particularly the federal government. A host of explanations are available for the public's cynicism about government and elected officials. There is the traditional American ethic of individuality and a limited role for government, coupled with the current "postmaterialist" skepticism about authority from an increasingly affluent and educated public (see Clark and Inglehart, 1998; Greenberg, 1995; Inglehart, 1998; Lipset, 1996; Samuelson, 1995; Sandel, 1996). There are the damages to trust caused by the traumas of the Vietnam War and Watergate, public disappointment with the performance of big government programs, and a negative tone about government set by the candidates for national office and the news media (see Bok, 1996; Garment, 1991; Orren, 1997; Weisberg, 1996). In all likelihood, these factors and others have worked together to reduce confidence in government (see Citrin, 1974; Craig, 1996; Dionne, 1992; Lipset and Schneider, 1983; Miller, 1974; Nye, Zelikow, and King, 1997; Tolchin, 1996).

Political distrust first surfaced in national public opinion surveys in the late 1960s. Americans who think that the federal government can be trusted to do what is right "just about always" or "most of the time" declined from 65 percent in 1966 to 39 percent in 1998. The number who think the government is run for the benefit of all the people declined from 53 percent in 1966 to 32 percent in 1998. Those who think that quite a few people in government are crooked has jumped from 25 percent in 1966 to 39 percent in 1998 (National Election Studies, 1996, 1998).

DISTRUST IN THE FEDERAL GOVERNMENT

The distrust of government among Californians is consistent with recent national trends. The results for four questions taken from the "Trust in Government Index" used by the University of Michigan in the National Election Studies and repeated in our surveys are exemplary

TABLE 2-10   TRUST IN THE FEDERAL GOVERNMENT

	California	U.S.
Trust in Government		
Always/most of the time trust government to do what is right	33%	39%
Government run by a few big interests	70	63
Government wastes a lot of taxpayers' money	65	61
Quite a few people in government are crooked	39	39
Government Responsiveness		
Government pays a good deal of attention to what people think	15%	18%
Elections make the government pay a good deal of attention	44	46
Political Efficacy		
Agree: Public officials don't care what people like me think	54%	60%
Agree: People like me don't have any say in government	47	40

SOURCE: PPIC Statewide Surveys, September and October 1998, all adults; National Election Studies, 1998.

NOTE: These percentages include "don't know" responses.

(see Table 2-10).[5] Only one-third of Californians think the federal government can be trusted to do what is right either all or most of the time. These results are more negative than those in the national survey, where 39 percent said they had trust in the federal government either all or most of the time.[6]

There are some major differences by political affiliation. Interestingly enough, those who don't even register to vote have more trust than those who are registered and affiliated with major parties. Forty-four percent of those who are not registered trust the federal government all or most of the time, compared with only 31 percent of registered voters.

5. The four questions that are part of the "Trust in Government Index" have been used in national surveys for 40 years. We consider the separate answers in this analysis.

6. Multiple regressions controlling for age, gender, income, region, and race and ethnicity indicate that nonvoters were significantly different from voters. Those who are not registered to vote had more trust in government, as indicated by the following B's and significance levels (in parentheses) in the final equations with all variables: government trust = .12 (.001), government waste = −.09 (.001), government crooked = −.12 (.001).

Democrats (37%) express a higher degree of trust than Republicans (25%) but still trail the unregistered.

The lack of trust is reflected in perceptions of government motivation. Is the government in Washington run for the benefit of all the people? Only 25 percent of Californians think so, whereas 70 percent assume that it is "pretty much run by a few big interests looking out for themselves." These results are more negative than those in the national survey, which found 63 percent of Americans believing that the government is run for and by a few big interests. Again, registered voters tend to be more cynical about the federal government's motives. Seventy-two percent of registered voters think that the federal government is run by a few big interests, compared with 57 percent of those not registered. Nevertheless, a solid majority in all political groups believe that the federal government is not run for the benefit of all the people.

Californians are as untrusting as Americans at large when it comes to the federal government's fiscal performance. Two-thirds of Californians think that government wastes a lot of the money we pay in taxes; only 3 percent say it does not waste money. In the national survey, a similar share of Americans said that government wastes a lot of money.

Political involvement again relates to higher levels of political distrust. Sixty-five percent of registered voters believe that the federal government wastes a lot of taxpayer money, compared with 55 percent of those who are not registered. Democrats (62%) are only slightly less likely than Republicans (68%) to fault the federal government for its fiscal performance, indicating little difference across parties.

Many Californians not only question the motivations and fiscal responsibility of the federal government; they also think that many officials in Washington are downright dishonest. Thirty-nine percent went so far as to say that quite a few of the people running the government are crooked. Only 14 percent believe that hardly any are crooked. In the national survey, an identical 39 percent said that quite a few people in government are crooked. On this score, there is also agreement across groups. Democrats (37%) and Republicans (36%) are similar in opinion to the unregistered (40%) in thinking that quite a few people in the government are crooked.

Evidently, Californians make some distinction between all people in government and elected officials. Fifty-five percent of Californians agreed that "most elected officials are trustworthy" while 44 percent did not. In fact, they are about as charitable toward elected officials as Americans at large. In a national survey by the Pew Research Center (1998a), 51 percent of Americans thought that most elected officials were trustworthy while 48 percent did not.

The lack of trust also correlates with a belief that government simply isn't interested in what the people want. As shown in Table 2-10, only 15 percent believe that government pays a "good deal" of attention to what the people think when it decides what to do, but 44 percent think it pays a good deal of attention to elections. Both of these results closely track the findings on "government responsiveness" from the 1998 National Election Studies.

Some more hints about the distrust that Californians feel toward their federal government are seen in the relative confidence they have in other levels of government. When asked which level of government is best at solving their problems, only county government (18%) fared worse than Washington (20%). People had more confidence in city (27%) and state (26%) government.

As noted previously, people believe the government wastes a lot of the taxpayers' money. When Californians were asked more specifically about which level of government they trust the most in spending their money, the federal government once again fared badly. Only 10 percent named the federal government as the level of government they trusted the most to spend their tax money wisely. Trust was greater for city (31%), county (22%), and state (17%) government. Fifteen percent said they trusted no branch of government with their tax money, a number that actually exceeded those saying they most trusted the federal government. This attitude toward the federal government was consistent among voters and the unregistered, and between Democrats and Republicans.

About half of Californians believe that government and their public officials don't listen to them. This is evident in the response to two questions from the 1998 National Election Studies "External Political Efficacy Index" that were repeated in our surveys. When presented with the statement "People like me don't have any say in what the government does," 47 percent of Californians agreed. With regard to the statement "Public officials don't care much what people like me think," 54 percent of Californians agreed. Compared with the results of the national survey, Californians are somewhat less likely to say that public officials don't care what they think but are somewhat more likely to say that people like themselves don't have any say in government. Overall, the state trends again reflect the national discontent.

These feelings of political powerlessness were confirmed once again when I asked a question from the Pew Research Center Survey (1998a). Fifty-one percent of Californians agreed that "most elected officials care what people like me think" while 48 percent disagreed. In the national survey, 41 percent agreed that most elected officials cared what people like themselves thought, and 57 percent disagreed.

DISTRUST IN STATE GOVERNMENT

Do Californians trust Sacramento any more than they trust Washington? The growing use of the initiative process implies that they are disillusioned with the state government's performance and motivations.

Indeed, our surveys indicate that Californians deeply distrust their state government, although slightly less than they distrust the federal government. Table 2-11 presents their responses to three questions from the "Trust in Government Index," in which the survey changed the focus from the federal to the state government. Only one-third say they can trust the state government in Sacramento to do what is right either always or most of the time. The unregistered (42%) are slightly more likely than voters (37%) to trust the state government a great deal, and Democrats (40%) have a little more trust than Republicans (33%). However, in all voter categories, most people trust state government only some of the time.

As Table 2-11 also shows, just over half of Californians think that the state government wastes a lot of tax money. However, Californians are much less likely to say that about state government (52%) than about the federal government (65%). Although there are slight differences across voter categories, a majority in every group but the unregistered believe the state government wastes a lot of tax money.

Although they are less cynical about the motivation of the state compared with the federal government, 64 percent believe state government is pretty much run by a few big interests looking out for themselves. Recall that 70 percent see the federal government in this way. Again, voters are more distrustful: 67 percent of voters see the state government run by a few big interests, compared with 55 percent of those who aren't registered. Democrats (64%) and Republicans (66%) have similar views on this issue.

Do Californians have much trust that government can solve the state's problems? The overall trend is a lack of confidence in problem solving at all levels of government. Only 11 percent said they had a

TABLE 2-11   TRUST IN THE STATE GOVERNMENT

"How much of the time do you think you can trust the state *government in Sacramento to do what is right?"*

Always	4%
Most of the time	33
Only some of the time	60
None of the time	2
Don't know	1

"Do you think that the people in state *government waste a lot of the money we pay in taxes, waste some of it, or don't waste very much of it?"*

Waste a lot	52%
Waste some	41
Don't waste very much	5
Don't know	2

"Would you say the state *government is pretty much run by a few big interests looking out for themselves or that it is run for the benefit of all the people?"*

Few big interests	64%
Benefit of all the people	29
Don't know	7

SOURCE: PPIC Statewide Survey, December 1998, all adults.

great deal of trust and confidence in Governor Pete Wilson, and 45 percent had little or no trust in his ability to solve the state's problems. As for the California legislature, only 4 percent had a great deal of trust and confidence in these elected officials, while 35 percent had little or none. Although the number having a great deal of confidence in their County Board of Supervisors (8%) to solve county problems was only slightly higher, Californians trust their mayors and city councils (16%) more in solving city problems.

Because Wilson was a Republican, and Democrats controlled the California legislature, one might anticipate partisan differences in the level of distrust in state government officials, but a partisan trend was not very evident. Republicans (20%) were more likely than Democrats (6%) or the unregistered (10%) to say they had a great deal of confidence in Wilson; and equally sparse numbers of Democrats (3%), Republicans (4%), and the unregistered (6%) said they had a great deal of confidence in the California legislature. The public is not particularly swayed by party loyalty when they are evaluating trust in the state's elected officials. This is especially the case with the legislature, which all voters seem to hold in low regard.[7]

Other findings suggest that Californians trust their local governments more than they do their state government. When asked what level of government they trust the most to solve problems, 45 percent mentioned their city and county governments, while 26 percent named their state government. When asked what level of government they trusted the most to spend their money wisely, 53 percent mentioned their city and county governments, while 17 percent named their state government.

Another way of looking at the issue of trust and confidence in state government is to assess the views of the public in how well the governor and legislature work together. Apparently, California residents don't think much of their joint efforts at governing the state. Only 11 percent said they had a great deal of confidence in the governor and legislature when it comes to the ability to solve the state's most important problems, while 30 percent had very little or no confidence. The low level of confidence is consistent across voter categories. Thus, it is little wonder that initiatives are popular avenues for policymaking.

Survey results suggest that the public's confidence in state government is not likely to improve just because divided government ended with the 1998 election of a Democratic governor. Californians do not seem to infer that it is partisan divisions that hamper problem solving at the state level. California had a Republican governor and a Democratically controlled legislature for most of the 1980s and 1990s. One of our survey questions asked whether it was better if the governor comes from the same political party that controls the California legislature or better to have a governor from one party and the legislature controlled by another. Californians were closely divided on this issue, with 39 percent saying it was better if they were from the same party, 36 percent saying it was better if they were from different parties, and 25 percent saying it depends or they weren't sure.

Nor do Californians hold themselves responsible for the lack of ability of the legislature and the governor to handle the state's problems. As a result of an initiative passed in 1990, the California legisla-

7. The job performance ratings also suggest that state elected officials are not held in high regard. In the May survey, 30 percent of the respondents gave the California legislature excellent or good ratings, while 34 percent offered similar evaluations of Wilson. In the September survey, 36 percent gave excellent or good ratings to the California legislature, while 42 percent said that Wilson was doing an excellent or good job. By comparison, six in ten Californians were optimistic about the direction of the state, and six in ten gave Clinton either excellent or good ratings.

ture and the state constitutional officers, such as the governor, have operated under term limits for almost a decade. Some observers have said that the lack of experience in key state positions has harmed state policymaking, blaming the constant turnover for creating a lack of institutional knowledge about the process of passing laws. But most Californians do not agree. Two-thirds think that term limits are a good thing for California, while only 14 percent think they are bad for the state. Republicans (77%) and Democrats (63%) overwhelmingly see term limits as a good policy for the state. Even though Californians are apparently pleased with themselves for imposing term limits, the policy has not boosted their confidence in the state officials they have elected.

DEFINING A ROLE FOR GOVERNMENT

Given their political apathy and distrust, what role does the public want government to play in their lives? Because many Californians think their governments are not prone to do the right thing, are not very good at solving problems, are likely to waste a lot of money, and are influenced more by special interests than by the public good, they want government to have a very limited role. Middle-class Americans, and suburban residents in particular, have expressed similar opinions. Their political philosophy tends to be moderate to somewhat conservative, and their policy preferences have been dubbed "the New Political Culture"—liberal on social issues and conservative on fiscal issues (Clark and Ferguson, 1983; Clark and Hoffman-Martinot, 1998). What seems at first glance politically schizophrenic is logically consistent. People do not want the government to have much involvement in either their private lives or in the large public issues of the day. This is totally consistent with a lack of confidence in government and with the popularity of the initiative process in California.

In fact, Californians fit the "New Political Culture" profile very well. Most describe themselves as centrists or just to the right of center in their political philosophy. About one-third call themselves liberals, one-third say they are middle-of-the-road, and one-third describe themselves as conservatives (see Table 2-12). But 60 percent fit into the categories of middle-of-the-road and somewhat conservative, making this the largest political grouping. This pattern is also similar to that for the nation (National Election Studies, 1998). Although Democrats are the most inclined to call themselves liberal (42%) and Republicans are more likely to say they are conservative (58%), a majority of

TABLE 2-12   POLITICAL ORIENTATION

	California	U.S.
Liberal	29%	24%
Middle-of-the-road	35	37
Conservative	36	39

SOURCE: PPIC Statewide Survey, April, May, September, and December 1998, all adults and National Election Studies, 1998.
NOTE: California percentages were from a 5-point scale and U.S. percentages were from a 7-point scale of liberalism to conservatism.

Democrats (52%) and Republicans (71%) describe their politics as middle-of-the-road to somewhat conservative. The prevalence of the right-of-center orientation has important implications for the evolution of government's role in the foreseeable future.

Many Californians do not want the government making decisions that affect their private lives. Attitudes toward abortion are a good example (see Table 2-13).[8] Sixty-one percent say that decisions about abortion should be left up to the woman and her doctor; only 12 percent think that it should be illegal in all cases. The results are almost identical for the same question asked in a national survey conducted by NBC News/Wall Street Journal (1998).

A majority of Democrats (73%) and Republicans (53%) and close to half of the unregistered (47%) hold this view about government intervention in the abortion decision. How important is this issue to Californians? In the 1990s, the winners in the presidential, U.S. Senate, and governor's races all favored leaving the decision on abortion up to the woman. In the 1998 governor's race, the Democrats constantly reminded voters in television commercials that Gray Davis was pro-choice while Dan Lungren was not. The Davis campaign saw the pro-choice abortion stand as one of their most effective issues.

A pro-civil-liberties attitude also extends to homosexual rights, but not so strongly. Fifty-five percent of Californians said that homosexuality is a way of life that should be accepted by society, but 40 percent thought it should be discouraged by society. A majority of Democrats (64%), many Republicans (40%), and most of the unregistered (57%) stated that homosexuality as a way of life should be accepted. When this question was asked in a national survey by the Pew Research

8. Multiple regressions indicate no significant differences between voters and nonvoters for specific policies involving the role of government after controlling for age, gender, income, region, and race and ethnicity.

TABLE 2-13   THE ROLE OF GOVERNMENT

	California	U.S.
Abortion		
Choice left up to woman and her doctor	61%	60%
Legal in some cases, such as rape or incest	26	26
Illegal in all circumstances	12	11
Don't know	1	3
Spending and Taxes		
Reduce taxes, spend less	44%	31%
Spend more, raise taxes	51	47
Don't know, it depends	5	22
Environmental Regulations		
Stricter environmental laws worth the cost	58%	63%
Stricter environmental laws cost too many jobs	38	30
Don't know	5	7

SOURCE: PPIC Statewide Survey, May 1998, all adults; NBC News/Wall Street Journal (1998); National Opinion Research Center (1996); Pew Research Center (1996a).

Center (1998a), 46 percent of Americans said that homosexuality should be accepted by society. This indicates a stronger pro-civil-liberties stand in California than in the rest of the nation.

Liberal attitudes are not in evidence, however, when it comes to issues such as government involvement in poverty programs. Even in the wake of welfare reform and declining welfare rolls, many Californians continue to believe that the poor are too dependent on government assistance programs and that the government is spending too much money to help the poor. Seventy-seven percent of Californians agree that poor people have become too dependent on government assistance programs. This nearly matches national trends: 79 percent of Americans said the poor were too dependent on government programs when the question was asked by the Pew Research Center (1998a) in a national survey.

The vast majority of Democrats (71%), Republicans (89%), and the unregistered (73%) hold this view. Moreover, almost half of Californians (44%) agree that the government is spending too much money on programs to help the poor. This statewide trend is 9 points higher than when this question was asked in a national survey by the Gallup Organization in 1996. A sizable number of Republicans (59%), one-third of Democrats (33%), and almost half of the unregistered (41%) feel that the government is spending too much money on the poor.

Most Californians believe that their state is divided into two economic groups, the "haves" and the "have-nots." However, this view does not translate into support for government efforts to reduce income inequality. About 60 percent said that the state was divided into haves and have-nots, while 40 percent disagreed. In fact, about one-third of Californians placed themselves in the have-not group, including more than half of those earning under $40,000 a year. But fewer than half (45%) said the government should do more to make sure that all Californians have an equal opportunity to succeed. Most Democrats (63%) and many Republicans (46%) see the state as divided into haves and have-nots, but only half of Democrats (55%) and few Republicans (28%) want to see more government action to alleviate the differences.

The conservative side of Californians shows itself most forcefully in the area of government taxes and spending. Even popular programs such as Social Security are not immune to the antitax fever. About half of Californians (44%) said they would like to see the government reduce taxes, even if it means spending less on the more popular social programs such as health care, Social Security, and unemployment benefits. Compared with respondents to a 1996 national survey by the National Opinion Research Center, Californians are more likely to favor reducing taxes (44% vs. 31%).

Republicans and Democrats hold nearly opposite views on the trade-off between tax cuts and social spending. The Republicans want lower taxes, even if it means cutting social programs, by a 2-to-1 ratio; the Democrats favor more programs, even it requires a tax hike, by the same margin. The unregistered are evenly divided on this tax-and-spend issue involving social programs.

Californians remain committed to the tax restrictions they have imposed through initiatives and do not favor provisions making it easier to pass local taxes. Proposition 13 requires a two-thirds vote instead of a simple majority to pass local taxes. Two-thirds of residents believe that this super-majority vote requirement has had either a good effect or no effect on local government services. Only 20 percent believe it has had a negative effect. Moreover, 60 percent oppose measures allowing local special taxes to pass with a simple majority instead of a two-thirds vote. A similarly large majority are against the passage of school bonds with a simple majority vote.

Voter support for changing the supermajority requirement to a simple majority does not reach 50 percent among Democrats, Republicans, or the unregistered for either local taxes or local school bonds

How important are state tax cuts to residents? The governor and state legislature passed a $1.4 billion tax cut for the 1998–1999 fiscal year, including a reduction in the state vehicle license fee. In the September 1998 survey, 75 percent of Californians said the tax cut was important to them, half describing it as "very important." Across the political spectrum, residents said this tax cut was something they personally valued. Following the tax cut, Governor Wilson's job ratings jumped 8 points. The tax revolt is alive and well in California.

Many Californians do see a role for government in regulating the private sector for workers and consumers. A majority (54%) of Californians believe that government regulation of business is necessary to protect the public interest; 43 percent believe that government regulation of business does more harm than good. When we compare the statewide results to the national survey by the Pew Research Center (1996a), we see that Californians are more likely than Americans in general to believe that government regulation of business is necessary (54% vs. 45%). Moreover, 58 percent of Californians believe that stricter environmental laws and regulations are worth the cost, while only 38 percent think that stricter regulations cost too many jobs and hurt the economy. The results of a Pew Research Center survey (1996a) show that the nation is similar to California in its views on this issue. These findings indicate that Californians want their government to protect them from harms they may face as consumers and workers. However, they are not interested in paying more taxes for social programs or having the government do more to help the poor. These are consistent themes of the middle class in the "New Political Culture."

MAKING ELECTION CHOICES

How do Californians decide what to do in what they view as the imperfect world of elections? As we saw in Chapter 1, many simply have chosen not to vote. Many of those who do vote are uneasy. They are more cynical about politics than those who stay home. They are not inclined to spend a lot of time researching the candidates, nor do they find the election information essentially truthful. So what did they take into consideration during the 1998 gubernatorial primary and general election?

Two powerful forces were at work in the June primary: the new open-primary voting rules and the millions spent by two wealthy candidates.

These factors should have changed the shape of the election. They did not. The losers—businessman Al Checchi and U.S. Representative Jane Harman—were the wealthy political outsiders who promised to shake up the Sacramento political establishment. The winners—Attorney General Dan Lungren and Lieutenant Governor Gray Davis—were the conventional candidates, the kind who would have won an old-fashioned party primary. The two-term governor, Pete Wilson, was termed out of office. The voters chose the next-highest-ranking Republican and the highest-ranking Democrat in statewide elected office for the November election.

Why did voters make these choices? Were Californians suddenly enamored with career politicians and the people holding high state offices? Not according to the surveys. The evidence suggests that they made these choices because they did not want to risk any changes that might rock the boat.

Californians were in an upbeat mood in the spring of 1998. Sixty percent said the economy was in excellent or good shape, and only 10 percent said it was poor. Seventy percent rated the quality of life in California in positive terms. When they were asked whether they thought the state was headed in the right direction, 60 percent said it was. Moreover, many thought it likely that the good times would continue. More than 40 percent thought they would be better off financially in the year ahead, and only 6 percent expected to be worse off.[9]

The "angry voter" of the 1994 election had been replaced by the "status quo voter" in the 1998 election. When Californians were voting for governor in 1994, the voter surveys I conducted for KCAL-TV News in Los Angeles showed that only one-third thought the state was headed in the right direction, while 60 percent believed it was going the wrong way. One-third thought the quality of life in the state was good, while 60 percent described it in negative terms. Only 16 percent said they were better off than they had been the year before.

Voters went into the June 1998 primary in a risk-averse mood. They wanted choices that would maintain the status quo of good economic times and keep them from slipping back into the deep recession of the not-so-distant past. Under these circumstances, there would be no Jesse "The Body" Ventura emerging as the next governor of California.

Given all the political distrust, it came as a surprise when, as Table 2-14 shows, 46 percent of voters said they preferred statewide candi-

---

9. The percentages from the statewide survey reported in this section are based on the total sample of registered voters, rather than all adults or likely voters.

TABLE 2-14   CANDIDATE QUALIFICATIONS
AND ELECTION CHOICES

"People have different ideas about the qualifications they want when they vote for candidates for statewide office, such as governor or U.S. senator. Which of these is most important to you?"

Before the June primary

Experience in elected office	46%
Experience running a business	38
Other	10
Don't know	6

Before the November general election

Stands on issues	54%
Character	20
Experience	19
Political party	5
Don't know	2

SOURCE: PPIC Statewide Survey, May and October 1998, all adults.

dates with a track record in elected office. Democrats (51%) were more likely to prefer experienced politicians than Republicans (32%), but all of the responses are in stark contrast to the professed deep distrust of elected officials. In another rebuke of outsider politicians, 53 percent said they favored the candidates who raised money from their supporters to pay for their political campaigns, while only 35 percent said they preferred candidates who spend their own money.

The voters' wish list for candidate qualities gave both Lungren and Davis a big advantage in June. Voters were unwilling to take a chance with untested politicians, specifically Al Checchi and Jane Harman, who greatly outspent their rivals on paid television commercials. Most Republicans stayed with Lungren, while most Democrats voted for Davis. But the voters had spoken. They didn't want a radical change in their state's leaders to get in the way of the good times that were under way in California. Once again, a limited role for government seemed better than the risk of government intrusion.

In the November matchup, neither of the candidates had a track record that fit the profile of the ideal candidate. Most Californians describe themselves as politically moderate to somewhat conservative, with liberal views on issues of personal freedom and conservative views on taxes and spending. Lungren was suspect for his highly conservative tendencies, especially his support for restricting abortions. Davis had worked for liberal Democratic Governor Jerry Brown, which raised questions about where he stood on increasing taxes and state spending. In the fall election, voters would have to weigh their conflicting sentiments and make a choice. They ultimately opted for Davis over Lungren, breaking the 16-year domination of the governor's office by Republicans.

Why Davis? The bottom line is that voters gravitated to the candidate who seemed to offer the least potential for change. Lungren worried some voters because he presented himself as a conservative politician who might shake things up a bit. Davis won because he was the more successful of the two candidates in crafting the image of a safe choice, and he portrayed Lungren as an agent of change without mainstream sensibilities. And Davis succeeded through television advertising. Time and again, his commercials emphasized that his opponent was not a middle-of-the-road thinker on issues ranging from guns to abortion to schools. On abortion in particular, Lungren's views raised the unpopular prospect of increased government intrusion in people's lives. To voters looking for a steady politician who wouldn't make waves, Lungren seemed like more of a risk.

California voters were also highly distracted by the media attention surrounding the Clinton-Lewinsky affair. During the fall, the Starr report and the congressional hearings were ever present, sapping the political interest of the electorate and dominating print and television news coverage. Yet Californians gave President Clinton high ratings. Though they were deeply split along partisan lines, 60 percent thought the president was doing an excellent or good job. Democrats (81%) gave the president high marks, while few Republicans (27%) felt he was doing a good job. Polls at the time showed that most Americans and Californians thought that the president should not resign.

These feelings about the president reflect a cynical but deeply held sentiment. Politicians are viewed as "ethically challenged" by most Californians. Thus, they should be judged on what they do for the voter rather than on the basis of their already suspect moral character. The economy was great, and most Californians thought that the president was doing a good job for them. He should therefore stay in office, even though he appeared to be morally bankrupt.

The president's approval ratings did not deter Republicans from taking the high road and, at times, sounding like they were waging a moral crusade in the fall election. Their thinking was that they could take advantage of the Democrats' troubles, what with their top leader embroiled in a sex scandal. Lungren in particular focused on the issue of "character." He portrayed himself as more upstanding and honest than his Democratic opponent (see Jacobs, 1999). But Davis brushed off these claims as groundless allegations and focused instead on the differences between the candidates' stands on the issues. The voters weren't buying Lungren's approach, since they don't see politicians as morally upstanding. In the statewide surveys before the November election, more than half said that a candidate's stands on the issues mattered the most to them, while only 20 percent said that character was the most important consideration in their vote for governor. A majority of both Democrats and Republicans said that stands on the issues mattered most in choosing a candidate. After the election, Lungren's pollster was quoted as saying that the focus on character rather than issues in the gubernatorial campaign was a "strategic fatal error" (Skelton, 1999).

CONCLUSIONS AND IMPLICATIONS

As California enters an era when it will face some of the toughest challenges in its 150 years of statehood, most of its public has become disengaged from the political process and highly cynical about their elected leaders. This political climate will make it truly difficult for the public to reach consensus about how to address the issues confronting the state as it continues to grow rapidly—let alone reach some general agreement on the solutions and sacrifices that may be needed to keep the California Dream alive. This political dilemma is all the more difficult because the state is basically reflecting national trends that draw their strength from causes that extend beyond the Golden State's borders.

There is plenty of evidence that political apathy and distrust are the overarching themes of elections and policy debates in California today. Many Californians apparently no longer treat voting as a civic duty, skipping elections with increasing regularity. Only about half of the eligible adults are participating in presidential elections, while only 40 percent cast ballots in the gubernatorial elections. Both figures reflect sharp declines from the early 1970s. Not only are the turnouts down, but the voting population is highly skewed. The California electorate is older, whiter, and more affluent relative to the total adult population. As a result, an unrepresentative minority is choosing representatives and making decisions that affect all Californians (see Schrag, 1998).

At a time in the state's history when the stakes have never been higher, people are paying surprisingly little attention to government and politics. Few express much interest in politics. Many spend little time following government affairs in the news. Even during the course of major events, such as a governor's election, there is not much of an increase in interest in California political news.

The lack of political attentiveness fits into a broader pattern of civic disengagement. Very few Californians are highly involved in state and national issues or even issues that are closer to home. Because of their limited attention span when it comes to politics, most people spend little time and effort gathering news and information on this topic. Television has become the principal source of information on politics and elections as newspaper readership has declined. Yet, ironically, in response to market research that shows little public interest in this topic, most television news broadcasts are now giving sparse coverage to politics and elections. News coverage from Sacramento about the issues facing the state government is even rarer. During the elections, television commercials by the candidates filled the information void. Californians overwhelmingly recall seeing the paid advertisements, although the commercials do not seem to have encouraged people to go out and vote.

Even though residents confess to paying little attention to politics, what they do know has led them to harbor negative feelings about government and elected officials. Many Californians do not trust Washington and the federal government to do what is right. They think the federal government wastes taxpayer money, believe that it works in the favor of special interests rather than average citizens like themselves, and feel that many of its politicians are crooked. The public's distrust of government is not limited to Washington; Californians also hold cynical views toward Sacramento and the state government. Few express a great deal of confidence in the governor and legislature. Most believe their local governments are more trustworthy, but only relatively so.

Given their lack of trust in government and elected officials, Californians prefer a limited role for government. They are moderate to somewhat conservative overall, but liberal on social issues and conservative on fiscal issues. They don't want the government to interfere with the personal decisions in their lives, such as choices on abortion. They don't want the government to spend a lot more money and effort on poverty programs. They are not inclined to raise taxes or to make it easier for the government to pass tax increases. Yet they are supportive of government intervention to protect them from corporations and environmental problems.

Political apathy and distrust played an important role in Californians' ballot choices in the 1998 election. Most eligible adults stayed home. Those who voted were bombarded with commercials from the major-party candidates from the June open primary until the November election. Ultimately, voters made what they thought were "safe" choices during this particular election cycle. They rejected candidates who they feared would add to government interference in people's private lives. They were disbelieving of candidates who made claims of superior character and integrity, assuming all politicians to be untrustworthy. With the economy going so well, California voters wanted candidates who would maintain the status quo and who would focus on a few issues of importance to them, such as education. After the election was over, nearly half of the Californians we surveyed could not name the new governor. This lack of basic knowledge about state elections perhaps best reflects the depth of public apathy at the heart of California political life and policy discussions.

CHAPTER 3

The Voters' Revolt

The public's distrust has had real consequences for California politics and elections. It has led people to search for answers outside mainstream politics, apparently guided by a desire to reform their governments and to punish the elected officials they see as failing them. Upset with the status quo, many no longer have strong attachments to the major political parties who run their candidates for state and federal office and then take up the majority and minority leadership positions in legislatures. Having low expectations for what their governments can do, they are not shy about taking into their own hands the business of creating laws and public policies.

This chapter explores two of the most dramatic manifestations of the voters' revolt. The first is the growth of independent voters in California elections. Americans are showing a greater tendency to describe themselves as independents, at the same time that their opinions of politicians and government have been declining.[1] Some say that independent voters are partisans in disguise—some Democrats, others Republicans—while others believe that they reflect a political movement whose members are very volatile in their political choices. I tend to agree with those who see independent voters as part of the "New Political Culture" that places issues-oriented coalitions ahead of partisan

1. See discussions about the partisan leanings of independents in Craig (1996), Greenberg (1995), Keith and co-authors (1992), Lipset and Schneider (1983), Miller and Shanks (1996), and Polsby and Wildavsky (1996). Clark and Inglehart's (1998) review of the "new Political Culture" fits with my profile of the independent voter.

politics. California has had a phenomenal growth in independent voters in recent decades. Their influence has extended from being the much-sought-after "swing voters" who determine general elections in a state where no party has a majority to now being active players in the partisan primaries through the California open primaries that debuted in June 1998.

The second, and even more important, manifestation of the voters' revolt is the increasing use of citizens' initiatives in making public policy. There is a strong "direct democracy" element in the California system of state government that originated in early-twentieth-century reform movements and that enables voters to take decisionmaking responsibility out of the hands of their elected representatives.[2] It is unlikely that the creators of the initiative process expected it to evolve into a powerful tool of citizens and special interests that represents a constant threat to the legislative and executive branches of state government. Such has been the result, however. As the number of state initiatives reaching the ballot has skyrocketed, the amount of money spent on initiative campaigns has become astronomical, and the public policies that have been approved by the voters are far-reaching. Between 1976 and 1996, Californians voted on 106 statewide ballot initiatives. In the two decades proceeding 1976, only 29 initiatives were placed on the ballot. Spending on initiatives reached $140 million in 1996 (Gerber, 1998).

As noted in Chapter 2, California is fairly representative of the nation in the level of distrust the people have toward politics and government. However, Californians have been much quicker than other states to express their pent-up frustrations in dramatic ways through the initiative process. In addition, they have now added the dimension of open primaries to further sap power from the major parties.

INDEPENDENT VOTERS

THE INCREASE IN INDEPENDENT VOTERS

Over the past three decades, there has been a steady growth of independent voters in California—people who register to vote but do not choose a party affiliation. If they wish, voters can register as Democrats, Republicans, or members of another officially recognized party. For the 1998 election, there were the American Independent, Green, Libertarian,

2. See discussions of the history of the citizens' initiative process in California in California Commission on Campaign Financing (1992), DeBow and Syer (1997), Field and Sohner (1999), Lee (1997), and Schrag (1998).

TABLE 3-1   REGISTRATION TRENDS FOR VOTERS

	Independents	Democrats	Republicans
1970	278,284	4,388,052	3,274,967
1980	959,236	5,786,806	3,703,515
1990	1,206,039	6,453,186	5,072,331
1998	1,863,590	6,830,530	5,225,686

SOURCE: California Secretary of State (1998a).

Natural Law, Peace and Freedom, and Reform parties. Independent voters are those who officially "decline to state" a party affiliation.

In the focus groups, independent voters gave a variety of reasons for their registration status. They appear to be motivated by issues. Many have negative or ambivalent opinions about the major political parties and the election process. "If an issue affects me, that's when I start to vote. I guess I don't have strong feelings about any political party," remarked one San Diego resident. An Orange County resident said, "I focus more on the issues, not so much on the individuals." "I've been a Democrat for years but I recently went independent. Sometimes there's people on the ballot that you don't really want to vote for," remarked another San Diego resident.

Table 3-1 charts the considerable growth of independent voters since 1970. In that year, there were just over one-quarter of a million independent voters in California. By 1998, the number had grown to nearly 1.9 million. The growth in this voter group in the 1990s was particularly impressive, because this was the time when the California secretary of state was purging the voter rolls of "deadwood," or ineligible voters.

Over time, the percentage of all voters who register as independents has increased. In 1970, only 3 percent of the voters were independents, while 54 percent were Democrats and 41 percent were Republicans. By 1998, the independents had grown to 13 percent, while the number of Democrats declined to 47 percent and the number of Republicans to 36 percent. One in six voters was independent or belonged to a minor party in 1998. Independent voters are now the "swing votes" in California elections, since neither the Democrats nor the Republicans have a simple majority of the state's registered voters.

Independent voters have been the fastest-growing group since 1970. By 1998, they had gained 1,585,306 people, for a growth rate of 570 percent. The Democrats increased by 2,442,478, for a growth rate of 56 percent. The Republicans gained 1,950,719, for a growth rate of 59 percent. Even more remarkable is the period of the 1990s. Both numerically and proportionally, independents outgained Republicans and Democrats. Independents increased by 54 percent, while Democrats increased by 6 percent and Republicans by 3 percent.

The independent voter status got a boost from the November 1996 election, when Californians approved the open-primary initiative. Beginning with the June 1998 primary, voters would be able to vote for any candidate they choose. Prior to this time, independent voters did not have a say in the selection of party candidates for president, governor, U.S. senator, and other federal, state, and local elected offices. One would expect the ranks of independent voters to grow even more, now that one of the most important incentives for registering as a Democrat or a Republican had been eliminated.

National studies have also indicated the growth of independent voters in recent decades, but some have insisted that most independents have strong leanings toward either the Democrat or the Republican party (see Keith et al., 1992). Such is not the case in California, where independent voters have become not only a significant group but also one that shows no signs of having any partisan loyalty. In recent years, there have been dramatic shifts in support from one statewide election to the next. Independents were divided between Bill Clinton and Ross Perot (41% to 39%) and gave little support to George Bush (19%) in the 1992 presidential election. Four years later, they divided their vote between Clinton and Dole (42% to 35%) and deserted Perot (20%). Independents strongly favored Pete Wilson over Kathleen Brown (56% to 35%) in the 1994 gubernatorial election. Four years later, they made a sharp reversal and supported Democrat Gray Davis over Republican Dan Lungren (60% to 28%). In the 1994 election, when they were supporting Wilson, they also narrowly favored Dianne Feinstein over Michael Huffington (44% to 40%), thus helping her to keep her U.S. Senate seat in this close race. In the 1998 election, while they were overwhelmingly favoring Davis, they gave only a narrow edge to Democrat Barbara Boxer over Republican Matt Fong (48% to 43%) as she went on to keep her U.S. Senate seat (Los Angeles Times Poll, 1992, 1994, 1996, 1998).[3] Many independent voters in California are thus truly independent. The evidence from the first-ever open California primary in June 1998 provides some insight about how independent voters and partisan voters react to their new independence

---

3. The results for the governor's race and the U.S. Senate race were similar in the exit polls conducted by the Voter News Service (1998).

from the two-party closed-primary system. First, independent voters were present in greater numbers than would normally be expected. In previous primaries, they could vote only in local and state nonpartisan races and for local and state propositions. Independents were estimated to have doubled their participation rate, from about 7 percent to 14 percent (Field Poll, 1998). Also, independents split their vote among a number of candidates competing for their attention through a heavy dose of television commercials leading up to the June primary. In the end, they supported Gray Davis (42%) over Dan Lungren (21%), Jane Harman (15%), and Al Checchi (13%). Three in ten Republicans crossed over to vote for one of the Democrats, while one in ten Democrats crossed over to vote for a Republican (Los Angeles Times/CNN Poll, 1998). Contrary to the fears of party leaders, few people seemed to vote "strategically" for weak candidates in the party they wanted to lose (see Walters, 1999). As respondents told us in our focus groups and reiterated in preelection polls and exit surveys, they voted for the candidates they liked the most. In sum, the open primary had the effect of increasing the independent voter turnout and fostering independence among the major-party voters (see Jeffe, 1998c).

DEMOGRAPHIC AND IDEOLOGICAL
PROFILE OF INDEPENDENT VOTERS

Little is known about the demographic profile of California's independent voters. They represent only a small proportion of most voter surveys, so their characteristics are usually not available in the summary statistics. However, five waves of our survey gave us a large sample of independent voters.[4] As Table 3-2 shows, these voters are most distinct in their youthfulness: 42 percent of independents are under 35, while only one in four Democrats and Republicans are in this age group. As a result of their youthfulness, independents tend to have lived in California and their current residence for a shorter period of time compared with the major-party voters. Their educational levels indicate a high proportion of college educated, similar to other voter groups. Their incomes and home ownership rates show a comparable level of affluence. Independents are mostly men (57%), while Democrats are mostly women (58%) and

---

4. The findings are based on responses coded "independent or other party," except in the December survey, where we coded both "independents" and "other parties." In the latter survey, very few people identified themselves as other-party members, which is consistent with voter registration figures. There were no major differences in the demographic and political profiles of independent voters and other-party members.

TABLE 3-2   DEMOGRAPHIC PROFILES OF VOTERS

	Independents	Democrats	Republicans
18 to 34	42%	26%	23%
35 to 54	41	44	43
55 and older	17	30	34
College graduate	41	36	44
Some college	34	34	38
Less education	25	30	18
White	66	59	81
Latino	19	25	11
Black	5	10	1
Asian/other	10	6	7
Men	57	42	49
Women	43	58	51

SOURCE: PPIC Statewide Survey, 1998, all adults.

TABLE 3-3   POLITICAL ORIENTATION OF VOTERS

	Independents	Democrats	Republicans
Liberal	32%	42%	12%
Middle-of-the-road	39	38	30
Conservative	29	20	58

SOURCE: PPIC Statewide Survey, 1998, all voters.

Republicans are evenly split between men and women. Two-thirds of independents are whites, similar to the Democrats (59%) and much less so than the Republicans (81%). Sixty percent of independents say they live in the suburbs, which is similar to other voter groups.

One way to better understand why the independent voters are such an unpredictable group in California elections is to look at their political orientation, shown in Table 3-3. Three in ten independents describe themselves as liberals, four in ten are middle-of-the-road, and three in ten say they are conservatives. Democrats more often describe themselves as liberals. Republicans are more likely to call themselves conservatives. Independents are more likely to be centrists and stay away from ideological labels, compared with registered Republicans or Democrats. This allows independents to support candidates from either party who voice the themes and issues that connect with them. It probably also drives them away from the party structures that often accentuate liberal causes or conservative values. Independents (56%) mostly describe themselves as middle-of-the-road to somewhat conservative in their political views, which is also the frequent self-categorization of Republicans (71%) and Democrats (52%). So independents tend to have much in common with the mainstream from both major parties.

In sum, the independent voters fit the demographic and ideological profile of the "New Political Culture" voters. They are young, educated, and affluent. They tend to be whites, homeowners, and suburbanites. Independents appear to avoid labels, such as liberal and conservative, and show no party loyalty in their ballot choices.

POLITICAL BEHAVIOR OF INDEPENDENT VOTERS

Independent voters have been dubbed as not politically focused and easily swayed by issues-oriented messages. Polsby and Wildavsky (1996, p. 21) noted, "The most attentive are generally committed to a party and that party's position, whereas the least attentive are unavailable to persuasion: since they don't take in political information, they cannot be influenced by it. This leaves the middle ground as most open to persuasion. . . . They are not previously committed, but they learn enough so that it is possible for them to be swayed by new information about issues and by campaigns." The authors go on to dismiss the independents as a small group. Although the independent voters fit this information-seeking profile, they are not insignificant in California. Recognizing their importance, the candidates from both major parties spend a lot of effort gearing their messages to this voter block as well as to the small number of marginally loyal voters from their party and the opposition party.

As Table 3-4 shows, independents are not highly attentive to politics. Few show a high level of interest in politics, and many do not closely follow government issues.[5] They are more different from Republicans than from Democrats. This reflects the fact that Republicans tend to have higher socioeconomic status than other voters.

---

5. Multiple regressions controlling for age, gender, income, region, and race and ethnicity indicate that the slight differences in political interest reported between independents and the major-party voters are not significant. This means that the lower attentiveness of independents is explained by their relative youthfulness and lower incomes. Thus, as long as independents have these demographic qualities, they will as a group show less interest in politics than major-party members. Independents did pay less attention to the news than did major-party voters when other factors were accounted for, as indicated by the following B's and significance levels in the final equations: watch television news = −.17 (.001), read newspapers = −.28 (.001).

TABLE 3-4   POLITICAL INTEREST OF VOTERS

	Independents	Democrats	Republicans
Interest in Politics			
A great deal	17%	19%	22%
Fair amount	49	52	52
Little or none	34	29	26
Follow Government Affairs			
Most of the time	37%	39%	45%
Some of the time	39	41	38
Now and then,			
hardly ever, never	24	20	17

SOURCE: PPIC Statewide Survey, 1998, all adults.

Independents are more likely to admit that they vote only when the issues and candidates move them. In each survey, we asked people how often they vote, with answers including "always," "nearly always," "part of the time," and "seldom or never." Fewer than half of the independents said they always vote in elections (47%), compared with almost two in three Republicans (65%) and Democrats (61%). When asked why they don't vote all of the time, independent voters are most likely to answer that they don't know enough about the choices (37%), that they are too busy (25%), or that nothing changes by voting in elections (24%). Independents are more likely to give the cynical reason for not voting—"nothing changes"—than either Republicans (12%) or Democrats (13%).

There was evidence that independents were not very tuned in to politics, although voters in the major parties were not much involved either. Throughout the entire course of the 1998 election cycle, 8 percent of the independent voters said they were very closely following the election news, 34 percent were somewhat closely following it, and 58 percent were not closely following it. By comparison, half of Republicans (49%) and Democrats (52%) said they were "not too closely" or "not at all closely" following the 1998 California election news.

One of the major differences between independents and the major party members is that they pay less general attention to the news. About four in ten independent voters say they read a local newspaper every day, compared with more than half of the Democrats (50%) and Republicans (54%). Four in ten independent voters read a newspaper less than once a week. Over half of independent voters (55%) watch television news every day, compared with about two in three Democrats (65%) and Republicans (62%). In these media responses, the fact that independents are a younger group probably accounts for their lower news involvement.

The relative lack of attention to news does not mean that independents are more disengaged from civic life in general; they just don't care about politics as much as others do. Independents (44%) are as likely as Republicans (46%) and Democrats (43%) to be involved in work on local and neighborhood problems. Independents (22%) are also as likely as Republicans (22%) and Democrats (23%) to do work on state or national problems. Independents (66%) are between Democrats (61%) and Republicans (69%) in their level of involvement in volunteer and charity work. It is only in their lack of involvement in politics, party, election, and campaign work that independents (87%) stand out as even more disengaged than Democrats (80%) and Republicans (79%). Californians, in general, are not very actively involved in politics compared with the rest of the nation, as was reported in Chapter 2.

One area of civic life in which independents distinguish themselves from other voters is their low level of religious involvement. As others have noted, independent voters are intensely secular, a trend that has implications for their political choices (Greenberg, 1995). About one-third of independent voters (38%) said that religion is a very important part of their daily life, compared with about half of Democrats (48%) and Republicans (54%). Only about one-quarter of the independents attend religious services at least once a week, compared with 33 percent of Democrats and 41 percent of Republicans. More than half of independents attend religious services a few times a year or less. As a result, very few independents (13%) say that the clergy or religious groups tell them how to vote. Nearly two in three (63%) disapprove of candidates talking about their religious values, compared with 60 percent of Democrats and 45 percent of Republicans.

How much did independent voters remember the televised commercials by the gubernatorial and U.S. Senate candidates during the 1998 elections? Their level of recall was similar to that of the major-party voters, although consistently slightly lower. Seventy-three percent of independent voters remembered the gubernatorial candidates' commercials before the June primary, compared with 78 percent of Republicans and Democrats. Fifty-seven percent of the independent voters remembered the gubernatorial candidates' commercials before the November election, compared with 63 percent of Republicans and Democrats. As for the U.S. Senate race in the fall, 43 percent of independent voters recalled the paid advertisements, while 49 percent of Republicans and Democrats said they saw the candidates' commercials.

The trends that national surveys have found with independents are evident in California. Independent voters are not highly attentive to politics and elections. They are not much tuned in to the news. Because this large block of voters is capable of swinging a close election in either direction and have not made up their minds based on partisan loyalty, they are highly sought after by Republicans and Democrats. But it is no easy task to reach out to the independent voters. They are not inclined to spend a lot of time and effort seeking information about the elections, and they are not highly motivated, because many feel that voting does not change anything.

INDEPENDENTS' DISTRUST OF GOVERNMENT

One of the reasons that independents shy away from political news may be that the whole topic of government has been a big disappointment to them. In fact, political scientists have often pointed to a relationship between increases in political distrust and the growth of independent voters. Lipset and Schneider (1983) found that the time in which Americans began to voice deep distrust in government was the 1970s, the same decade when people started to gravitate away from the parties and into independent status. Keith and co-authors (1992) have disputed that claim, indicating that there is an unimpressive correlation between Americans' distrust of government and their self-characterization as independent voters. But more recently, Stanley Greenberg's *Middle Class Dreams* (1995) has shown that many of Ross Perot's supporters in the 1992 presidential campaign were independents with a deep distrust of government. Greenberg (p. 254) describes the Perot voters in this fashion: "They stood out, however, in their intense antigovernment and antiestablishment views. Neither Democrats nor Republicans will reach these voters unless they find a way to break through the fog of populist, political alienation."

We can look to independents themselves for evidence of their relatively negative attitudes toward government. The four-question "Trust in Government Index" of the University of Michigan offers a good

TABLE 3-5   TRUST IN GOVERNMENT BY VOTERS

	Independents	Democrats	Republicans
People Running Federal Government			
Quite a few are crooked	49%	37%	36%
Not many are crooked	38	45	50
Hardly any are crooked	11	15	13
Don't know	2	3	1
How Federal Government Is Run			
Few big interests	77%	72%	70%
Benefit of all the people	17	23	25
Don't know	6	5	5
Federal Government Wastes Tax Money			
Wastes a lot	69%	62%	68%
Wastes some	29	33	29
Doesn't waste very much	2	5	3

SOURCE: PPIC Statewide Survey, September, October, and December 1998, all adults.

starting point. As Table 3-5 shows, independents are highly distrustful
of government.[6] They are more negative than major-party voters in
their views about honesty in government. Nearly half of independents
(49%) think that quite a few people running the government are
crooked. Democrats (37%) and Republicans (36%) are much less likely
to believe this. Independents are slightly more likely than Democrats
and Republicans to say that the government is pretty much run by a
few big interests looking out for themselves, and they are just as likely
as Republicans and a little more likely than Democrats to say that the
government wastes a lot of the taxpayers' money. As for overall trust,
28 percent of independents say they can trust the federal government to
do what is right always or most of the time, compared with 38 percent
of Democrats and 25 percent of Republicans.

Similar questions on distrust from the Pew Research Center showed
the same pattern of responses. Independents here also gave low ratings

6. Multiple regressions controlling for age, income, region, gender, and race and ethnicity indicate that independents are significantly more distrustful of government than
major-party voters. This trend is evident in the following B's and significance levels from the
final regression equations including all variables: trust government = −10 (.001); government is crooked = −.16 (.001); government waste = −.10 (.001); trust government = −.15
(.001); government run for people = −.09 (.001).

to the trustworthiness of elected officials. Only 44 percent agreed with the statement "Most elected officials are trustworthy," while 55 percent did not agree. By contrast, a majority of Democrats (58%) and Republicans (54%) felt that most elected officials were trustworthy. Moreover, 67 percent of independents agreed with the statement "When something is run by the government it is usually wasteful and inefficient." Democrats (58%) were less likely to hold this view of the federal government, while the Republicans (69%) were just as likely as independents to have negative perceptions.

Next, we look at two questions from the "Government Responsiveness Index" of the University of Michigan. Independents have a distinctly negative opinion about the government's responsiveness to its citizens. Independents (64%) are less likely than Republicans (75%) or Democrats (75%) to think that the government pays a good deal or some attention to what the people think when it decides what to do. About one-third of independents (36%) feel that having elections makes the government pay a good deal of attention to what the people think, compared with 46 percent of Republicans and 48 percent of Democrats. These results fit with earlier findings on why independents don't vote as regularly in elections, with many indicating that "elections don't change things." Their perception of government unresponsiveness explains their disinterest in politics.

Responses to the two questions from the "Political Efficacy Index" of the University of Michigan indicate that independents do not feel more powerless than the major-party voters, although it is notable how negative all of the respondents are. Forty-four percent of independents agreed that "people like me don't have any say about what the government does," similar to the Republicans (47%) and Democrats (44%). Fifty-six percent of independents agreed that "public officials don't care much what people like me think," and a slight majority of Republicans (53%) and Democrats (52%) also viewed themselves as having very little influence over the government's actions.

The reactions of independents were negative when the political efficacy issue was directed toward elected officials. Using a question from a national survey by the Pew Research Center (1998a), we found that 44 percent of independents in California agreed that "most elected officials care what people like me think"; about half of the Democrats (49%) and Republicans (52%) held this view. Similar to the results for the government responsiveness issue, independents hold elected officials in low regard.

I also considered the possibility that independents might be more likely than others to distrust their state government. The evidence was mixed, as it was for the questions on the level of trust in federal government. Independents (74%) are more likely to think that the state government is run for the benefit of a few big interests looking out for themselves, compared with the Republicans (66%) and Democrats (64%). Only about one in five independents believes that the state government is run for the benefit of all the people. However, independents (55%) are no different from Republicans (56%) in believing that the people in state government waste "a lot" of the taxpayers' money, and Democrats (50%) are just about as cynical in this regard. As for trusting the state government in Sacramento to do what is right, 38 percent of independents said they feel that this is true "always" or "most of the time," which is similar to the response for the Democrats (40%) and actually a little more upbeat compared with the Republicans (33%).

Further evidence that independents are no more cynical than others about state government is found in the response to a question we asked about performance. When asked, "How much confidence do you have in the governor and state legislature when it comes to their ability to solve the state's most important problems?" two in three independents said they had a great deal (7%) or only some (59%) confidence, and one-third said they had very little (23%) or none (10%). Two in three Republicans also said they had a great deal (9%) or only some (61%) confidence in the state government's problem-solving abilities, while three in four Democrats had a great deal (15%) or only some (58%) confidence.

Independents are distinctly different from major-party voters in the level of government they trust the most. They appear to favor the local level, where elections are required to be held on a nonpartisan basis, over the state and federal levels, where the races are dominated by Republican and Democratic candidates jockeying for political power. One of the statewide surveys asked, "What level of government do you trust the most to solve problems of concern to you?" Fifty-two percent of the independents named their city or county government, 37 percent mentioned their state government or federal government, and 10 percent gave other responses. By contrast, Democrats were more confident in the state and federal governments (51%) than in city and county governments (42%). The Republicans were evenly split between favoring city or county government (47%) and the federal or state government (45%).

There are more indications of the fact that many independent voters are uncomfortable with the power of the major parties in their responses to questions about the state legislature and governor. We asked respondents if they thought it was better for California to have a governor who comes from the same political party that controls the state legislature or better to have the governor from one party and the state legislature controlled by another. Voters are generally ambivalent about having a divided government, and the findings are not statistically significant. However, independents show a slight preference for divided government (38% to 32%), while Democrats and Republicans would slightly prefer to have one-party ruling. Most independents (63%) also feel that term limits for state legislators has been a good thing for California; one in five believes it has made no difference, and very few think that term limits has been a bad thing for the state. Republicans are also very supportive of term limits, while Democrats are the most likely to feel that it has been a bad thing. Of course, the Republicans thought they would gain seats and the Democrats believed they would lose seats in the Democratically controlled legislature. For independents, many believe that shaking the status quo of political power by the parties is beneficial in and of itself.

Overall, independent voters are quite cynical about politicians, political parties, and elections. They are more likely than Democrats or Republicans to call politicians crooked and to perceive them as untrustworthy. They are more likely to feel that the state and federal governments are run by a few big interests. They are less likely to think that elections make the government more responsive to the people. They are not consistently different from the major political parties on all measures of distrust, but then Californians as a whole are quite disenchanted with government. The independent voters' negative views on government are a disincentive to spending time and energy on learning about politics and voting in elections.

INDEPENDENTS AND GOVERNMENT INVOLVEMENT

The cynical views held by independent voters should translate to a certain perspective on what level and type of government involvement they prefer. As stated earlier, they fit the demographic profile of the "New Political Culture" (Clark and Inglehart, 1998). They tend to be young, affluent, highly educated homeowners with suburban residences. By definition, they are not attached to any political party. We have also identified them as politically centrist, with the strongest tendency to be middle-of-the-road to somewhat conservative. Independents choose their policy preferences on an issue-by-issue basis rather than according to a political ideology. However, their distrust of politicians and government suggests that they prefer a limited role for government that does not interfere in their daily lives. We thus expect independents to be liberal on social issues and conservative on fiscal issues. The "New Popular Culture" is known for its liberal-conservative mix of policy preferences, including pro-environment, anti–welfare spending, and pro-choice on abortion. This political profile, as noted in Chapter 2, reflects Californians in general. Independent voters have consistent political leanings in this direction, with views on specific issues often falling between the more liberal Democrats and the more conservative Republicans.

Independents do in fact feel very strongly that government ought not to be involved in limiting personal freedom.[7] As shown in Table 3-6, seven in ten independents say that the choice on abortion should be left up to the woman and her doctor. Democrats (73%) are equally pro-choice on abortion, reflecting their liberal orientation, while only half of Republicans (53%) think that the choice on abortion should be left up to the woman and her doctor. Independents hold similar positions on other civil liberties as well, such as feeling strongly that homosexuality as a lifestyle should be accepted by society (58%). Again, these attitudes are more aligned with the Democrats (64%). Among the Republicans, 55 percent think that homosexuality should be discouraged.

On some issues of government involvement, the independents show more ambivalence in their responses. For instance, independents have mixed feelings about the need for government regulation of business, while Republicans and Democrats are more polarized on this issue. As shown in Table 3-6, an equal number of independents say that government regulation of business is necessary to protect the public interest (48%) as say that government regulation of business does more harm than good (47%). The majority of Democrats (60%) say that regulations are necessary for the public good, while the majority of Republicans (55%) say regulations do more harm than good. However, independents are much more definitively in favor of environmental protection than ei-

7. Independents did not have significantly different attitudes toward the role of government after age, income, region, gender, and race and ethnicity were accounted for in multiple regressions. These findings of nonsignificance reflect the fact that the independents' policy preferences often fall between the more liberal views of Democrats and the more conservative views of Republicans.

TABLE 3-6   ROLE OF GOVERNMENT FOR VOTERS

	Independents	Democrats	Republicans
Abortion			
Choice left up to woman and her doctor	68%	73%	53%
Illegal in some cases	20	19	34
Illegal in all circumstances	10	8	12
Don't know	2	0	1
Government Regulation of Business			
Regulation necessary to protect public	48%	60%	43%
Regulation does more harm than good	47	37	55
Don't know	5	3	2
Increasing Taxes versus Social Spending			
More on social programs, increase taxes	49%	65%	31%
Reduce taxes, less on social programs	43	31	64
Don't know	8	4	5

SOURCE: PPIC Statewide Survey, May 1998, all adults.

ther the Democrats or the Republicans. Nearly seven in ten independents (68%) say that environmental laws and regulations are worth the cost, with three in ten (29%) saying that environmental laws and regulations cost too many jobs and hurt the economy. Fewer Democrats (62%) and Republicans (52%) think that environmental laws are worthwhile. In terms of environmental attitudes, independents once again fit the profile of the "New Political Culture."

As shown in Table 3-6, independents are also divided on the issue of reducing taxes versus increasing spending on social programs such as Social Security and health care. Independents are more fiscally conservative than Democrats, most of whom want spending increased (65%), while more Republicans want to reduce taxes (64%).

The ambivalence of independent voters on tax and spending issues is also evident in attitudes toward government assistance for the poor. Three in four independents agree that "poor people have become too dependent on government assistance programs," yet six in ten agree that "it is the responsibility of government to take care of people who can't take care of themselves." When they are asked if "the government is spending too much on programs to help the poor," about the same number of independents think it is (42%) as think it is not (46%). By contrast, most Republicans (59%) think the government is spending too much on the poor, while most Democrats (65%) think it is not. Clearly, many independents see a role for government in helping out individuals who are in poverty.

As for government involvement in another controversial arena, affirmative action, the opinions of independents are more divided than those of the major-party voters. Republicans (43%) are the most likely to want affirmative action programs to end, independent voters (23%) are less likely to want them to end, and the Democrats (14%) are the least likely to want them to end. Almost half of the Democrats (48%) want affirmative action to continue, compared with 39 percent of independents and only 17 percent of Republicans. The major-party voters are more likely to have reached consensus, either for or against affirmative action. The independents are divided between immediately ending, phasing out, and continuing these programs.

Independents are more likely to say that all people in California have an equal opportunity to get ahead than to want the government to become involved in guaranteeing all Californians an equal opportunity to succeed (53% to 43%). By contrast, most Democrats say the government should do more (55%), while most Republicans believe that all Californians have an equal opportunity to succeed (70%). Thus, independents are once again ambivalent about government involvement in social issues.

There is strong support among independents, however, for outreach efforts that fall short of the conventional definition of affirmative action programs. Independents (63%) agree with Democrats (67%) in favoring employer and college outreach programs for minorities, while a majority of Republicans (52%) are opposed to such efforts. Likewise, Democrats (74%) and independents (65%) want special programs to assist minorities in competing for college admissions, while most Republicans (52%) do not.

Independents have much in common with Democrats and Republicans when it comes to tax and spending issues related to public education. Schools were among the top policy issues when we were conducting the surveys, so they offer a good test of public sentiment about a state fiscal issue (see Jeffe, 1998b). Voters give high priority to state spending on public schools. All of the voter groups are also in favor of the school vouchers concept. Republicans (63%) are strongly behind state tax-supported vouchers, so that parents can send their children to any school they choose, and a majority of Democrats (52%) and independents (53%) are also in favor of vouchers. However, voter support for moderating the supermajority requirement (i.e., two-thirds vote) to raise local school taxes does not reach a majority among independents (40%), Republicans (32%), or Democrats (46%).

All three groups also place a high value on state tax cuts. When asked about the $1.4 billion tax cut that was approved by the governor and state legislature for 1998–1999, four in ten Republicans (42%), independents (39%), and Democrats (39%) said it was very important to them. About four in ten independents said the state tax cut was somewhat important, while two in ten said it was not important. The independents are thus similar to other voters in wanting tax cuts and in opposing a relaxation of tax restrictions.

In sum, independent voters are liberal on social issues and conservative on fiscal issues. Their attitudes are generally in line with those of average California voters. But they do not fit a political pattern and appear to be more concerned about issues than ideology. Their opinions on a range of subjects are moderate, making them more conservative than Democrats and more liberal than Republicans. The more ideological positions of either party would offend the centrist politics of many independents, which explains why many candidates from the two major parties moderate their positions to attract these "swing voters."

INDEPENDENTS AND THEIR CHOICES

The survey responses show that California's independent voters are not very enthusiastic about politics. They don't trust government, and they don't care what the big or small political parties say. Many are dubious that their showing up to vote in elections will make a difference. In 1998, they were confronted with their first ever open primary in June and a chance to determine the outcome of the November election. Candidates from both parties tried to woo their votes. We look now at how the independents went about making choices in the high-profile race for governor.

When we first checked in with independents, most were paying little or no attention to the California election news.[8] In the early spring,

---

8. The percentages from the statewide survey reported in this section are based on the total sample of registered voters, rather than all adults or likely voters.

only 6 percent were very closely following California political stories, while 25 percent were fairly closely following the election news. They apparently knew of little else but television ads by Al Checchi and Jane Harman; these were seen by two-thirds of the independents, and they are probably the main reason one-third of the independents told us they would vote for Checchi or Harman. At that time, more independents preferred an outsider with business experience over an insider with experience in elected office (44% to 33%), similar to Republicans (50% to 35%) but different from Democrats, who favored insiders over outsiders (55% to 30%). Most independents also told us that they didn't mind the fact that wealthy candidates, such as Checchi and Harman, were using their own millions to fund their political campaigns.

The attentiveness of independents was slight even a month before the primary. In the May 1998 survey, only 6 percent were closely following the election news, while one-third were now fairly closely following these stories. Most of what they knew was still what they saw on television from Checchi and Harman. Seven in ten recalled these ads the most, while only 5 percent said they remembered the Davis and Lungren ads the most. However, commercials were no longer making a positive impression on independents. They were now divided as to whether they preferred outsider (41%) or insider (41%) status as a candidate quality, and they slightly favored candidates collecting campaign contributions (44%) as opposed to spending their own money (39%). They now favored the insiders—Davis and Lungren—over the outsiders—Checchi and Harman—by a 2-to-1 margin.

Independent voters who went to the open primary gave three-quarters of their votes to the Democratic gubernatorial candidates. Four in ten supported Davis, one in five voted for Lungren and Harman, and 13 percent voted for Checchi. When asked what they thought of the open primary, most said they liked it because it allowed them to vote for the candidate of their choice (59%) or because they thought it was fairer to allow all voters to vote in all races (33%). Only about one-third said the governor's race had brought them out to vote. The same number cited Proposition 227 (28%), while fewer mentioned Proposition 226 (21%) and the U.S. Senate race (11%). One clue as to why they wanted to stay with the insider politicians lies in the fact that two in three thought that the state was going in the right direction. But in keeping with their antigovernment image, two in three also said that it was time for a change to the Democrats, rather than having the Republicans hold the office for four more years. Independents wanted to rock the boat in 1998, but only a little (Los Angeles Times/CNN Poll, 1998).

By the early fall, independent voters were again oblivious to the news about the upcoming general election. Only 6 percent were very closely following the election news, and 17 percent were fairly closely following it. Three in ten had seen ads for the governor's race in the past month. Only 20 percent said that the recent debate by the candidates had helped them in deciding whom to vote for in the governor's race. Independents slightly favored Davis (37%) over Lungren (31%) at the time, but one-quarter had not made up their minds. In typically independent-minded fashion, six in ten said that the candidate's stand on the issues is what mattered most to them in deciding whom to vote for in the governor's race. Only one in six ranked "character" as their primary concern. This was a rejection of the theme that Lungren and the Republicans were try-ing to use against the Democrats in the wake of the Clinton scandal and impeachment. For independents, with their consistently negative views of politicians, hearing one politician claiming to have higher moral charac-ter than another probably just sounded like foolishness.

A month before the general election, more independents were focus-ing on the governor's race. Still, half of them were not closely follow-ing the election news. Only 8 percent were very closely following the election news, while 36 percent said they were fairly closely following it. More than half recalled seeing the television ads by the candidates, with equal numbers saying they mostly recalled the commercials for Davis (23%) and for Lungren (24%). Only about one in five said that the ongoing debates were helping them to determine whom to support. Independents continued to overwhelmingly cite "stand on the issues" (59%) rather than "character" (19%) as the reason they would favor one statewide candidate over another. They overwhelmingly cited the schools (33%) as the issue they most wanted the candidates to talk about before the November election, with all other issues ranking a dis-tant second. Independents were particularly undisturbed by the Clinton-Lewinsky sex scandal, with most saying it would make no dif-ference in their inclination to vote or their support for Democratic ver-sus Republican candidates. By this point, Davis was heavily favored over Lungren (48% to 31%), although 18 percent of independents were still undecided.

Independent voters were in a positive mood as they went to the polls in November. Seven in ten thought the state was going in the right di-rection, and most thought the California economy would stay the same

(50%) or get better (36%) in the year ahead. They chose Davis over Lungren by more than a 2-to-1 margin, citing a focus on education issues and candidate qualifications as factors in their choice, with the Clinton-Lewinsky matter not a factor. Independents were most likely to say that the governor's race (50%) was the motivating factor for turning out for the election; one-third said it was the U.S. Senate race, one-quarter named Proposition 5 (the Indian gaming initiative), and another quarter named other state propositions (Los Angeles Times Poll, 1998).

The 1998 election for governor provides an enlightening case for studying the voting behavior of independents. They are not very focused on elections. As a reflection of their relative youthfulness, they do not read newspapers or watch television news as much as older voters. Many gain their negative views and positive impressions from paid commercials rather than objective news sources. Independents are more interested in having the candidates discuss the issues of concern to them, and they reject those who focus on character and personality or partisan differences. In good economic times, independents will go with political insiders who are likely to rock the boat only gently. But they also have an antigovernment inclination that could lead them, in bad economic times, to favor the outsiders who use their own money to challenge the political establishment. This explains why independent voters have become such a powerful force in California.

THE INITIATIVE PROCESS

One of the distinguishing features of California elections is the important role played by citizens' initiatives. California is not the only state where residents can vote on policy initiatives placed on the ballot by interested citizens. But in recent times, in nowhere else in the United States have there been as many controversial initiatives appearing on the ballot and so much money spent trying to pass or defeat them. The importance of this issue is reflected in a vast new scholarly literature on initiatives (see Bowler and Donovan, 1998; Bowler, Donovan, and Tolbert, 1998; Cain and Noll, 1995; Cain et al., 1995; Ferejohn, 1995; Gerber, 1995, 1998; Lupia, 1998). The use of initiatives has grown rapidly since the passage of Proposition 13 in 1978. Distrust in government has also been increasing over the past two decades. Indeed, the growing use of initiatives seems to be a major consequence of the feeling by California voters that their elected officials are not capable of solving the state's problems. But as initiatives have increased in use, so have complaints about the initiative process itself.

INITIATIVES AND HOW THEY GREW

The citizens' initiative was created during the "progressive era" of state government. In a special election in the fall of 1911, voters passed a series of reforms to the state constitution, including the initiative, the referendum, and the recall. The reforms were passed in response to the widespread corruption that was perceived in relation to the strong influence over state politicians by the powerful railroads. The initiative allowed the voters to pass new state laws or amend the state constitution, the referendum provided voters with an opportunity to repeal existing state laws, and the recall allowed voters to remove an elected official. By far, the initiative has been the most commonly used tool of state government reform. To appear on the ballot, an initiative must be reviewed by the attorney general; then petitions are circulated and a minimum number of signatures are needed. A statutory initiative requires fewer signatures than a constitutional amendment. An initiative can then qualify for a state primary, a general election, or, in rare circumstances, a special election (Schrag, 1998).

Initiatives were used quite frequently in the early decades after this process was instituted. There were 100 state propositions between 1912 and 1939 (see Table 3-7). They were not very successful: only 28 of the 100 were passed by the voters. Then, for three decades, the initiative fell out of favor as a tool for state policymaking. Only 42 propositions appeared on the ballot between 1940 and 1969, and they remained unpopular, with only 11 passed by the voters. The use of initiatives has climbed in each of the three decades since the 1960s. There were 24 propositions on the ballot in the 1970s, 44 in the 1980s, and 69 in the 1990s. Fewer than 1 in 3 passed in the 1970s, but the success rate was nearly 1 in 2 in the 1980s and 1990s.

During the 1990s, initiatives have played a much greater role in policymaking. There have been 279 state propositions since the process was begun in the early twentieth century. About half of all the state propositions have been placed on the ballot in the past 30 years. The 1990s alone account for one-quarter of all the state propositions that Californians have ever had the opportunity to vote on. Ninety-nine state propositions have passed since 1912, all but a few being citizens' initiatives that qualified through petitions signed by the state's voters as opposed to being placed on the ballot by the legislature (DeBow and Syer, 1997). Two-thirds of all of the initiatives that have passed have appeared on the state ballot in the past three decades. About half of all the

TABLE 3-7   STATE PROPOSITIONS ON THE BALLOT

	Number on Ballot	Number Approved
1912–1919	30	8
1920–1929	33	10
1930–1939	37	10
1940–1949	20	6
1950–1959	12	2
1960–1969	10	3
1970–1979	24	7
1980–1989	44	21
1990–1999	69	32
Total	279	99

SOURCE: Lee (1997); California Secretary of State (1998a, 1998b).

initiatives that have passed can be found on the ballot since 1980. Perhaps most impressive, the state propositions that have passed since 1990 account for one-third of all of the changes in state laws and amendments to the state constitution since voters began approving initiatives over 85 years ago.

The growth of initiatives has not gone unnoticed by the California public. In our focus groups, we heard Californians say they feel overwhelmed with the propositions on the ballot. "California runs too many initiatives," said a Sacramento resident. "I think they put too many on at a time," said a San Francisco resident. "It's very time consuming to read all of the initiatives and understand them. . . . I don't have time to do that . . . so I'll watch TV . . . so the TV does all of this for you," said an Orange County resident. The large number of initiatives has become another reason why many people don't like to vote.

Why there are more initiatives on the ballot today than in the past is a point of contention. There are probably many reasons. Not the least among them is the feeling on the part of grassroots citizens' groups that the governor and state legislature are not responsive to their needs and are not competent at solving the state's problems. Special-interest groups place initiatives on the ballot as a way to get the laws they want without having to subject them to legislative scrutiny and compromise. Businesses have submitted "dueling propositions" whose purpose is to siphon off money and votes from initiatives that might cause them financial harm. State elected officials and candidates sometimes gather signatures and place initiatives on the ballot as a way of raising their profile as populist leaders and grandstanding their support for popular causes. Then there is the growth of the initiative business, a year-round industry of collecting signatures for initiative qualification, raising money, polling, producing commercials, and reaching voters through phone banks (see DeBow and Syer, 1997).

The initiatives that are appearing on the ballot differ significantly in their intentions and sponsors. Jack Citrin has identified these categories of initiatives among others: grassroots, program protection by government agencies, partisan conflict by the Republican and Democratic parties, self-promotion by politicians, and self-defense by industries. Of course, these vary in their popularity and support among voters. Initiatives can also vary in their political motivations, according to Citrin, including the "Trojan Horse," or hidden agenda; the pork barrel; "shootouts," or attempts by one industry to hurt another; the poison pill, or counterinitiative; and the preemptive strike against existing regulations (Lee, 1998, pp. 119–120). Many of these initiative efforts make voters even more cynical about elections.

The growth of initiatives in the 1980s and 1990s, and their increasing role in setting state policies, has corresponded with a phenomenal rise in expenditures. Gerber (1998) reports that spending reached a record $127 million in 1988, declined to $49 million in 1992 and to $45 million in 1994, and then set another record of $140 million in 1996. This was not only a function of the presence of more initiatives on the ballot; average spending on state propositions more than doubled between 1976 and 1996. In the November 1998 election, the California Voter Foundation reported that the campaigns raised more than $195 million to pass or defeat twelve state propositions (Associated Press, 1998). Nearly $89 million was spent to pass or defeat one measure (Proposition 5), with Indian tribes spending $63.2 million to pass it and Nevada gambling interests and labor unions spending $25.4 million to defeat it (Morain, 1999a). The vast majority of the funds are spent on 30-second television commercials, which have become a major source of information for the many California voters who think there are too many initiatives on the ballot to read and research on their own.

The "voter revolt" initiatives have flourished in an era in which big money and an "initiative industry" seem to have taken control of the electoral process (see Table 3-8). These grassroots efforts have shaken the state government, its elected officials, and the political establishment to the core. There seems to be little that special interests, even those with deep pockets, can do against the populist and antigovernment messengers. The voter revolt era began when Proposition 13 passed in June 1978. A little-

TABLE 3-8   VOTER REVOLT INITIATIVES

1978	Proposition 13	Sets tax limits for local governments
1988	Proposition 98	Earmarks spending for education
1990	Proposition 140	Sets term limits for state elected officials
1994	Proposition 187	Reduces public services to illegal immigrants
1996	Proposition 198	Establishes open primaries
1996	Proposition 209	Ends government affirmative action programs
1996	Proposition 218	Limits tax and fee increases by local government
1998	Proposition 227	Restricts bilingual education in public schools

SOURCE: Baldassare (1998); California Secretary of State (1998a); Legislative Analyst (1995a, 1995b, 1996a, 1996b).

known antitax activist, Howard Jarvis, was able to convince voters that their local governments should roll back property taxes and restrict tax hikes. But that was merely the beginning of the use of initiatives to extend the voter revolt into state and local government reform. A decade later voters passed Proposition 98, which forced the state legislature to set aside a specified amount of funding every year for the voters' favorite program—the public schools. In 1990, the voters turned their rage on the state legislators and constitutional officers, enacting consecutive-term limits in an effort to eradicate career politicians and entrenched power in Sacramento. In 1994, in an angry mood about a depressed economy and severe budget crisis, they voted for Proposition 187, which required their governments to severely restrict the public services received by illegal immigrants. The court ultimately ruled against this initiative, much to the disappointment of the voters. In 1996, voters passed Proposition 209, ending affirmative action programs in local and state government. The voters struck again in 1996 with Proposition 218, which closes some of the loopholes left by Proposition 13 by making it more difficult for local government to increase taxes and fees. In the 1998 election, voters took school policy into their own hands by passing Proposition 227, restricting bilingual education programs in public schools.

CALIFORNIANS' LOVE-HATE
RELATIONSHIP WITH INITIATIVES

Californians have an abiding faith in the citizens' initiative process, despite all of its flaws. This comes from their deep distrust of government and dislike of elected officials. When asked which is the best way to address the most important problems facing the state today, Californians by a 3-to-1 margin chose initiatives over reliance on the governor and

TABLE 3-9   INITIATIVES AND STATE GOVERNMENT

"What do you think is the best way to address the most important problems facing California today? (a) The governor and the state legislature should decide what to do and pass state laws. (b) California voters should decide what to do by bringing citizens' initiatives to the ballot box and passing them."

	Total	Democrats	Republicans	Independents
Governor and legislature	21%	22%	27%	16%
Citizens' initiatives	75	75	69	80
Don't know	4	3	4	4

SOURCE: PPIC Statewide Survey, December 1998, all adults.

the state legislature to pass laws (see Table 3-9). Although every voter group favors the initiative process, independents (80% to 16%) favor initiatives over legislative action by a larger margin than the Republicans (69% to 27%) or the Democrats (75% to 22%).

Latinos have had more unpleasant experiences with the initiative process than any other ethnic or racial group in recent years. They opposed three initiatives that the state's voters passed into law: Proposition 187, which reduced public services to illegal immigrants; Proposition 209, which ended affirmative action programs in state and local government; and Proposition 227, which restricted bilingual education programs in the public schools. Nonetheless, only 18 percent of Latinos chose reliance on the governor and legislature as the best way to address the state's important problems; 79 percent preferred the initiative process.

The initiative process receives this strong support because in addition to their general distrust of government and dislike for elected officials, voters believe that the governor and legislature simply can't get the job done. When it comes to solving the state's most important problems, only 11 percent of the people have a great deal of confidence in the state's executive and legislative branches of government. Six in ten say they have only some confidence, while three in ten have little or no confidence. Independent voters (34%) are more likely than either Democrats (27%) or Republicans (28%) to say they have very little or no confidence in the problem-solving abilities of the state's elected officials.

Californians have a love-hate relationship with initiatives, however, when asked to evaluate them solely in terms of the voting process and without relation to the legislative alternative. They value initiatives for addressing important public policy issues but readily admit that the process has problems and shortcomings.

TABLE 3-10   CONFLICTING FEELINGS ABOUT INITIATIVES

	Agree	Disagree	Don't Know
Citizens' initiatives bring up important public policy issues	73%	22%	7%
Citizens' initiatives are often complicated and confusing	79	17	4
Citizen's initiatives reflect the concerns of special interests, not average residents	78	18	4

SOURCE: PPIC Statewide Survey, October 1998, all adults.

Seven in ten residents agree that citizens' initiatives highlight important public policy issues that the governor and state legislature have not adequately addressed (see Table 3-10). However, as a signal of their lukewarm endorsement, fewer than one-quarter strongly agree with this view, while half agree only somewhat that initiatives tackle important issues. Among voters, the independents (70%), Democrats (74%), and Republicans (76%) agree equally that initiatives bring up important unresolved issues.

But negative opinions also arise, indicating that the recent experiences with initiatives have not always been good. Eight in ten residents think that the ballot wording for citizens' initiatives is often too complicated to provide an understanding of exactly what will happen if an initiative passes. Nearly half strongly agree with this criticism. Among the voters, there are no differences in agreement with this criticism of the initiative process among the independents (80%), Democrats (80%), and Republicans (83%).

Sounding another negative note, and reflecting the reality of many recent state propositions, eight in ten residents believe that citizens' initiatives usually represent the concerns of organized special interests rather than the concerns of average California residents. One in three strongly hold this view, and about half somewhat agree with this perspective. Among voters, there is uniformity of opinion that initiatives reflect special interests among the independents (80%), Democrats (83%), and Republicans (77%).

In focus groups, we also heard that Californians like the initiatives concept but find their recent experiences with them to be troubling. "It's a good process for the people to vote rather than have the legislature do it," said a Los Angeles resident. "I think sometimes it's confusing . . . a yes means a no and a no means a yes," said a Fresno resident.

"It should be just plain language that somebody can read and you understand and you make your decision," added a San Francisco resident. "It seems we all get excited about something passing . . . then it doesn't come true," said a San Diego resident.

AMBIVALENCE TOWARD INITIATIVE REFORMS

There has been no shortage of proposals aimed at reforming the state's initiative process as the complaints about the process have surfaced. The California Constitution Revision Commission (1996) called for three changes: (1) After an initiative has qualified for the ballot, allow the legislature to have a short period of time to add technical and clarifying amendments; then, if the proponents of the initiative agree, the measure is submitted to the voters as amended by the state legislature. (2) Provide fuller public review by placing constitutional amendments on the November ballot, when voter turnout at the polls is higher. (3) Allow the legislature, with gubernatorial approval, to amend statutory initiatives after they have been in effect for six years. To date, none of these reform proposals has been implemented.

The California Commission on Campaign Financing (1991) had these recommendations for change: limit the number of words in an initiative; require public hearings when an initiative qualifies for the ballot; make it more difficult to amend the state constitution; identify the major campaign contributors in all paid advertisements; improve the voter pamphlet information on initiatives; and reform the state court's review procedures. Again, these reform proposals have not been enacted to date.

We know from our surveys that Californians strongly favor involving the legislature in drafting citizens' initiatives. However, they are divided about allowing the legislature to change initiatives once they are passed. Both of these reforms were recommended by the State Constitution Revision Commission. By a 2-to-1 margin (63% to 29%), Californians favor allowing the legislature to hold hearings on an initiative and to adopt changes once the initiative has qualified for the ballot. There are no differences between independents (59%), Democrats (65%), and Republicans (61%) on this reform issue. Forty-four percent would allow the legislature to amend initiatives after they have been in effect for six years. About half of the independents (51%), Democrats (50%), and Republicans (53%) are opposed to this proposal for legislative review.

In general, Californians appear to view the initiative process as in need of some fixing. They would like to make it easier for voters. They don't want to go through the disappointing process of having something pass and then be struck down by the courts. But few see the initiative process as badly broken. Californians are certainly not prepared to let the governor and state legislature alter what the voters have passed.

PROPOSITION 13 IS STILL POPULAR

There is probably no better-known citizens' initiative in California history than Proposition 13. Not only has it reshaped the landscape for state and local government in California, but its presence has also changed the way people in other states and the nation as a whole have thought about government taxes and spending for the past 20 years (see Citrin, 1979; Lo, 1990; Sears and Citrin, 1982). We were interested in attitudes toward Proposition 13 because residents' perceptions of this antitax ballot measure will continue to affect people's general impressions about the initiative process in the state.

Proposition 13 touched off populist and antigovernment sentiments when it was discussed in our focus groups. But some see it as unfair. "It was wonderful . . . finest thing that ever happened," said a Los Angeles resident. "It keeps my taxes lower. . . . A lot of people who buy houses now don't think it's fair . . . but it works really well for me," said a Sacramento resident. "They said it would destroy our police, fire department, the library. . . . Well, it went through, and we still have the police, the fire, the library," observed a San Francisco resident. "I want it to continue . . . simply because I'm selfish. I'd like to keep my taxes at the rate they're at, but I don't think it's fair that I pay one-fourth the amount of taxes as someone who moves in now," remarked an Orange County resident.

Twenty years later, Californians evidently still strongly support Proposition 13 and its perceived effects. This measure limited the property tax rate to 1 percent and the growth of property tax increases to 2 percent annually until the property is sold. It also constrained the abilities of local governments to raise revenues. Some local government officials claim this constraint on tax revenues limits their abilities to provide residents with public services. Californians, however, do not share this perception.[9]

---

9. These results are generally confirmed in a survey reported by the Field Institute (1998), which found that voters would support Proposition 13 if it were up for a vote again (53% to 30%). Most voters also said they would oppose changing the supermajority vote needed for raising local taxes to a simple majority vote (53% to 40%).

TABLE 3-11   PROPOSITION 13
AFTER 20 YEARS

Effect of Property Tax Limitations	
Good effect	38%
No effect	27
Bad effect	23
Don't know	12

Effect of Two-thirds Vote to Pass Local Taxes	
Good effect	38%
No effect	28
Bad effect	22
Don't know	12

SOURCE: PPIC Statewide Survey, October 1998, all adults.

As Table 3-11 shows, only one in four Californians believes that the tax limits imposed by Proposition 13 have negatively affected the services provided by their local governments. The vast majority of residents, two in three, say that this tax-limiting feature has had no effect (27%) or a positive effect (38%). Republicans (47%) are more likely than independents (40%) and Democrats (32%) to believe that tax limitations have had a good effect on their services. Homeowners and renters have similar views on the effects of Proposition 13, even though homeowners benefit more directly from it.

Since the passage of Proposition 13, the state government has had the responsibility of dividing the property tax funds among the local governments that provide services. Some local government officials claim that this has taken away important local powers and has created a system that lacks fiscal accountability. Again, most Californians disagree with this view. A majority favor the arrangement of having property taxes collected at the local level and then having the state legislature and governor be responsible for dividing the tax money among local governments. Only one in three is opposed to the current system. Republicans (60%) strongly favor this Proposition 13 adaptation, while the Democrats (54%) and independents (48%) are more ambivalent.

Proposition 13 further limited the abilities of local governments to raise revenues by requiring that two-thirds of the voters rather than a simple majority approve all new taxes. Some local government officials argue that this high hurdle makes it virtually impossible to pass local taxes and to raise revenues needed to provide local services to residents. Once again, average Californians have a different perspective. Two-thirds of Californians believe that the supermajority vote for local taxes has had a neutral effect (28%) or a positive effect (38%) on the services provided to local residents, while about one in five say it has had a bad effect. Republicans (47%) are more likely than Democrats (33%) and independent voters (34%) to say that the supermajority has had a good effect on local services. The vast majority in all voter groups, however, think the two-thirds vote has been beneficial or made no difference.

Some have called for changing the supermajority vote so that local governments can have more control over their revenues. Given the widespread perception of its neutral or positive effects, it is not surprising that six in ten Californians strongly oppose changing the supermajority vote while four in ten are in favor of this reform. A majority of Republicans (59%), independents (59%), and Democrats (52%) do not want to make it easier for governments to raise local taxes at the ballot box.

Despite the general approval of Proposition 13, Californians readily admit that they have problems with its fairness. This was evident in both our focus groups, as noted earlier, and in responses to our survey questions. Because housing prices have escalated sharply in the 20 years since the passage of Proposition 13, recent home buyers often pay much more in property taxes than long-term homeowners in the same neighborhood. For this reason, new home buyers in older neighborhoods have complained that Proposition 13 has been unfair to them. Californians are generally sympathetic to this injustice. Six in ten say they are opposed to the fact that recent homeowners will pay much higher property taxes. Only about one in three are in favor of the way the property taxes are calculated. Republicans (48%) are evenly divided on this feature of Proposition 13, while independents (59%) and Democrats (63%) are strongly opposed. A narrow majority of homeowners (51%) oppose this aspect of the property tax system, while renters (72%) are strongly opposed. Those who bought their homes in the past five years (61%) are much more opposed to this feature of Proposition 13 than those who have owned their homes for 15 to 19 years (53%) or 20 or more years (38%).

The findings related to length of home ownership point to the uphill battle in reforming even a highly unpopular feature of Proposition 13. Many Californians consider the current system of unequal property tax payments for similar homes unjust, but most residents who bought their homes years ago simply do not want to pay higher taxes. In most cases, these are the white, older voters who tend to vote frequently and in high numbers in California elections. Whenever politicians talk about making changes to Proposition 13, as candidate Jane Harman

did briefly in the gubernatorial primary, they learn that they risk alienating a large group of likely voters. Proposition 13 remains a formid-
able force in California politics.

MAKING CHOICES ABOUT INITIATIVES

Californians are having a difficult time with citizens' initiatives these
days. They are confronted with too many of them on the ballot, and the
initiatives are hard to decipher, particularly for voters who admit to
being disinclined to study the issues deeply. Moreover, Californians have
become suspicious of those who draft the initiatives. They recognize, in
many cases, that special interests are trying to manipulate them and use
the initiative process to their own advantage. In the election season, voters are faced with a barrage of commercials attempting to sway their
opinions on a wide range of issues. In the 1998 elections, the state's voters encountered nine propositions in the June primary and twelve in the
November election. How do California voters make choices?

We look for answers in the survey questions concerning four of the
state propositions in the 1998 elections. We asked about two measures
on the June ballot, Propositions 226 and 227, and two measures on the
November ballot, Propositions 1a and 8. The voters' responses reveal
their struggles with these measures, which have become a part of the initiative process. The powerful influence of commercials is also evident.

Proposition 227, the "English Language in Public Schools" initiative,
was placed on the June ballot by a conservative Republican named Ron
Unz. It requires that all public school instruction be conducted in English.
It provides short-term placement in English immersion programs, for up
to a year, for children not fluent in English and $50 million for 10 years
for English tutoring. The initial reactions to this initiative from focus
group respondents were overwhelmingly positive. Simply put, they liked
Proposition 227 because they had strong feelings that all Americans
should speak English. "I think that people who immigrate to this country
should speak English," a San Francisco resident said. "I believe in an
English-speaking country," remarked a Fresno resident. "I feel this is
America and you should speak English," said an Orange County resident.

In our statewide survey in the early spring, Proposition 227 was supported by a 3-to-1 margin (75% to 21%).[10] It was widely favored

---

10. The percentages from the statewide survey reported in this section are based on
the total sample of registered voters, rather than all adults or likely voters.

TABLE 3-12   PROPOSITION 227: MAKING DECISIONS ON
                        SCHOOL POLICY

	April	May
Knowledge about Current Bilingual Education Programs in California's Public Schools		
Great deal	16%	18%
Fair amount	37	38
Little or nothing	47	44
Local School Districts Deciding on Bilingual Education Programs		
Approve	55%	52%
Disapprove	41	42
Don't know	5	6

SOURCE: PPIC Statewide Survey, April and May 1998, all adults.

among Democrats (69%), Republicans (85%), and independents (71%). The Latino voters were the most ambivalent (57%). It was also evident that the voters were responding to their desire to promote the speaking of English, rather than from knowledge about what represents sound educational policy. Only one in six knew a great deal about bilingual education programs in California's schools, about one-third a fair amount, and almost half little or nothing. Moreover, the voters supported the statewide mandate for bilingual education reform while saying that they believed discussions about bilingual education should be made at the local level (see Table 3-12).

Proposition 227 was winning by more than a 2-to-1 margin a month before the election. Democrats (57%), Republicans (80%), and independents (64%) were still overwhelmingly in favor of this initiative; Latinos (48%) were now equally divided. What was most remarkable is that the survey showed that the initiative had not significantly stimulated knowledge about the pros and cons of bilingual education in California. When people were asked how much they knew about bilingual education, the results were virtually the same as they were in the earlier survey. Nor were residents any more inclined to support the state government over the local government in deciding school policy, although they favored Proposition 227. It was all about wanting Californians to speak English.

On election day, Proposition 227 passed by 61 percent to 39 percent. Democrats narrowly opposed Proposition 227 (53%), but its victory was secured because independents (59%) and Republicans (77%) were strongly in favor. The Latinos turned against this initiative by almost a 2-to-1 margin (63%), but the more numerous whites supported it by a similar margin (67%). Only liberals opposed the measure, while both moderates and conservatives favored an end to bilingual education by wide margins (Los Angeles Times/CNN Poll, 1998).

Proposition 226, the "Political Contributions by Union Members" initiative, placed on the June ballot by Governor Wilson and other Republicans, required unions to obtain permission from their members before using dues for political contributions. Because unions are a major funding source for Democratic candidates, and Republicans get little money from unions, this was a campaign reform measure with an agenda. Proposition 226 had received a mixed reaction in our focus groups, with some liking the freedom to choose, others suspicious of the motives, and some admittedly unaware of the political impact. "I don't think employees or unions have the right to decide where I give my money," said a San Diego resident. "This does not provide an equal playing field, because some candidates do get money from corporations," said a San Francisco respondent. "I would want to know who is funding it," said a Sacramento respondent.

Proposition 226 was supported by more than a 2-to-1 margin (67%) in the early spring. Californians obviously liked the idea of union members having control of how their money was being used and did not seem to be focusing on the political implications. Democrats (58%), independents (71%), and Republicans (69%) all strongly favored Proposition 226. But there were signs that the voters were ambivalent about this issue. For instance, when asked whether they would favor a similar requirement that corporations obtain permission from their stockholders before using corporate funds for political contributions, voters were strongly in favor (76%). Moreover, they were divided about placing restrictions on labor unions' contributions to political candidates and ballot measures (50% to 43%), even though that was the effect of Proposition 226.

Support for Proposition 226 showed a decline a month before the election. This was largely because a partisan split had surfaced. Fifty-nine percent were now in favor and 33 percent were opposed. Fewer than half of the Democrats now said they would vote yes on Proposition 226 (48% to 43%), while it was still strongly supported by the Republicans (73% to 20%) and the independents (58% to 33%). Only a bare majority thought it was a good idea to place restrictions on labor unions' contributions to political candidates and ballot initiatives

(50% to 44%). Once again, more Californians wanted restrictions on corporate contributions in elections (55% to 39%). Certainly, these would be the campaign messages to use, if the Democrats and unions wanted to sow seeds of doubt. Money was no object for either side in this high-stakes political battle.

Proposition 226 was defeated by a relatively narrow margin, 47 percent to 53 percent, in the June primary. Most notable is the fact that the campaign advertising had created a highly partisan split, with overwhelming support by Republicans (72%) and similarly strong opposition by Democrats (72%), with independents narrowly more opposed (55%). Liberals strongly opposed the measure, moderates were divided, and conservatives were very supportive. The initiative had been redefined from its original perception of having to do with "fairness" and "personal control" to its real purpose of political gains for the Republicans at the Democrats' expense. Independents were thus the most ambivalent about the outcome (Los Angeles Times/CNN Poll, 1998).

We also followed Proposition 1a, the $9.2 billion bond measure for construction and repair of public schools, colleges, and universities that was placed on the November ballot by the state legislature. It was intended for the primary, but a political battle over some of its provisions delayed its appearance on the ballot. Throughout 1998, Californians rated education as their top issue. The response to this proposition was very positive in our focus groups, as many recognized the importance of better schools and few questioned the need for more school funds. "I think it would facilitate the goal of smaller class sizes," said one San Francisco respondent. "It's needed. Schools are falling down," said a Fresno resident. "I'm not even sure what a bond is, but these kids need money," said a Sacramento resident. "There's a great need," said an Orange County resident. But, as might be expected, there were those who were against more government spending. "Nine zeros is a lot of zeros," said a Los Angeles resident regarding the multi-billion-dollar bond. "I have an inkling to vote no because so much of the school's money has been misused," said a San Diego resident.

Support for Proposition 1a was more than 2-to-1 (70%) two months before the election. Democrats (82%) and independents (73%) were strongly in favor of the school bond, while a majority of Republicans (56%) said they would vote yes. The strong support was fueled by the perception that the current state funding for public schools was inadequate. Two in three said that the public schools are not getting enough funding from the state. About one-quarter said there was just enough funding, and only 10 percent thought that the current level of funding was more than enough. The perception of inadequate funding was found in all voter groups.

A month before the election, supporters still outnumbered opponents of the proposition by a 2-to-1 margin (66% to 22%). There were no signs of weakening support among the Democrats (76%), independents (69%), or Republicans (55%). While $6.7 billion of the $9.2 billion would go to the public schools, about $2.5 billion was earmarked for public colleges and universities. Although Californians are most concerned about K-12 public schools, the prospect of increased funding for higher education appeared to be helping rather than hurting support for Proposition 1a. Half said that higher education was not getting enough funding, about one-quarter said it had just enough, and fewer than one in ten said it had more than enough money.

In the November election, Proposition 1a won by 63 percent to 37 percent. Californians overcame their antigovernment feelings and supported the largest state bond measure in history for several reasons. First, this was about issuing state bonds and not raising taxes, so it did not elicit an extreme reaction from fiscal conservatives. Second, this state measure called for the bond money to be spent for the sole purpose of improving schools, the issue most Californians perceived as the state's biggest problem. Finally, there was hardly any visible opposition to Proposition 1a through television commercials, so the voters had little negative information to move them to vote no.

We also followed Proposition 8, the "Public Schools" initiative on the November ballot. Its overwhelming defeat offers a stark contrast to the success of Proposition 1a. Supported by Governor Wilson, this initiative called for permanent class size reduction, parent-teacher councils, improvements in teacher credentialing and evaluation, a state office of chief inspector of public schools, and student suspension for drug possession.

Two months before the election, there was overwhelming support for Proposition 8 (72%). The reason this measure was so popular with the voters was because two in three Californians thought that class size reduction was making a "big difference" in helping children learn reading, writing, and arithmetic. However, only one month later, fewer than half (48% to 43%) said they would vote yes on Proposition 8. The reason for the declining support was that fewer than half of Californians thought that the other elements of this multifaceted initiative would make a big difference in improving the quality of education. These included the provisions to impose new teacher credential requirements

(48%), establish parent-teacher councils (38%), and create a chief inspector of public schools (12%).

Proposition 8 lost by 63 percent to 37 percent in the November election—a reverse image of the huge win by Proposition 1a. How could a
school reform initiative that included popular class size reductions
draw such a negative reaction when a school bond measure won on the
same ballot? It is because the teachers' unions disliked certain elements
of the measure and spent millions of dollars on television commercials
pointing out the unpopular aspects of the initiative, such as the schools
inspector, while the Proposition 8 supporters did not match their efforts
with television commercials. The opponents were able to raise doubts,
even for a popular issue. One reason they were able to do this was because the voters had become suspicious of the motives and implications
of any multifaceted initiative.

CONCLUSIONS AND IMPLICATIONS

Californians' lack of confidence in government is representative of the recent national trends. What is unique is that the political distrust is expressing itself in ways that have profound implications for how decisions
will be made about the state's future. The voters have shown a strong desire to disengage themselves from the political parties who choose their
statewide candidates and the governor and legislature who make their
state laws. Specifically, they have opted for "open primaries" to select the
party standard-bearers for statewide office, have increasingly chosen to
register as independents, and have relied on a dizzying array of citizens'
initiatives to create new and far-reaching state policies. The voters have
taken on more of the burdens of governing from the established political
institutions—just at a time when many demanding issues are confronting
a growing and changing California. The future is more in the hands of the
people now than ever before, with political parties and elected representatives playing a diminished role. Has the latest incarnation of the voters'
revolt turned an alienated and cynical public to an electorate that is willing to commit the time and energy to governing California? Unfortunately,
no. And this adds to the litany of challenges facing the state.

The number of voters who are registered as independents has grown
at a rapid rate in the past three decades as voters have fled the two-
party structure. More people registered as independents than as either
Republicans or Democrats in the 1990s. In a state where neither of the
major parties has a majority, independents play a crucial role in elec-

tions. Independents tend to be young, affluent, highly educated, and suburban. They have not shown any party loyalties in the 1990s, switching back and forth between Republicans, Democrats, and representatives of other, smaller parties. Independents are driven to vote by issues rather than political ideology. They have a strong antigovernment sentiment and a negative opinion of politicians and elections. They stake out the middle ground between Republicans and Democrats on tax and spending issues, while they tend to be liberal on personal freedom and environmental issues. Most disturbing for the state's future, they are not highly tuned in to politics and they vote irregularly, based on the belief that "nothing changes" through elections.

Looking at their attitudes and voting behavior in the 1998 governor's race, we see that independents were only moderately interested in the news coverage and were highly affected by television commercials. They supported Gray Davis, citing the candidate's attention to issues as opposed to character or party. From now on, independents will play an important role in choosing party candidates because of the open primary, and this disaffected and tuned-out group will hold the balance of power in state elections.

Initiatives have grown at an explosive rate in recent decades, and special-interest spending on commercials for state propositions has reached astronomical proportions. State ballots have been jammed with initiatives in the 1980s and 1990s, some reflecting the voters' revolt and others reflecting attempts by special interests to circumvent the legislative process. Californians believe that initiatives are better able than their elected officials to tackle the problems that are most important to them. However, initiatives today get mixed reviews. Californians overwhelmingly agree that they bring up important policy issues that would otherwise not be addressed, but they also find them complicated, confusing, and prone to reflect special interests rather than the concerns of average residents. Still, Californians favor only modest initiative reforms, such as having the legislature review initiatives before they are placed on the ballot. Proposition 13, the best-known of all initiatives, remains highly popular more than 20 years after it was passed by voters. Californians balk at any suggested changes to Proposition 13, and most refuse to believe it has had bad consequences—despite complaints by elected officials and some policy experts. Many still see Proposition 13 as "sending a message" to politicians.

Several conclusions can be drawn from the four state propositions that we closely followed in the 1998 election. Two were passed by the voters, and two were not. Voters respond to general populist themes and often remain uninformed when it comes to the specifics of the policies they are voting on. This was evident in the case of Proposition 227. Voters are suspicious of campaign reform measures and can be easily convinced that initiatives are designed for partisan gains. This is why Proposition 226 was soundly rejected. Voters can overcome their antipathy toward increased spending if it is limited to funding areas where they think the money is truly needed. This is why Proposition 1a passed by a large margin. Finally, voters are prone to vote against a multifaceted initiative—even if the initiative contains favorable items—if they find something in it they don't like. This is what happened to Proposition 8.

In all, the initiative process has become a trying ordeal for voters, with too many initiatives and too many motives. This has introduced an element of unpredictability into policymaking, because voters often devote only limited attention to very complex issues and frequently depend on information that comes from biased sources.

CHAPTER 4

Racial and Ethnic Change

Racial and ethnic change is creating a new California—one that is unsettling to the state's traditional majority. Residents are keenly aware that many immigrants have been moving to California from Asia and Latin America. They know that the large Mexican immigration has significantly altered the population composition of the state. Indeed, the growing Latino population is the dominant force in the state's demographic change.

The growth in diversity has been both dynamic and controversial. In the past three elections, three citizens' initiatives have been placed on the ballot to address issues related to race and immigration. In 1994, the voters passed Proposition 187, an anti–illegal immigrant initiative. In 1996, they passed Proposition 209, an anti–affirmative action initiative. In 1998, they passed Proposition 227, an anti–bilingual education initiative. All have been high-profile events, and each has created some racial and ethnic divisiveness.[1]

By and large, however, the 1998 election told a different story about the effects of demographic change. There were signs that a political changing of the guard was occurring in state politics. It was a watershed year for Latino political power. At the time of the June primary, there were about 2.3 million Latino voters (Latino Issues Forum, 1998). The gubernatorial candidates had a first-ever Spanish-language debate, and they all opposed Proposition 227. Candidates ran television commercials in Spanish. Four Latinos ran for state

---

1. See the discussion of the racially divisive nature of these initiatives in Chavez (1998), Maharidge (1996), and Schrag (1998).

constitutional offices in the November election. Cruz Bustamante, the former Speaker of the Assembly, was elected lieutenant governor. Latinos increased their membership in the state legislature from 18 to 24. Two Latinos were selected for top positions in the state assembly after the election, Speaker Antonio Villaraigosa and Republican minority leader Rod Pacheco. The city of San Jose elected a Latino, Ron Gonzales, as its mayor. The County of Los Angeles elected a Latino, Lee Baca, as its sheriff. Loretta Sanchez was reelected to Congress in Orange County.[2]

Many questions are being raised about Latino politics as a result of the increasing electoral successes of this group. How many Latinos vote today, and what future participation rates can we expect? Do Latinos differ from other Californians in their political profile and partisan leanings? Will Latinos' public policy preferences shift the state to the left or to the right? Relatively few researchers have examined Latino politics in any detail (see Cain et al., 1986; Cain, Kiewiet, and Uhlaner, 1991; Moore and Pachon, 1985; Pachon, 1998; Pachon and DeSipio, 1995; Uhlaner, Cain, and Kiewiet, 1989; Uhlaner and Garcia, 1998). This is because most preelection polls and voter surveys have proven to be relatively uninformative, either ignoring the responses of this group altogether or offering only scant data about Latino policy preferences and ballot choices. Moreover, the survey subsamples of Latino voters are usually too small to allow valid generalizations.[3]

The purpose of this chapter is to address two large questions related to California's demographic change: How is the change reshaping the issues raised in elections and policy debates? How is the growth of the Latino population likely to affect the state's political profile and election outcomes? The chapter reviews the state's changing demographics and Latino voting trends in the 1990s and examines the future projections for each. The discussion is based on analysis of more than 2,000 interviews with Latinos, a minimum of 400 in each of the five survey waves, during the 1998 election cycle. The size of this sample of adult residents permits comparison of Latino political attitudes with those of whites.

---

2. See the reviews of November 1998 election successes by Latino politicians in California by Covarrubias (1998) and Tobar (1998).

3. See the discussion of the limitations of general population surveys for understanding the Latino community in De la Garza (1987).

TABLE 4-1   POPULATION SIZES OF ETHNIC
AND RACIAL GROUPS IN CALIFORNIA
(*in millions*)

	Latino	Asian	Black	White	Total Population
1980	4.5	1.2	1.8	15.9	23.7
1990	7.8	2.7	2.1	17.1	29.9
1998	10.0	3.7	2.3	17.3	33.5
2000 (est.)	10.7	4.0	2.4	17.4	34.7

SOURCE: California Department of Finance (1992, 1998a).
NOTE: Other ethnic and racial groups account for less than 1 percent of state population and are not included.

THE STATE'S CHANGING
DEMOGRAPHICS: NATURE AND RESPONSE

Latinos are the key to understanding the rapid growth and changing demographics in California; thus, this chapter focuses on the Latino profile and its political effects. The state gained about 6 million residents between 1980 and 1990. At the same time, the Latino population grew from 19 percent to 26 percent of the state's total population. The Asian population increased from 7 percent to 10 percent. The black population stayed at 7 percent. The white population shrank from 67 percent in 1980 to 57 percent in 1990. This demographic shift continued in the 1990s, as Latinos continued to gain share rapidly. The Asian share grew less dramatically. The black population remained stable, and the white percentage continued to decline. Sometime soon after 2000, if these trends persist, the white population will drop to below 50 percent of the state's total population. By the middle of the twenty-first century, Latinos are expected to constitute about 50 percent of the state's population, and whites will account for one in three Californians. This scenario is the opposite of the state's demographic composition in 1998 (California Department of Finance, 1998a).

The influence of the Latino population on California is even more impressive when we consider the population sizes of the ethnic and racial groups. As Table 4-1 indicates, California gained about 3.6 million residents between 1990 and 1998. The Latino population contributed about 2.2 million residents to this total, while the Asian population contributed about 1 million. The white and black populations each gained only 200,000 residents. Latinos numbered about 10 million in California in 1998, a group large enough to be considered a major state within a state. The white population, meanwhile, held steady at around 17 million residents.

The estimates for growth and change between 2000 and 2010 are equally dramatic. The state is expected to gain 5.3 million residents. The Latino population will increase by 3.3 million, accounting for most of the state's growth. The Asian population will increase by 1.3 million, representing the second largest component of population increase. At the same time, the white population is expected to grow by 500,000 and the black population by 100,000. Latinos will account for two-thirds of the state's growth, Asians for 25 percent, and whites and blacks together for only 11 percent.

According to demographers, the state's dramatic racial and ethnic changes are fueled by immigration trends. The state gained 2.8 million residents from legal immigration between 1980 and 1994 (California Department of Finance, 1997). These immigrants arrived from every part of the globe, but the largest single group came from Latin America. Mexico alone accounted for about 40 percent of the immigrants to California in the late 1980s and early 1990s. About 1.5 million people came from Mexico between 1985 and 1995 (Clark, 1998, pp. 22–24). These figures do not include illegal immigrants. Estimates are that between 1.4 million and 2 million illegal immigrants came to California during this same time (Johnson, 1996), most of them from Mexico.

Immigration to California has been occurring at a rapid pace since 1980, during good and bad economic times, and there is no indication that these trends will end any time soon. About half of the immigrants are locating in Los Angeles and Orange Counties. The other major immigrant destinations are San Diego, the Central Valley, the San Francisco Bay area, Riverside County, and San Bernardino County.

Natural increase was the chief factor in population growth in the 1990s and a large component of the Latino growth in California (California Department of Finance, 1998b). Latinos are a youthful population compared with whites and blacks. This is a function of the kinds of people who tend to immigrate. Latinos also have a higher birth rate, which is in part explained by religion and culture as well as by the fact that women who immigrate from developing countries such as Mexico tend to have more children.

The differences in natural increase across racial and ethnic groups are dramatic. The Latino population grew by 1,228,000 from natural increase between 1990 and 1995. Despite being more than twice as large as the Latino population in 1990, the white population grew by only 333,800 from natural increase. The Asian population grew by 246,300 and the black population by 140,100. In sum, between 1990 and 1995, Latinos accounted for about two-thirds of the California population growth due to natural increase.

One concrete way of demonstrating the dominance of Latino natural increase in the state lies in the choice of names for the newborn. According to records from the Social Security Administration, José was the leading choice of baby boys' names in California in 1998, displacing the traditional favorites such as Daniel and Michael (*San Francisco Chronicle,* 1999).

A host of concerns have arisen as the Latino population has grown in California. Some observers worry about whether or not the Latinos will move into the economic mainstream. They point to the relatively low wages of Latino workers, the low level of educational achievement, and the high poverty rates (see Clark, 1998). Others, however, demonstrate that the Latino middle class is growing in California. Latinos are becoming homeowners, major consumers, and small business owners and are showing many signs of economic success (Rodriguez, 1998).

CALIFORNIANS' ATTITUDES TOWARD IMMIGRATION

During the 1998 election, Californians were not feeling as nervous about immigration to the state as they were four years earlier, when they voted for Proposition 187, the anti–illegal immigrant initiative. Yet, beneath the calmer exterior was a sense of uneasiness about the profound effects of immigration on the state. There were also deep racial and ethnic divisions over those effects.

In the focus groups, people from every region talked openly and concretely about immigration. "The population is growing in California and there's nothing you can do about it because you can't stop people from coming in," said a Los Angeles resident. "It seems like Hispanics, especially, are being used as scapegoats here in California, yet when we get cheap labor, we don't complain at the supermarket," said a San Diego resident. "People get nervous when they see foreigners come in," said a San Francisco resident. "Our welfare system is strained enough, and then to have any immigrant come here and use it puts it in a bigger strain," said a Sacramento resident.

Still, hardly anyone put immigration at the top of the list in 1998 when they were asked about the biggest problems facing California. Twice during the election cycle, we asked survey respondents to think about the public policy issues in California and then tell us what they thought was the most serious problem. In a survey before the June primary, only 7 percent mentioned either illegal or legal immigration. In the early fall, only 5 percent named immigration. Before the November election, we asked residents which one issue they wanted the candidates for statewide office, such as the governor and U.S. senator, to talk about before the election. Only 2 percent named immigration. After the election, we asked Californians, "Which one issue facing California today do you think is most important for the governor and state legislature to work on in 1999?" Again, only 5 percent named immigration.

As a point of comparison, in the fall of 1994, when I was conducting statewide surveys for KCAL-TV News, I asked voters what they thought was the most important issue facing California. About 20 percent named immigration—fourfold more than in 1998. At that time, immigration outranked crime and the economy as the state's top issue. But over the next four years, the issue of immigration lost its urgency as the California economy marched steadily from deep recession to prosperity.

Although fewer California residents rank immigration as the most pressing policy problem today, the majority still believe that the immigrant population has been growing rapidly. Seventy-three percent said that the overall immigrant population has increased over the past few years, with 47 percent maintaining that it has grown "a lot" and 26 percent saying it has been increasing "somewhat." Moreover, at least seven in ten residents in all of the major regions of the state say the immigrant population is growing. Latinos (63%) are a little less likely to say this than blacks (77%), whites (76%), and Asians (73%). What is most remarkable is that Californians in all groups and regions see a growing immigrant population as an ongoing trend in the state.

Although they agree that the immigrant population is growing, Californians are divided in their opinions about its effects. As Table 4-2 shows, 46 percent believe immigrants are a benefit to the state because of their hard work and job skills. However, 42 percent think they are a burden. Looking deeper into this ambivalence, we see a public that is sharply divided along racial and ethnic lines. Two in three Latinos and Asians—the groups that have grown the most through recent immigration—consider immigrants a benefit to the state. Blacks are evenly divided. Nearly 50 percent of whites think immigrants are a burden. Since most voters in California are white, those with negative views about the effects of immigration are overrepresented at the ballot box.

TABLE 4-2   CALIFORNIANS' ATTITUDES
TOWARD IMMIGRATION

"Which of these two views is closest to yours? (a) Immigrants today are a benefit to California because of their hard work and job skills. (b) Immigrants today are a burden to California because they use public services."

	Latino	Asian	Black	White	All Adults
Benefit	66%	68%	45%	37%	46%
Burden	25	23	45	49	42
Don't know	9	9	10	14	12

SOURCE: PPIC Statewide Survey, April 1998, all adults.

Given that Mexican immigration is, and is perceived as, the largest component of immigration to California, how do Californians feel about Mexican immigrants specifically? A narrow majority of Californians (52%) say that they consider Mexican immigrants a benefit to the state because of their hard work and job skills, while about one-third (36%) describe Mexican immigrants as a burden because they use public services and schools. Beneath the surface of this overall sentiment are large differences across racial and ethnic lines. Latinos (70%) are much more likely than blacks (55%) and Asians (52%) to describe Mexican Americans as beneficial to California. Whites are more likely to say that Mexican immigrants are a burden (45%) than to say they are a benefit (42%). As evidence of political differences, Republicans (35%) are much less likely than Democrats (57%) to describe Mexican immigrants in positive terms.

Forty-four percent of Californians say that *illegal* immigration from Mexico has been a big problem since 1994, when Proposition 187 was passed. Again, this aggregate figure masks large differences across groups. More than half of whites (53%) think that illegal immigration has been a big problem in recent years, and about four in ten Asians (40%) and blacks (42%) believe it has been a big problem. In contrast, only 29 percent of Latinos consider illegal immigration as a big problem. Again, there are differences between political parties, with Republicans (53%) more likely than Democrats (41%) to call illegal immigration a big problem.

In the year before Proposition 187 was put on the ballot, 75 percent of Californians described illegal immigration as a major problem (Los Angeles Times Poll, 1993). Seventy-eight percent of whites and 44 percent of Latinos saw illegal immigration as a big problem at the time. Thus, it appears that serious concerns about illegal immigration have declined considerably in recent years. Still, nearly half of Californians think that illegal immigration from Mexico is a big problem and few think it is not a problem. For many, then, the issue was not resolved when Proposition 187 was passed by the voters.

In 1994, one of the most controversial elements of Proposition 187 was that it would prohibit illegal immigrant children from attending public schools. Some saw this as a heartless policy that would hurt innocent children, while others focused on the heavy financial costs to taxpayers. In our statewide survey, 22 percent of the respondents thought that illegal immigrant children should not be allowed to attend public schools in California. Whites (27%) and Asians (22%) were more likely than Latinos (14%) and blacks (10%) to say that illegal immigrant children should be excluded from the public schools. Republicans (35%) were more likely than Democrats (22%) to favor this restriction, but neither group showed much interest in this policy. In the fall of 1994, by contrast, a KCAL-TV News survey that I conducted found that about 40 percent of the voters favored prohibiting illegal immigrant children from attending public schools.

Californians are more accepting of immigration than they were when they passed Proposition 187 in 1994—the "year of the angry voter." However, it is likely that their attitudinal changes are more the result of a healthy economy than of any newfound tolerance. Indeed, many white Californians continue to hold negative views about immigration. The strong support for Proposition 227, the anti–bilingual education initiative of June 1998, offers confirmatory evidence that white voters still feel strongly about immigration issues. Moreover, while the white anti-immigrant constituency has shrunk in good times, it could return in force when the state's economy deteriorates and the state's budget surplus disappears in the next downturn (see also Schrag, 1999).

CALIFORNIANS' ATTITUDES
TOWARD RACIAL AND ETHNIC CHANGE

Californians are as ambivalent about racial and ethnic change as they are about the immigration responsible for that change. The state is now well on its way to becoming a truly multiethnic state, with large concentrations of Asians, blacks, Latinos, and whites. Many accounts have focused on whites' reactions to the changes under way, but a much broader view is needed. Rather than focusing on one group, we need to consider the interrelations, tensions, and conflicts between the various groups. For instance, many have speculated that blacks are becoming displaced economically and politically by the new immigrant groups. Others have sensed growing tensions in the workplace and marketplace between Asians and Latinos. We saw this interracial strain surface explosively in the Los Angeles riots of 1992 (Baldassare, 1994).

In the focus groups, we found mixed feelings about the effects of California's increasing social diversity. "The demographics are changing to the point where there's really not going to be any one group as a majority or a minority. I think it will be good," said a Sacramento resident. "No matter where you are, there's that racial tension, discrimination," said a Fresno resident. "It seems like we've got our little pockets where everybody keeps themselves segregated," remarked an Orange County resident.

How pervasive do Californians think racial and ethnic change is, and how do they feel about it? Two-thirds of residents find that an appreciable amount of racial and ethnic change has occurred in their region in recent years, according to our statewide survey. One-third say that the racial and ethnic composition has changed a lot. More than 60 percent of the residents in all of the major regions say that the change around them has been significant, and we found similarities in this perception across racial and ethnic groups.

Among those who have noticed change, the results are evenly split among those who see it as good (22%) and as bad (20%). Fifty-five percent of Californians report that ethnic and racial change has made no difference for their region. There are, however, important differences in attitudes across racial and ethnic groups. Those who see the change in diversity as a good thing outnumber those who see it as a bad thing among Latinos (30% to 13%), blacks (30% to 13%), and Asians (25% to 14%). Whites are more ambivalent, with slightly more saying racial change is a bad thing than a good thing (23% to 19%).

How do people think racial and ethnic groups in their region are getting along? Twenty percent say that racial and ethnic relations are going very well, another 20 percent say that they are going badly, and the rest say they are going "somewhat well." Asians (29%) are the most likely to say that racial and ethnic relations are going well, while blacks (23%), whites (21%), and Latinos (18%) give less-glowing reports.

Californians strongly favor the idea of racial and ethnic groups assimilating rather than maintaining their separate identities. Sixty percent say it is better if groups change so that they blend into the larger society, but 30 percent believe that racial and ethnic groups should maintain their distinct cultures. Once again, there are significant differences across groups. Whites favor the assimilation of ethnic groups over their maintaining separate racial and ethnic identities by a large margin (64%). Most Latinos (58%) and blacks (53%) think that it is better if groups blend into the larger society, but there are large numbers who think otherwise. Asians prefer the "melting pot" idea to maintaining distinct identities by only a small margin (48% to 42%).

As Table 4-3 shows, two years after Proposition 209 passed, Californians continue to be deeply divided along racial and ethnic lines on the issue of affirmative action. Overall, almost 40 percent think that affirmative action programs should continue and 25 percent think they should be stopped immediately. In fact, the preference for ending affirmative action at once is stronger in California than in the rest of the nation. In a CBS/New York Times survey (1997), only 12 percent of Americans wanted affirmative action programs to end immediately, while 41 percent wanted them to continue.

As Table 4-3 also shows, the differences in support for this policy across racial and ethnic groups are dramatic. Almost 75 percent of blacks and over 60 percent of Latinos want affirmative action programs to remain. The percentage drops sharply for Asians (43%) and even more dramatically for whites (25%). The racial order is reversed on the choice to end affirmative action programs immediately. Along party lines, Republicans (43%) are much more likely than independent voters (23%) and Democrats (15%) to want an immediate end to the programs.

When voters passed Proposition 209, public officials said that affirmative action programs would be replaced by special efforts targeted at encouraging more applications to colleges and for employment from underrepresented racial and ethnic groups. How do the state's residents feel about that? Sixty percent favor outreach programs to hire minority workers and find minority students. Support for minority outreach programs is about the same in California as in the nation. For example, a CBS/New York Times survey (1997) also found that 60 percent of Americans favor minority outreach programs. Once again, reactions to such policies differed across racial and ethnic groups. Blacks (83%), Latinos (75%), and Asians (68%) showed overwhelming support for minority outreach programs. Whites (50%) were almost evenly divided on the issue. A split between the major political parties is also evident, with Democrats (67%) overwhelmingly supporting minority outreach programs and a majority of Republicans (52%) against them. The pattern of public support was similar for special educational programs to assist minorities in competing for college admissions.

TABLE 4-3   CALIFORNIANS' ATTITUDES TOWARD
AFFIRMATIVE ACTION POLICIES

*"What should happen to affirmative action programs—should they be ended
now, should they be phased out over the next few years, or should affirmative
action programs be continued for the foreseeable future?"*

	Black	Latino	Asian	White	All Adults
Continued	74%	61%	43%	25%	38%
Phased out	19	20	29	37	31
Ended now	4	12	17	32	25
Don't know	3	7	11	6	6

SOURCE: PPIC Statewide Survey, October 1998, all adults.

The newly elected Governor Davis announced that the era of
"wedge politics" would be over as soon as Governor Pete Wilson left
office and his administration took the helm in 1999. This may be wish-
ful thinking by a governor with little or no control over the citizens' initiative process. The public opinion surveys that we conducted two years
after Proposition 209 was passed indicate that affirmative action and
other racial policies are still powerful issues. The public is sharply divided along racial and ethnic lines as to whether special efforts should
be made to help certain groups achieve work and college admissions.
Large numbers of whites and Republicans continue to oppose affirmative action and other post–Proposition 209 efforts to "level the playing
field," perhaps seeing such efforts as representing too much government involvement or too much effort to help other groups. Whites hold
a big majority in the electorate, and thus it should not be surprising to
see citizens' initiatives or candidates that focus on racial policy issues.
As Latinos ascend in political power, we may also see efforts to reverse
the anti–affirmative action policies of recent years through political
coalitions with blacks, Asians, and more liberal whites. These two
likely scenarios point to the uncertain future for this multicultural state.

THE LATINO POLITICAL
PROFILE AND ITS POTENTIAL EFFECTS

Because Latinos are the fastest-growing racial and ethnic group in the
nation, their voting behavior has naturally been a topic of great interest in political circles. Earlier studies have focused on differences between Latinos and other racial and ethnic groups in political attitudes,

participation, and partisanship (see Cain et al., 1986; Cain, Kiewiet, and Uhlaner, 1991; Uhlaner, Cain, and Kiewiet, 1989; Uhlaner and Garcia, 1998). Some of the differences are partly explained by Latino citizenship rates, length of stay in the United States, and the youthfulness and lower socioeconomic status of the Latino population. In California, Latinos have been voting in greater numbers and in highly defined patterns in recent elections. There are many reasons for this trend, including the rapid growth and aging of the Latino population, increasing citizenship rates, targeted voter registration drives, strategic efforts on the part of candidates and parties to reach Latino voters, and the political mobilization of this group as a result of the perception of hostile citizens' initiatives. The surveys provide considerable insight into voter turnout, partisan trends, and responses to initiatives during the 1990s, and they offer a rather good foundation for speculating about the effects of increased Latino voting.

VOTER TURNOUT AND PARTISAN TRENDS

Many Latinos in the focus groups seemed genuinely enthusiastic about voting in the 1998 election, especially the new citizens. Some were also eager to participate because they felt that their lack of involvement in earlier statewide elections had been harmful to Latinos. "I like to raise my voice for what I believe in," said a Los Angeles resident. "In order to have changes made, you need to vote for what you want," said a Sacramento resident. "We need to express our desires," remarked a San Diego resident. "My vote could make a difference for this crazy world," exclaimed a Fresno resident. However, a few admitted that voting was not a priority for them. "I don't involve myself enough in politics to make decisions that will affect others," said a Fresno resident. "I just don't feel comfortable voting because I don't know what I'm doing," admitted an Orange County resident. "Sometimes I don't have enough time to go out and vote," remarked a Fresno resident.

There is no question that the share of the Latino vote has been increasing in recent elections. As seen in Table 4-4, in the 1990 gubernatorial election, only 4 percent of the electorate were Latino. By the 1998 gubernatorial election, the Latino share had increased to 14 percent, according to Voter News Service exit polls. The trend of increasing Latino participation in elections is also found in the primary election. Latinos accounted for 6 percent of all voters in the June 1994

TABLE 4-4   ETHNICITY AND RACE OF VOTERS IN THE
GENERAL ELECTIONS

	Latino	Asian	Black	Other	White
1998	14%	4%	7%	1%	74%
1996	12	4	6	2	76
1994	9	4	8	2	77
1992	8	4	7	2	79
1990	4	4	8	2	82

SOURCE: Voter News Service, 1990, 1992, 1994, 1996, 1998.

primary and 12 percent in the open primary of June 1998 (Los Angeles Times/CNN Poll, 1998).[4]

Although whites still represent the vast majority of voters in California, the white vote has shown the greatest proportional decline in the 1990s. Whites made up 82 percent of the electorate in the 1990 election and 74 percent in the 1998 election. The share of the Asian vote has not changed, despite the fact that this group has been growing rapidly in population size. The black vote also has not changed over time.

Latino voters in California are strongly Democratic in their party affiliation. Across the five surveys, 2,301 Latinos gave us their voting status, and two-thirds said that they were registered to vote. As Table 4-5 shows, 63 percent of Latinos identify themselves as Democrats, 22 percent as Republicans, and 15 percent as independents (see also Latino Issues Forum, 1998). Among racial and ethnic groups, only blacks (79%) were more likely than Latinos to be Democrats, while whites and Asians were fairly evenly split between the two major parties. As Table 4-5 also shows, Latinos are distinct from white voters in their youth and lesser education. Asians are similar to Latinos in their youthfulness and similar to whites in their level of education. Blacks are most similar to Latinos in their educational achievement and more similar to whites in their older age.

Latinos have been strongly supportive of Democratic candidates in the state's major races. In recent elections, Latino voting preferences have been similar to blacks' and distinct from whites', while Asian patterns are more difficult to categorize. Latinos supported Feinstein

4. Exit polls (Los Angeles Times Poll, 1990, 1992, 1994, 1996, 1998) also show an increase over time in the Latino vote and a decrease in the white vote.

TABLE 4-5   VOTER PROFILES BY ETHNICITY AND RACE

	Latinos	Whites	Asians	Blacks
Democrats	63%	41%	37%	79%
Republicans	22	44	41	6
Independents	15	15	22	15
18 to 34	56	23	53	40
35 to 54	34	44	39	38
55 and older	10	33	8	22
College graduate	20	42	56	29
Some college	31	36	27	40
Less education	49	22	17	31

SOURCE: PPIC Statewide Survey, all voters.

over Wilson by a 2-to-1 margin in the 1990 gubernatorial election. They favored Clinton over Bush (65% to 23%) in the 1992 presidential election. They supported Brown over Wilson (71% to 27%) in the 1994 gubernatorial race, an election marked by Wilson's ties to Proposition 187. Latinos voted for Bill Clinton over Bob Dole by more than a 2-to-1 margin in the 1996 presidential election (65% to 28%). The largest landslide was in the 1998 gubernatorial election, where Davis received 78 percent of the Latino vote compared with only 17 percent for Lungren (Voter News Service, 1990, 1992, 1994, 1996, 1998).

Latino voters appear to strongly support Democratic candidates further down the election ballot as well. They are similar to blacks in their partisan support, though they do not display quite the same level of intensity, and distinct from whites. In the 1998 election, 69 percent supported Boxer for U.S. senator, 74 percent voted for Bustamante for lieutenant governor, and 66 percent voted for Lockyer for attorney general. In the 1992 election, 67 percent of Latinos supported Feinstein and 65 percent favored Boxer in the U.S. Senate races (Los Angeles Times Poll, 1992, 1994, 1998).

Latino voting on state initiatives has also been an issue of intense interest. Three controversial initiatives—Propositions 187, 209, and 227—provide good evidence of how Latino voters have responded to measures aimed at racial and ethnic groups. The Latino vote has been against these measures, and at odds with the white vote, in all three cases. Asians and blacks have not always voted like Latinos, highlighting once again the complex racial and ethnic divisions in the state.

California voters passed Proposition 187, the anti–illegal immigrant initiative, in November 1994. The statewide vote was 59 percent in favor and 41 percent opposed. Latinos were the only racial and ethnic group to oppose this initiative, according to Los Angeles Times exit polls. Sixty-three percent of whites voted for the measure, as did a majority of blacks (56%) and Asians (57%). Only 31 percent of Latinos voted for the measure (Clark, 1998).

The November 1996 vote on Proposition 209, the anti–affirmative action initiative, was strongly divided along racial lines. Overall, the initiative passed 55 percent to 45 percent. According to Los Angeles Times exit polls, 63 percent of whites voted in support of the initiative. However, 76 percent of Latinos, 74 percent of blacks, and 61 percent of Asians voted against it. The high proportion of white voters in the November 1996 election ensured the victory of the initiative, even though the measure was strongly opposed by minority voters. Proposition 209 was credited with drawing a large turnout of Asians, blacks, and Latinos to the polls, who voted overwhelmingly for the Democrats. This surge in minority voting helped Clinton to win over Dole, 51 percent to 38 percent (Chavez, 1998).

Proposition 227, the anti–bilingual education initiative, was placed on the ballot in November 1998. Overall, the initiative passed by 61 percent to 39 percent. White voters supported it by a 2-to-1 margin, with 63 percent in favor. Asian voters supported the measure by a solid margin, 57 percent to 43 percent. Blacks were divided, with 48 percent voting for the measure and 52 percent voting against it. Latinos were solidly against it, with 63 percent voting no and 37 percent voting yes (Los Angeles Times/CNN Poll, 1998).

Clearly, Latinos have not reached their full potential for political participation. One in seven voters in the November 1998 election was Latino. However, one in five adults eligible to vote in California is Latino (Latino Issues Forum, 1998). These demographics indicate that there is much more potential to the Latino vote (see Stiles et al., 1998). In addition, Latinos will become a larger share of the pool of adults eligible to register to vote, as the relatively young immigrant population ages and as more immigrants qualify to vote by becoming U.S. citizens.

At this point, California politicians are concerned about both the current and the future Latino vote. The 14 percent of Latino voters could tip the outcome of close state races, if they vote strongly in favor of one candidate. The Democratic and Republican parties are also trying to court the new Latino voters in the hope of establishing ethnic voting patterns that will carry forward to when the Latino vote is large enough to determine election outcomes. The Republicans' big fear is that they may have alienated Latino voters for many years because of Governor Wilson's support for Proposition 187.

There is considerable uncertainty about how much the Latino vote will actually grow. Based on projections, Latinos will constitute 32 percent of the voter-eligible adult population in 2010 and 41 percent of the voting-age population in 2040 (Skelton, 1998). Those would be very substantial, almost insurmountable voting blocks that would ensure Latinos political power. But the demographic characteristics of the Latino population may be an impediment to the achievement of such high numbers of Latino voters (Chao, 1998). For instance, there is the low income and low educational attainment of this population, both of which characterize nonvoters. Only 20 percent of the Latinos in our statewide surveys were college graduates. If the educational attainment level and socioeconomic status of Latinos do not improve much over time, it is likely that considerable and sustained political mobilization will be necessary to achieve the turnout levels found among white voters.

LATINO POLITICAL INTEREST

Latinos did become more politically mobilized after the sting of Proposition 187's passage in November 1994. But the growth of this voting block must be placed in perspective. Latinos still make up a much larger share of the adult population than they do of the electorate, which suggests that many Latinos are not interested in politics and elections.[5]

Table 4-6 compares the political attentiveness of Latinos and whites as summed across all five of our surveys. It is evident that few Latinos are highly interested in politics. Only 13 percent described themselves as having a great deal of interest in politics, and half said they had little or no interest in politics. Their political interest is much lower than that of whites. For instance, Latinos lead whites by a 15-point margin in saying they have little or no interest in politics (44% to 29%).

To place the level of political interest exhibited by Latinos in a larger context, Californians are less likely than Americans in general (20% to

5. Multiple regressions controlling for age, income, gender, region, and voter registration found that Latinos were not significantly different in political attentiveness, as measured by political interest and following public affairs. Latino trends in political attentiveness are thus explained by age and socioeconomic status. Still, Latinos will continue to lag behind whites in political attentiveness so long as youthfulness and lower socioeconomic status distinguish this population.

TABLE 4-6   POLITICAL INTEREST
OF LATINOS

	Latinos	Whites
Interest in Politics		
A great deal	13%	20%
Fair amount	43	51
Little or none	44	29
Follow Government Affairs		
Most of the time	26%	42%
Some of the time	39	39
Only now and then	24	14
Hardly ever, never	11	5

SOURCE: PPIC Statewide Survey, 1998, all adults.

25%) to say they have a great deal of interest in politics (Pew Research Center, 1996a). Truly, then, political interest is significantly lagging among Latinos.

The level of interest in public affairs also appears to be much lower among Latinos than among whites. There is a 16-point difference between them in following government affairs "most of the time," with 42 percent of whites and 26 percent of Latinos expressing this high level of interest. Thirty-five percent of Latinos—compared with 19 percent of whites—say they follow what's going on in government and public affairs only now and then, hardly ever, or never.

Another measure of Latinos' lower political interest is their knowledge of political events. Recall that when all adult residents in the post-election survey were asked to give the name of the new governor of California, 53 percent knew that the correct answer was Davis. Only 40 percent of Latinos named Davis. The results were the exact opposite for whites, among whom 61 percent named Davis.

The lack of political attentiveness among Latinos is reflected in the fact that many are not registering to vote or are not voting in elections. When Latinos who do not frequently vote were asked why they don't participate in elections, 32 percent said it was because they didn't know enough about the choices, 22 percent said it was because they were too busy to vote, 16 percent said it was because voting didn't change things, and 11 percent said it was because they were not interested in politics. The pattern of these answers mostly matches that of whites, except that a higher proportion of Latinos have found these to be reasons not to participate in elections.

The demographic profile of Latinos helps to explain this low level of political interest. We know that adults who are younger, have lower incomes, and have less education are less tuned in to politics. Latinos are much more likely than whites to have these characteristics, and that creates constraints to raising their level of political interest.

LATINOS' POLITICAL INFORMATION

Californians as a whole rely more on television than on newspapers for political information. This tendency is even stronger among Latinos. As Table 4-7 shows, television is by far the primary source of political news for Latinos, with newspapers a distant second (46% to 30%). In contrast, whites are evenly divided between relying on newspapers and television.

Latinos mention newspapers as their major source of political information much less often than do whites because they are much less likely to read a newspaper for any reason. Fewer than one in three Latinos read a newspaper every day. By contrast, more than half of whites read a newspaper daily. To place these findings in perspective, whites are about as likely as all Americans to read a newspaper daily (53% to 51%), while Latinos are much less likely to do so (American Association of Retired Persons, 1996). Again, the low percentage of Latinos holding college degrees may account for much of the difference. Other contributing factors may be the difficulty some have in reading written English and the availability of Spanish-language newspapers.

More than half of Latinos (53%) say that they watch television news every day. In fact, Latinos appear to spend more time than whites watching television. A recent study found that 64 percent of Latinos watch television at least four hours a day compared with 45 percent of whites (DeSipio, 1998). In our survey, when we controlled for demographic differences such as age and income, Latinos were found to be significantly more likely than whites to watch local television news.[6]

---

6. Latinos were significantly more likely to say they watch local televisions news, after we controlled for the effects of age, income, gender, region, and voter registration. The B was .21 with a significance level of .001 in the final equation. Latinos were not any different from whites with respect to reading the newspaper after other factors were controlled for.

TABLE 4-7   POLITICAL INFORMATION
SOURCES FOR LATINOS

	Latinos	Whites
Source of Political Information		
Television	46%	36%
Newspapers	30	37
Radio	8	11
Talk to people	8	7
Other	8	9
Reading the Newspaper		
Every day	31%	53%
Few times a week	24	18
Less often	45	29
Watching Television News		
Every day	53%	61%
Few times a week	32	21
Less often	15	18

SOURCE: PPIC Statewide Survey, April, May, and October 1998, all adults.

The fact that Latinos watch a great deal of television means that it is possible to reach this group effectively through paid political commercials. Chapter 2 describes efforts by the Republican and Democratic candidates for governor and the U.S. Senate in the 1998 California election to reach the Latinos and other voting groups through television commercials. In fact, Al Checchi spent millions trying to reach Latinos through advertisements on Spanish-language television in the June primary. The evidence suggests that he succeeded. In our preprimary surveys, two in three Latinos said they noticed advertisements for the governor's race. The commercials they recalled the most were those paid for by Al Checchi. The results were very similar for the number of whites who recalled seeing ads before the primary. In our pre–general election surveys, 42 percent of Latinos recalled seeing advertisements for the governor's race, compared with 48 percent of whites.

The central role of television advertising among Latinos was confirmed by the results of the June primary. Al Checchi had his best showing among Latinos, winning 30 percent support from that group, compared with 9 percent of white voters (Los Angeles Times/CNN Poll, 1998). It is important to reiterate that there is no correlation between the record amounts that the candidates spent on television advertising and increased voter participation. In the Latino community, this was particularly evident: many people who were seeing and recalling the candidates' television advertisements were evidently not motivated to register to vote or go to the polls.

LATINO TRUST IN GOVERNMENT

One of the more interesting findings to emerge from the surveys is that Latinos are more trustful of government than Californians in general. This may partly reflect the fact that Latinos are more likely than whites to be nonvoters. In Chapter 2 we noted findings that the unregistered are more trusting in government than are voters. However, Latinos express more trust on several dimensions even after voter status is controlled for.[7]

Latinos today are injecting a more positive and less jaded view of government into the political process. Many of the Mexican immigrants have left a country where politics has been historically dominated by one-party rule and corruption scandals, so the American system may look good by comparison. This is most evident in the "trust in government" questions about the federal government. As Table 4-8 indicates, nearly half of Latinos (48%) think you can trust Washington to do what is right always or most of the time. This is a considerably higher level of trust than the 28 percent of whites who hold this view. Latinos are also less likely than whites to say that the federal government wastes a lot of the money we pay in taxes, less likely to say that the federal government is run by a few big interests, and more likely to say that it is run for the benefit of all the people. However, on the issue of government corruption, there are no differences. Latinos (38%) are just as likely as whites (38%) to say that quite a few people in government are crooked.

Latinos are also more trusting of their government in fiscal matters. When asked if they agreed or disagreed with the statement "When something is run by the government it is usually wasteful and ineffi-

---

7. Latinos were significantly more likely to say they trust government most of the time (B = .15, significance .001) and significantly less likely to say that government wastes the taxpayer's money (B = -.15, significance .001) in results of final regression equations including age, income, region, gender, and voter registration. Other "trust in government" questions, however, showed no significant differences.

TABLE 4-8   TRUST IN GOVERNMENT BY LATINOS

	Latinos	Whites
Trust Washington to Do What Is Right		
Always, most of the time	48%	28%
Only some of the time	50	67
None of the time	2	5
Federal Government and Tax Money		
Wastes a lot	58%	65%
Wastes some	32	32
Doesn't waste very much	8	3
Don't know	2	0
How Federal Government Is Run		
Few big interests	61%	72%
Benefit of all the people	34	22
Don't know	5	6

SOURCE: PPIC Statewide Survey, September 1998, all adults.

cient," 50 percent of Latinos thought so compared with 67 percent of whites. Latinos were as likely as whites to believe that "most elected officials are trustworthy" (59% to 56%).

Latinos also give the president and Congress better marks. In combined results of four of the surveys, 72 percent of Latinos, compared with 52 percent of whites, said that Clinton was doing an excellent or good job as president. Latinos (43%) were also more likely to say the U.S. Congress was doing an excellent or good job than whites (32%).

The findings were similar when people were asked how much trust and confidence they had in the president and Congress when it comes to solving national problems. Latinos (80%) were more likely than whites (63%) to say they had confidence in the president. Although Latinos might be expected to give high ratings to Clinton because of their Democratic leanings, they also had more positive views than whites of the Republican-led Congress, suggesting that their trust goes beyond partisan sentiment.

Latinos and whites gave similar answers to "government responsiveness" questions. This is despite the fact that Latinos vote less often. Latinos are about as likely as whites (67% to 72%) to say the government pays attention to what the people think when it decides what to do. As many Latinos as whites (42% to 44%) think that having elections makes the government pay a good deal of attention to what the people think.

There are no differences between Latinos and whites in feelings of political powerlessness, despite the lower participation levels among Latinos. When asked if they agreed that "public officials don't care what people like me think," the same number of whites and Latinos said yes (53% each). Latinos and whites agreed (47% each) with the statement "People like me don't have any say in what the government does." Latinos were also as likely as whites to agree that "most elected officials care what people like me think" (53% to 50%). On all of these questions about political powerlessness, the attitudes of white Californians and Latino Californians are relatively positive compared with the responses of all Americans.

Latinos' trust in state government is also similar to whites'. Less than half of Latinos and whites (43% and 36%) say you can trust the state government in Sacramento to do what is right all of the time or most of the time. A little over half of Latinos (55%) and whites (52%) think that the state government wastes a lot of the taxpayer's money. Two in three Latinos (62%) and whites (65%) believe that the state government is run for the benefit of all the people.

There is one area in which trust in state government has been affected by the recent controversies over Proposition 187 and Proposition 209. That is in the approval ratings of then-Governor Pete Wilson in the statewide surveys. Latinos were less likely than whites (27% to 45%) to say that Wilson was doing an excellent or good job in office. A negative view of Wilson was also found in the level of confidence in the governor to handle state problems. Latinos were much less likely than whites (39% to 61%) to say they had confidence in Wilson.

Latinos' negative feelings about state elected officials are limited to Wilson. When asked to rate the job performance of the state legislature, Latinos (39%) were more likely than whites (31%) to say they were doing an excellent or good job. When asked how much trust and confidence they had in the California legislature to handle state problems, about 60 percent in both groups said they had a great deal or fair amount of confidence. The level of trust that Latinos express toward government and elected leaders is all the more astounding in the wake of their experiences with Proposition 187 and Proposition 209. Perhaps this is because they blame the voters rather than the government for passing these measures, which they strongly opposed. A more compelling possibility, although difficult to prove, is that Latinos have a

TABLE 4-9   POLITICAL ORIENTATION
OF LATINOS

	Latinos	Whites
Liberal	29%	27%
Middle-of-the-road	34	36
Conservative	37	37

SOURCE: PPIC Statewide Survey, 1998, all adults.

more upbeat, less jaded attitude toward government because they are
less exposed to negative political messages. Perhaps their greater trust
in government is an indication of being more tuned out to news reports
and political campaigns, which have hammered on the negative themes
of government waste and inefficiency. If so, Latinos may become more
distrustful as they vote in larger numbers and pay more attention to
California politics.

LATINO PREFERENCES IN ROLES FOR GOVERNMENT

Two trends suggest that a larger and more politically active Latino population would swing the state's political pendulum to the left. First,
Latinos who have registered to vote are overwhelmingly Democratic.
Second, Latinos have a more positive and less fearful attitude toward
government. Together, these point to liberal voters willing to support a
more active role for government. Yet others have argued that the
Latinos have cultural ties and religious affiliations that may move the
state to the right. For instance, "ethnic" voters with Roman Catholic
backgrounds are often social conservatives on issues such as abortion
(Clark and Ferguson, 1983). Latinos have a complex political profile
that does not fit easily into the common political stereotypes.[8]

Latinos describe themselves as middle-of-the-road to somewhat conservative in their political philosophy. In this respect, they are just like
most Californians. As Table 4-9 shows, three in ten Latinos describe

8. Latinos were significantly less likely to support abortion rights (B = −.29, significance .001) and environmental regulations (B = −.10, significance .001), and more likely
to favor government regulations (B = .09, significance .001) and increased taxes for social programs (B = .06, significance .001) in results of final regression equations including age, income, region, gender, and voter registration. Other "role of government" questions, however, showed no significant differences.

themselves as liberal, one-third say they are middle-of-the-road, and one-third call themselves conservative. This is not that distinct from whites, which is surprising considering the large differences in party affiliation. Overall, though, what is more important is the fact that the majority of Latinos (59%) say they are middle-of-the-road to somewhat conservative. The Latino's right-of-center profile closely parallels the white's (63%). What truly distinguishes Latinos from whites has more to do with their specific policy preferences than their political philosophy.

The numbers in Table 4-10 show that Latinos hold more conservative views on abortion, a key indicator of how people feel about government involvement in decisions affecting their private lives. Fewer than half of Latinos (42%) want the decision on abortion left up to the woman and her doctor, while most (58%) say abortions should be illegal in some or all circumstances. In contrast, most whites (67%) want abortion to be left up to the woman and her doctor.

This streak of conservatism on civil liberty issues does not appear to extend to other private domains. The majority of Latinos said that homosexuality is a way of life that should be accepted by society. The number of Latinos (58%) who expressed tolerance for gays was similar to that for whites (54%). A strong majority of Latinos also said they were in favor of health insurance and other benefits for domestic partners of gay and lesbian employees.

Latinos have more liberal attitudes when it comes to taxes and spending. They lean more toward having the government spend more money on social programs (58%) such as Social Security and health care, even if it means higher taxes, than toward reducing taxes (38%) if that means making cuts in these programs. Whites are about evenly split between these preferences.

Latinos may want a more active role for government because of their lower socioeconomic status. In describing their financial conditions, most saw themselves as among the "have-nots" rather than the "haves" (50% to 42%). In contrast, most whites see themselves as among the "haves" rather than the "have-nots" (65% to 28%). It is not surprising, then, that Latinos are much more likely than whites (52% to 39%) to believe that "the government should do more to make sure all Californians have an equal opportunity to succeed."

Latinos do not, however, have more positive attitudes than whites when it comes to poverty programs. Latinos were as likely as whites to agree that "people have become too dependent on government assis-

TABLE 4-10 PREFERRED ROLES FOR GOVERNMENT OF LATINOS

	Latinos	Whites
Abortion		
Choice left up to woman and her doctor	42%	67%
Legal in some cases, such as rape or incest	37	24
Illegal in all circumstances	21	8
Don't know	0	1
Increasing Taxes versus Social Spending		
Spend more on social programs, increase taxes	58%	46%
Reduce taxes, spend less on social programs	38	48
Don't know	4	6
Government Regulations and Business		
Regulation necessary to protect public	63%	49%
Regulation does more harm than good	33	48
Don't know	4	3

SOURCE: PPIC Statewide Survey, May 1998, all adults.

tance programs" (75% to 77%) and that "the government is spending too much money on programs to help the poor" (43% to 45%).

In line with their strong support for government intervention, most Latinos favor an active regulatory role for the government. Two in three Latinos think that government regulation of business is necessary to protect the public interest, while one in three feels that government regulation of business usually does more harm than good. In contrast, whites are evenly divided in their opinions on this subject.

Latinos also have pro-environmental attitudes. The majority believe that environmental laws are worth the cost, rather than costing too many jobs and hurting the economy. Still, whites are more likely than Latinos to say that environmental laws are worth the cost (60% to 52%).

We find that it is not easy to categorize Latinos as either left or right. They do not fit the profile of most Californians—that is, liberal on social issues and conservative on fiscal issues—even though they, like the majority of Californians, describe themselves as moderate to somewhat conservative. On social issues, such as abortion, Latinos are more conservative than most Californians. But their social conservatism seems to be moderated, since there is no evidence that they hold more intolerant attitudes than others toward gays. On fiscal issues, such as government taxes and spending, Latinos are more liberal than most Californians. But their liberalism does not extend to more generous feelings about welfare programs for the poor. Overall, many Latinos hold attitudes toward the role of government that are often associated with immigrant groups. They reflect traditional or religious values. Many want government to provide a "safety net" and to help citizens succeed in getting ahead economically in American society.

NEW DIRECTIONS FOR CALIFORNIA POLICY?

The growth of the Latino vote at the ballot box raises questions about future policy directions. Latinos may have very different views from whites about the priorities for state government. For instance, we already know that they have opposed the race policy initiatives that whites have strongly favored, notably Propositions 187, 209, and 227. Moreover, since Latinos are not as strongly linked to fiscal conservatism, they may not be in agreement with the white voters who continue to favor tax cuts and spending limits. Do Latino preferences and priorities signal new policy directions?

There is agreement on the most important issues facing the state. When asked to name the issue they wanted the gubernatorial candidates to talk about the most before the election, one-third of Californians mentioned schools, and no other topic received more than 10 percent mention. Both Latinos (35%) and whites (28%) named schools as by far their biggest concern. In a postelection survey, we asked respondents to name the one issue they thought was most important for the governor and state legislature to work on in 1999. The top concern was again education, named by 36 percent of Californians. Latinos (37%) and whites (36%) both mentioned education more than any other topic, with fewer than 10 percent from either group mentioning other issues such as crime, immigration, the economy, or taxes.

There is also general consensus about how the state ought to be allocating its budget. The survey asked what priority should be given to each of the four major categories in the state budget, given that the state government faced a budget deficit in the next fiscal year. As Table 4-11 shows, about 67 percent of Latinos and whites want the public schools to have a very high priority, and about one-third want both public health and colleges and universities to be high priorities, while one-sixth believe that prisons and corrections should have a very high

TABLE 4-11   STATE FISCAL PREFERENCES OF LATINOS

	Latinos	Whites
"Very High" Priority for State Budget		
K-12 schools	72%	63%
Public health	38	27
Colleges and universities	43	20
Corrections and prisons	17	10
Simple Majority versus Supermajority Vote Requirement for Local Tax Increase		
Favor	32%	40%
Oppose	64	56
Don't know	4	4
Personal Importance of State Tax Cut		
Very important	54%	36%
Somewhat important	32	40
Not important	13	23
Don't know	1	1

SOURCE: PPIC Statewide Survey, September and December 1998, all adults.

priority. Latinos and whites both give public schools the highest rank-ing, they both place public health and colleges and universities in a sec-ond tier, and both groups give the lowest ranking to corrections and prisons. Latinos are more likely than whites to say that all state budget categories are very high priorities. They are most different from whites in the importance they place on higher-education spending.

Latinos are more likely to say that state spending on budget items is very important, but this does not mean that they have a different atti-tude toward taxes. Under Proposition 13, a two-thirds vote is required for passage of any new local special taxes. As the table shows, fewer than four in ten Latinos and whites favor allowing local special taxes to pass with a simple majority instead of a two-thirds vote. Latinos op-pose this effort to make it easier to pass local tax increases by a wide margin, as do whites (64% to 56%).

The results were similar in another survey that asked Californians about their willingness to allow local school districts to raise local taxes with a simple majority instead of a two-thirds vote. Despite the great im-portance that respondents place on state spending for schools, six in ten respondents were opposed to making it easier for local school districts to raise taxes. Once again, Latinos were opposed to the easing of tax restrictions, in agreement with whites (57% to 55%).

It is also evident that state tax cuts are very appealing to Latinos. The governor and state legislature approved a $1.4 billion tax cut as part of the 1998–1999 fiscal year budget in the summer of 1998. This included a reduction in the state's vehicle license fee. In the statewide survey, four in ten Californians said this state tax cut was very important to them. Latinos (54%) were more likely than whites (36%) to say that this tax cut was something they valued very much.

Education was the biggest campaign issue in the 1998 California election. A number of reform proposals were being discussed by the candidates, offering us an opportunity to test public opinion on these ideas and to see if the school policy preferences between Latinos and whites differ. Latinos are more likely to have children in the state's public schools because of their youthfulness. They are also more likely to live in lower-income neighborhoods, where schools are more likely to be performing poorly. Yet Latinos in our surveys were not as negative as whites about the public schools in California. While over half of the whites (51%) said that the quality of public school education was a "big problem" in California, only 36 percent of Latinos agreed. Whites were also much more likely than Latinos to know that California's student test scores were below average compared with other states (58% to 43%). These differences may reflect less knowledge about school quality, or they could point to lower expectations about the schools based on the parents' education.

The most controversial school reform issue is school vouchers—a concept that some see as having special appeal in the Latino community. Vouchers, for example, would allow lower-income parents to receive money from the state to send their children to private religious schools instead of their local public schools. When we asked Californians whether they favored or opposed providing parents with tax-supported vouchers to send their children to any public, private, or parochial school they chose, six in ten said they favored the concept. Latinos favor vouchers by a 2-to-1 ratio (63%), while a smaller number of whites support them (55%).

There was virtual agreement between whites and Latinos on almost every other proposal for improving California's public schools that was being discussed in 1998. As for teacher reforms, Latinos (84%) and whites (84%) want to increase teachers' pay based on merit to attract and retain more and better teachers, while Latinos (89%) and whites (82%) want to require that teachers be given more training and be subject to tougher credential standards before they teach in the classroom. Requiring students to pass achievement tests before they are promoted to the next grade is strongly supported by Latinos (88%) and whites (89%), as is requiring after-school and summer school programs for students who are not performing well (95% and 90%). There is an overwhelming belief that class size reductions have improved education in the lower grades, and thus Latinos (86%) and whites (83%) want to reduce class sizes to a maximum of 20 students from kindergarten through the twelfth grade.

One school reform proposal we asked about elicited a very different response between Latinos and whites. We asked people whether they would favor or oppose having the state take over a local public school when its students exhibit low test scores and show no signs of improving. Latinos (66%) are strongly in favor of this proposal, while whites (50%) are divided. This difference points to the general theme that we noted earlier: the greater trust in higher levels of government that is evident in the Latino population.

In all, the evidence suggests that Latinos are very similar to whites in their views about California policies. At this time, there is no reason to think that the increased participation by Latinos in the political process will result in significant shifts in citizens' policy preferences enacted through elections. Whites and Latinos hold the same views about the state policy issues that are considered important. They think alike with regard to how state funds should be spent. They generally agree on what needs to be done to improve the state's public school system. The differences between Latinos and whites are more subtle. Latinos are more enthusiastic about some reform proposals, such as school vouchers and state takeover of local schools. Latinos view state spending across all budget categories as more important. These trends probably reflect a more positive attitude among Latinos, and more cynicism among whites, about what the government can do for them. Neither Latinos nor whites support easing revenue-raising restrictions mandated through the initiative process, and both look very favorably on state tax cuts. In other words, there are no indications that the increasing involvement of Latinos in California elections will mean that the Proposition 13 era is over.

QUALITY OF LIFE DEFICITS

Latinos express policy concerns today that are very similar to the views of whites. But we also know that their socioeconomic characteristics are not close to being on a par with the conditions of the white population. They are less likely to have high-paying jobs, attend college, live in safe neighborhoods, own their own homes, or send their children to the better public schools. Although the life circumstances of Latinos are very different from those of whites in California, the Latino immigrants who compare their lives today with the lives they knew in their homelands may not be disenchanted with America. In this section, we examine whether Latinos and whites differ in their reports of the quality of their daily lives. If Latinos are deeply concerned about the quality of their lives, this could be reflected in their policy preferences as they become more politically active.

Our surveys show that Latinos, in fact, are upbeat about living in California. Two in three Latinos said they thought that things in California today were going in the right direction, while only three in ten said things were going in the wrong direction. Seven in ten said that they thought that the quality of life in California these days was going well, while only three in ten said it was going badly. Latinos' overall assessments were on a par with whites'.

There are no differences between Latinos and whites in their evaluations of the regions they live in. Latinos and whites are equally likely to say they are satisfied with their job opportunities (73% to 77%), the affordability of their housing (66% to 66%), and the cost of living (67% to 69%) in their regions.

They are also very positive about their personal finances. Latinos (40%) are more likely than whites (32%) to say that their financial situation has improved in the last year. Few Latinos (10%) say their finances have deteriorated. Latinos (54%) are also more likely than whites (37%) to say they expect their finances to improve in the next year. This is largely because most whites say their finances haven't changed in the past year and won't change in the next year. Latinos are also as likely as whites to say they are satisfied with their finances (77% to 75%). This is despite the fact that Latinos on average have lower incomes than whites.[9]

There are, however, important differences among the groups in their ratings of public services (see Table 4-12). Latinos are much less likely than whites to say they are receiving excellent or good police protection (58% to 73%). Latinos are also not as positive as whites about their pub-

---

9. Latinos are less likely than whites to say they have more than enough money to make ends meet (25% to 38%) and to say their standard of living is more than comfortable (8% to 17%). But relatively few Latinos complain that they are not comfortable financially and that they do not have enough to make ends meet. This, again, suggests that many Latinos may view their finances on the basis of relative improvement, rather than how they are doing compared with the white population.

TABLE 4-12   LOCAL SERVICE RATINGS
OF LATINOS
Percent Rating Excellent and Good

	Latinos	Whites
Police protection	58	73
Public parks and recreation	60	73
Local roads	48	46
Public schools	48	52

SOURCE: PPIC Statewide Survey, April and May 1998, all adults.

TABLE 4-13   LIFE SATISFACTION
OF LATINOS

	Latinos	Whites
Very Satisfied		
Housing	44%	60%
Leisure	42	50
Jobs	47	56
Feel Safe in the Neighborhood		
Very safe	23%	40%
Somewhat safe	33	32
Unsafe	44	28

SOURCE: PPIC Statewide Survey, April and May 1998, all adults.

lic parks and recreation (60% to 73%). However, it is important to note
that most Latinos say that their police and parks are excellent or good,
and very few say these services are poor. Latinos are simply not as glow-
ing about their police and local parks as the whites are in their evaluations.

Latinos' ratings of local roads and local public schools are similar to
those of whites. Fewer than half of Latinos (48%) and whites (46%)
say their local roads are in excellent or good shape. A similar number
of Latinos (48%) and whites (52%) believe their local schools are excellent or good. The fact that only about half of Latinos and whites
have positive things to say about their schools and roads indicates that
these public services—at least in the perceptions of respondents—merit
more attention and improvement than police and parks.

There are some important differences between Latinos and whites in
their satisfaction with the domains of their personal lives. As Table
4-13 shows, about four in ten Latinos are very satisfied with their housing,

compared with six in ten whites. This probably reflects a higher level of home ownership among whites. Latinos are also less likely than whites to be very satisfied with their leisure time (42% to 50%) or very satisfied with their jobs (47% to 56%). This explains, at least in part, why Latinos are a little less likely than whites to say they are happy with the way their lives are going (83% to 90%). Many of these differences seem to be attributable to income variations.

Because crime is still a major concern to most Californians, we asked people how safe they felt walking alone in their neighborhoods at night. About one-third said they felt very safe, one-third felt somewhat safe, and one-third felt unsafe. Latinos are much more likely than whites to feel unsafe (44% to 28%). These differences between whites and Latinos may be attributable to the fact that the latter are more likely to live in lower-income neighborhoods and inner-city areas, which have higher crime rates than the suburbs. Still, it is important to place these findings in perspective—in particular, the fact that over half of Latinos think their neighborhoods are very or somewhat safe at night.

Overall, Latinos seem quite satisfied with the way things are going with their lives. There is not much evidence to date of the kinds of widespread dissatisfaction that could alter the political landscape. They are upbeat about conditions in California and their own personal finances. Their ratings of local public services and the domains of their private lives are generally positive. However, the quality-of-life indicators in the survey also reveal that Latinos, relative to whites, are less satisfied in certain domains. It is likely that these perceived deficits in the quality of life exist because Latinos are less affluent than whites. These differences may become more salient among Latinos as they compare themselves with whites rather than against their own progress. And this might lead to disagreement among Latinos and whites in one key policy area—whether or not the government should play a major role in assisting Latinos' economic mobility.

LATINOS MAKING ELECTION CHOICES

What was the mood of Latinos during the 1998 elections, and how did they go about making ballot choices? One of the purposes of the focus groups was to see if there were any particular incentives that might bring Latinos to the polls. We found that there was indeed: Many Latinos took Proposition 187 very personally. They were still very unhappy with Wilson for his support for this anti–illegal immigrant initiative in 1994, and it seemed to be galvanizing them as they approached the 1998 election, based on what we learned when we asked Latinos about the upcoming election in focus groups. A Republican simply said, "I am changing party," while a Democrat concluded, "We need a new governor and a new administration." A Los Angeles resident said, "I think that Wilson has focused only on Hispanics in his advertisements. He's just focusing on criticizing the Hispanic community." There was also a perception that Latinos were being singled out unfairly in the implementation of immigration policy. "When Immigration comes to any restaurant or any factory, they only take Latinos. I never see them take other people," observed a Los Angeles resident. Many Latinos we talked to seemed energized by the ability to vote and to influence what they see as an injustice.

Yet our surveys early in the year showed that the election was a nonevent for many Latinos.[10] Two months before the June primary, only 4 percent of Latinos were very closely following the news stories about the California elections; 24 percent were following the election news fairly closely. Latinos were 10 points below the lackadaisical level of election news interest reported by whites. Yet seven in ten Latinos said they recalled seeing television commercials for the governor's race, mostly from Democrat Al Checchi. Latino attention to television commercials helps to explain the solid lead that Checchi (36%) had over Davis (9%), Harman (10%), and Lungren (8%) at this time, although more than one-third of Latinos were undecided. But Checchi's hold over the Latinos was built on a precarious foundation. Most Latinos said they valued experience in office over experience in business (54% to 32%), which distinguished them from whites, who narrowly favored experience in business over experience in office (43% to 40%). This preference helped to give Democrat Barbara Boxer (48%) a commanding lead over Republicans Matt Fong (5%) and Darrell Issa (9%) in the Senate primary. Latinos (55%) narrowly supported Proposition 227, the anti–bilingual education initiative, while whites overwhelmingly favored the proposition (80%). Yet Latinos were as likely as whites (46% to 45%) to say they knew little or nothing about the bilingual education programs in California's public schools.

One month before the primary, about 10 percent of Latinos were very closely following the news stories about the state's elections, and 24 percent

10. The percentages from the statewide surveys reported in this section are based on the total sample of all adults, rather than registered voters or likely voters.

were closely following them. This was only a slight gain from the preceding month and still 10 points below the level of attention paid by white voters. But two in three Latinos had seen television commercials by the candidates for governor, with most recalling advertisements by Checchi. Latinos continued to favor Checchi (40%) over Davis (14%) and Harman (5%) by a wide margin, but one-third were still undecided. Support for Boxer remained very high, but few could recall any commercials by the candidates for the U.S. Senate. Most Latinos still said that experience in office mattered to them more than experience in business. They were now less in favor of Proposition 227 (48%), while whites still strongly favored it (70%). Almost half of whites and Latinos continued to say they knew little or nothing about bilingual education programs in the public schools.

In the June open primary, Latinos constituted about 12 percent of the electorate. This was a higher participation rate than in previous years but still well below the levels that could be achieved if all Latinos who were eligible to vote did so. Latinos split their vote in the governor's race between Checchi (30%) and Davis (36%), with smaller percentages supporting Lungren (17%) or Harman (11%). This pattern was quite different for whites, who gave most of their votes to Lungren (43%) and Davis (30%), with few supporting Checchi (9%) or Harman (11%). In the U.S. Senate race, Latinos strongly supported Boxer (57%) over Fong and Issa (11% each), while whites gave fewer votes to Boxer (35%) and more support to Fong (26%) and Issa (24%). As mentioned earlier, Proposition 227 won by a wide margin in the state; although it was opposed by most Latinos, it was strongly favored by whites (Los Angeles Times/CNN Poll, 1998).

As the fall campaign began, there continued to be little interest in the election. Only 8 percent of Latinos said they were very closely following news stories about the California election; 24 percent were fairly closely following the elections. Three in ten had seen commercials on the governor's race, and two in ten had seen television advertisements on the U.S. Senate race. Whites were equally uninterested in the upcoming election.

In the governor's race, Latinos favored Davis over Lungren by a huge margin (55% to 20%), while whites were equally divided (40% to 39%). In the U.S. Senate race, Latinos supported Boxer over Fong by a landslide (59% to 23%), with whites once again split (40% to 41%). Latinos said that issues (43%) and experience in office (35%) mattered most to them in choosing candidates to support for statewide offices. Whites were more likely to mention issues (59%) and less likely to say that they were looking for experience (13%) when they vote for governor and U.S. senator.

A month before the November election, 7 percent of Latinos said that they were very closely following the elections; 35 percent were fairly closely following the political news stories. This was not much of an increase over the previous month and lower than the interest expressed by whites. More than half of Latinos had seen television commercials for the governor's race (55%) and one-third had seen advertisements for the U.S. Senate race (37%)—percentages somewhat lower than the number of whites who recalled seeing commercials for the governor's race (61%) and the U.S. Senate race (48%). Among the Latinos, Davis (58% to 19%) and Boxer (66% to 19%) continued to hold very large leads over their Republican opponents, while the white vote was evenly split between Democrats and Republicans. Latinos were nonplussed by the White House sex scandal. Similar to whites, most Latinos said that Clinton's troubles would not affect the party they voted for in the elections (74%) or their chances of voting in November (70%)

In the November election, Latinos represented 14 percent of the electorate. This was a record turnout for Latinos but well below the relative size of this voting block. The Latino electorate in 1998 was heavily Democratic. As mentioned earlier, Latinos voted overwhelmingly for the Democratic candidates for governor, U.S. senator, lieutenant governor, and attorney general. White voters were more evenly divided between Democrats and Republicans in all of the major statewide races (Los Angeles Times Poll, 1998). The lopsided nature of the Latino vote in the general election was instrumental in padding the margins of victory for the Democrats in the two major statewide races.

CONCLUSIONS AND IMPLICATIONS

In recent years, most of the discussion about the changing social and political landscape of California has really been about the dramatic racial and ethnic change taking place in the state. California is on the brink of becoming a "majority-minority" state. As the Latino vote becomes more prominent, many are predicting that this group will nudge the political pendulum to the left. The evidence suggests that this perception is misguided. Latinos are not much different from other voters in their political preferences. More important, the racial and ethnic change under way is having profound effects on the ability to achieve

consensus on crucial state issues. One troubling trend is the fissure that
has developed between whites, Latinos, blacks, and Asians over race
and immigration policies. The other troublesome issue is the political
nonengagement of the fastest-growing and someday-to-be-largest ethnic gre up in California. The state can hardly afford more public disengagement from the political process, or more episodes of racial and ethnic conflict like those that surfaced in the 1990s. Yet, given the current
trends, those are the likely scenarios of the future.

There is plenty of evidence that the demographic diversity of the
state has been increasing over time and that the public is aware of these
dramatic changes. The state's population growth is now largely a result
of immigration from Latin America and Asia and the natural increase
by immigrants from these countries. Whites will soon lose their majority status, while Latinos will be the single largest racial and ethnic
group in the state. Most Californians have noticed that the racial and
ethnic composition of their regions is changing, and a deep racial and
ethnic division sets in when people are asked about these changes.
Many whites and blacks hold negative opinions about the effects of immigration, while Latinos and Asians hold positive views. Most Latinos
and blacks think that affirmative action should continue, while many
whites and Asians want these policies to end. The divisions over racial
and immigration policy issues may well surface in elections and create
tensions and conflicts in the society at large. Indeed, we have seen some
of this already.

Latinos are bringing a more positive outlook toward government to a
state where white voters are notoriously cynical about politics. Latinos
are more likely to trust government, and they are more likely to approve
of government intervention in affairs that directly affect their personal
lives, as demonstrated in their attitudes toward abortion rights. Most
Latinos express contentment with the way their lives are going, even
though their current standard of living is generally not as high as that of
whites. Latinos have much in common with whites when it comes to
taxes. They are no more eager than whites to make it easier for local governments to raise taxes, and they are as pleased as whites with recent tax
cuts. In all, those looking for the Latinos to change the post–Proposition
13 status quo will be disappointed to learn that this group has conservative, "don't rock the boat" leanings.

The rapid growth of the Latino population is beginning to have a direct effect on the state's elections. Latinos have been voting in greater
numbers, and so far mostly for Democrats, although many who are el-

igible are still not voting. All Californians are heavily influenced by television commercials for candidates and initiatives, but Latinos are even more so because of their lower newspaper readership and their greater attention to television. The Latino vote should increase even more as a result of the aging of the immigrant population and increased citizenship. However, a low level of political interest and a limited interest in following government affairs are factors seriously reducing Latinos' chances of participating in California's future elections. It is likely that this disinterest is the result of their lower educational achievement and youthfulness, and the lower socioeconomic standing of Latinos relative to whites. While we know that the Latino population will age, it is less certain that Latinos will attain the educational and income levels achieved by whites. This raises the prospect of lower voter turnout rates and a less-engaged public as California makes the transition to a Latino-majority state. It also means that the largest group in the electorate may have a disproportionately small voice in shaping the outcome of elections.

The June primary and November general election in 1998 illuminated some unique patterns among Latinos. Many continued to stay away from the polls, even though as a group they voted in record numbers. Their interest in news and information about the election lagged well behind even the lackluster attention paid by white voters. Latinos were strongly opposed to Proposition 227, the anti–bilingual education initiative that white voters passed by a wide margin. Many Latinos seemed to equate this effort with an earlier anti-immigrant initiative. Latinos were highly supportive of Democrats, contributing to the overwhelming victory of Gray Davis in the governor's race. But the tendency to vote as Democrats may be only a temporary phenomenon. Latinos in focus groups told us that they wanted to send a message to Republicans about Wilson's support for Proposition 187. Their voting was deeply affected by the sting of perceived prejudice in the 1994 election, which serves as a reminder of the extent to which future politics in the state may be dictated by race.

CHAPTER 5

Regional Diversity

Many states have distinct regions and tensions among those regions, but in California the distinctions and tensions are intensified by the state's unique geography. The distance between the northern and southern borders, and the imposing internal boundaries of mountains and deserts, have made it difficult for Californians to develop a sense of oneness. The history of the state has exacerbated the regionalism. In the mid-nineteenth century, San Francisco became the political and economic powerhouse as banking and trade during the Gold Rush turned the city into an international port. Los Angeles came on strong a half-century later, when oil was discovered, and stronger still when the movie and television studios and then the defense industry took root in Southern California. The vast suburbs surrounding Los Angeles eventually upstaged the city, as Orange County and the Inland Empire became the new destination for Americans seeking the California dream. At the same time, the rich earth and vast expanses of the Central Valley were developing into farms that became the major producers of the nation's food.

As the north, south, and central regions grew in size and economic importance, they found themselves in a nasty political battle over the water flowing out of the Sierras into the nearby rivers. This bitter rivalry over water continues today. It serves as a constant reminder of the testy political, cultural, and social relationships between the state's regions. California is a large state where both the politicians and the people have a history of forming internal competitions and losing track of the common interests that link their destinies.

Californians have trouble considering the state as a whole but are quick to offer negative judgments about regions other than their own. Regional stereotypes largely go unchecked in a state that lacks statewide newspapers and television stations. In the focus groups, some said they would prefer to have the state just split up so that the regions would not have to deal with one another. "The problems in California are so different they should just go to San Luis Obispo and draw a line straight through to Fresno and separate the state," said a San Francisco resident. "California is basically two states, Northern California and Southern California," remarked a San Diego resident. "I always thought if they took the state of California and cut it in half maybe two states would be easier to govern than one state," said a Los Angeles resident. There is a tendency to blame other regions for problems. "I've heard we get Bay Area pollution and it gets stuck in our Valley," said a Fresno resident. Growth problems are the result of people "coming from the Bay Area and Southern California," according to a Sacramento resident. The desire to be distinct from other regions was summed up by a San Diego resident who said, "We definitely don't want to be Los Angeles."

Although these regional perceptions are largely based on historical rivalries and stereotypes, there is, in reality, considerable regional diversity in California. Regions are distinct in their populations, growth, economy, geography, politics, and public concerns. Yet there is no general agreement about the exact configuration of regions and where the dividing lines are. Some people simply divide the state into Northern and Southern California. Others talk about coastal California versus inland California, although the merging of the San Francisco and Los Angeles areas has more critics than supporters. Philip Fradkin (1995) divides the state into seven regions: Deserts (southeast), Sierra (east), Land of Fire (northeast), Land of Water (northwest), the Great Valley (central inland), the Fractured Province (central coast), and the Profligate Province (southern coast). This amounts to an environmental tour guide that gives equal weight to vast empty regions and densely populated areas. Dan Walters (1992) divides the state into fourteen regions, including several within the San Francisco, Central Valley, and Los Angeles metropolises. The state government at one time divided California into a dozen regions for economic and planning purposes, also splitting up some of the contiguous urban regions (Baldassare et al., 1996). California has also been divided into about a dozen media markets for the purpose of buying and selling television advertising.

This chapter focuses on the four regions defined in Chapter 1: Los Angeles County, the San Francisco Bay area, the Central Valley, and Orange County and the Inland Empire.[1] These four large, highly populated regions reflect both the historical regional conflicts in the state and the important regional trends that are currently under way. Today Los Angeles and the San Francisco Bay area are the dominant regions. But in due time, as a result of the uneven regional growth discussed in Chapter 1, the Central Valley and the Inland Empire and Orange County will be equals in population and political importance. This chapter provides an overview of growth patterns, demographics, and voting trends. It also explores regional differences in state perceptions, policy preferences, and political, social, and economic attitudes. As we shall see, the unique history of regional diversity in the state, combined with the ongoing regional shifts that are changing the balance of political power, present a precarious setting for the attainment of consensus on California's policy directions.

GROWTH PATTERNS, DEMOGRAPHICS, AND VOTING TRENDS

About 80 percent of Californians live in the four regions. Los Angeles County is the most populous and racially and ethnically diverse county in the state. The San Francisco Bay area is growing and changing as a result of immigration and the high-technology revolution. The Central Valley is one of the fastest-growing areas of the state, as farmlands give way to urban development. Orange County and the Inland Empire constitute the "mega-suburbs," where a huge and rapidly growing population has created a region distinct from nearby Los Angeles. These four regions have unique political, social, and economic profiles. They are all extremely important to elections and to the formation of public policy in the state. They each attract the separate attention of statewide candidates because of their size and distinctiveness.

1. I have separated Orange County and the Inland Empire of Riverside and San Bernardino Counties from Los Angeles County because the former three counties form a contiguous suburban region. The three-county area is defined as a suburban region because there is no dominant central city, and it is economically and politically separate from Los Angeles. See Baldassare (1986, 1992, 1998) and others (Fischer, 1984; Fishman, 1987; Garreau, 1991; Jackson, 1985; Kling, Olin, and Poster, 1991; Lewis, 1996; Logan and Molotch, 1987; Palen, 1995; Schneider, 1991; Teaford, 1997) for definitions of suburban regions and their political and economic importance. San Diego County is not considered to be part of this suburban region because it contains a city of over 1 million in population. The samples from the statewide surveys were not large enough to support a separate analysis of San Diego.

Map 5-1 Los Angeles County
SOURCE: Caliper Corporation (1997).

DISTINCT GROWTH PATTERNS

Los Angeles County, the San Francisco Bay area, the Central Valley, and Orange County and the Inland Empire are home to almost 28 million of the state's 33.5 million residents. Each has experienced a phenomenal increase in population over a 50-year period. Los Angeles County (Map 5-1), with about 10 million residents, is the most populous county in the nation. In the nine-county San Francisco Bay area (Map 5-2), the population will reach 7 million residents in the not-too-distant future, with the Silicon Valley in Santa Clara County propelling the region's growth.[2] The Central Valley, defined as the eighteen-county area stretching from north to the south through the middle of the state (Map 5-3), will soon contain 6 million residents, making it comparable to Los Angeles in the 1960s and the San Francisco Bay area in 1990s.[3]

2. This region includes the counties of Alameda, Contra Costa, Marin, Napa, San Francisco, San Mateo, Santa Clara, Solano, and Sonoma.
3. This area includes the counties of Butte, Colusa, Fresno, Glenn, Kern, Kings, Madera, Merced, Placer, Sacramento, San Joaquin, Shasta, Stanislaus, Sutter, Tehama, Tulare, Yolo, and Yuba.

Map 5-2 San Francisco Bay Area
   SOURCE: Caliper Corporation (1997).

The mega-suburb region of Orange County and the Inland Empire
(Map 5-4) has about 6 million residents and is equal in population size
to the Central Valley.

Table 5-1 charts the growth of the regions by decade from 1950 to
2000 (estimated). Los Angeles had about 4.1 million residents in 1950.
Its population grew by about 45 percent over the next decade, reaching
6.0 million in 1960. This was by far the fastest population growth it
would experience for the latter half of the century. Los Angeles experienced its lowest rate of population growth—6 percent—between 1970
and 1980, when the addition of about one-half million residents
brought the total population to 7.5 million by the end of the decade.
During this time, Los Angeles residents were moving out of the county
and into the surrounding suburban areas. But growth picked up again
sharply after 1980, as Los Angeles became a major destination for immigrants. Between 1980 and 1998, the county had a solid growth rate
of 28 percent, reaching a population of 9.6 million.

The San Francisco Bay area was not as heavily populated as Los
Angeles 50 years ago, and it has not gained as many residents since. There
was, however, a similar era of rapid growth in the 1950s and 1960s as the
population increased from 2.7 million to 4.6 million. After a slowdown
during the 1970s, the rate of population growth picked up as the area became one of the most popular destinations for new immigrants. Since

Map 5-3 Central Valley
    SOURCE: Caliper Corporation (1997).

1980, the San Francisco Bay area population has increased by 29 percent,
reaching 6.7 million residents as of 1998.

The Central Valley has a smaller population than either the San
Francisco Bay area or Los Angeles, but it has been steadily growing for
50 years. It grew from 1.7 million residents in 1950 to 2.8 million in
1970, a growth rate of 64 percent. Between 1970 and 1990, the growth
rate was 70 percent and the population reached 4.8 million. At this
point, the Central Valley began to show signs that suburban-style housing and employment were displacing farms. The Valley is on track to
add another 1.2 million people in the 1990s. It is growing at a faster

TABLE 5-1 POPULATION BY REGION
(in millions)

	Los Angeles	San Francisco Bay	Central Valley	Orange/ Inland
1950	4.1	2.7	1.7	0.7
1960	6.0	3.6	2.3	1.5
1970	7.0	4.6	2.8	2.6
1980	7.5	5.2	3.6	3.5
1990	8.9	6.0	4.8	5.0
1998	9.6	6.7	5.4	5.9
2000 (est.)	9.8	6.9	6.0	6.1

SOURCE: Johnson (1998); California Department of Finance (1998a).

Map 5-4 Orange County and the Inland Empire
SOURCE: Caliper Corporation (1997).

TABLE 5-2   RACE AND ETHNICITY BY REGION
(1998 est.)

	Los Angeles	San Francisco Bay	Central Valley	Orange/ Inland
Latino	44%	18%	25%	29%
Asian	12	19	8	8
Black	10	9	5	5
Other	—	—	1	1
White	34	54	61	57

SOURCE: Johnson (1998); California Department of Finance (1998a).
NOTE: Los Angeles and San Francisco Bay area have less than 1 percent "other."

pace now than either Los Angeles or the San Francisco Bay area and is gaining the same number of people as these regions.

The Orange County–Inland Empire region has been rapidly transformed in the last half-century. The population of the three-county area increased from two-thirds of a million in 1950 to 2.6 million in 1970 to 5 million in 1990. Thus, the total population nearly quadrupled between 1950 and 1970 and then doubled between 1970 and 1990. By 2000, the population of Orange County and the Inland Empire will be about 6 million residents. These population trends explain why local disputes over growth policies are so common to this region (Baldassare, 1986, 1991; Baldassare and Wilson, 1996; Glickfeld and Levine, 1990; Neiman and Loveridge, 1981).

DIVERGENT PATHS TO RACIAL AND ETHNIC DIVERSITY

As Table 5-2 indicates, the four regions are distinct in racial and ethnic composition. They are also all in demographic transition. Los Angeles is a "majority-minority" region, which makes it all the more valuable to study since it now has the racial and ethnic status that all of California is expected to have in the future. The San Francisco Bay area has equally large proportions of Asians and Latinos, and whites are close to losing majority status there as well. The Central Valley has the highest percentage of whites but also has a very large group of Latino residents. Orange County and the Inland Empire are gaining Asians and Latinos at a fast pace.

According to 1998 estimates, Los Angeles has a population that is 44 percent Latino, 34 percent white, 12 percent Asian, and 10 percent black. This is all the more remarkable considering that Los Angeles had a white population of 71 percent in 1970, 52 percent in 1980, and 42 percent in 1990. The Latino population increased from 15 percent in 1970 to 26 percent in 1980 and to 36 percent in 1990 before becoming the largest racial or ethnic group in Los Angeles. The Asian population has also been increasing, although not in as dramatic a fashion, rising from 3 percent in 1970 to 12 percent in 1990. The size of the black population, as a percentage of the total, is about the same today as it was in 1970 (Gabriel, 1996; Ong and Blumenberg, 1996).

The Central Valley has a 1998 population that is 61 percent white, 25 percent Latino, 8 percent Asian, 5 percent black, and 1 percent other. Over time, the white population has declined sharply, from 80 percent in 1970 to 66 percent in 1990. Meanwhile, the proportion of the population that is Latino almost doubled, from 12 percent in 1970 to 22 percent in 1990. The Asian population also doubled during this time, increasing from 3 percent to 6 percent. The black population has remained steady at about 5 percent. The rate of racial and ethnic change in the Central Valley has been slower because of the in-migration of whites from coastal metropolitan regions, such as the San Francisco Bay area and Los Angeles.

The San Francisco Bay area has a population 54 percent white, 19 percent Asian, 18 percent Latino, and 9 percent black. Like the others, this region has seen the whites' proportion in the population decline over time. As recently as 1990, 60 percent of the San Francisco Bay area was white, 15 percent Latino, and 15 percent Asian. In 1980, 69 percent of the population was white, 12 percent was Latino, and 9 percent was Asian. The region has experienced steady and equal gains in the Asian and Latino populations. The black population has remained about the same at less than 10 percent.

The stereotype that suburbs are home to mostly white residents does not apply to Orange County and the Inland Empire. As of 1998, the area population was 57 percent white, 29 percent Latino, 8 percent Asian, and 5 percent black. This region has also changed dramatically in ethnic and racial composition in just a few decades, pointing to the powerful role that immigration has played in changing California's suburbs. As recently as 1980, 75 percent of the population was white, 14 percent Latino, 3 percent Asian, 3 percent black, and 1 percent Native American. This mega-suburb is on course to become a "majority-minority" region soon, with whites projected to lose their majority status around 2010.

Although all four regions have been immigrant destinations, for the eight largest immigrant groups Los Angeles and the San Francisco Bay area stand out as among the top destinations in the United States. There is a significant amount of Latino and Asian immigration to the Orange

County and Inland Empire region (Clark, 1998) and, to a lesser degree, to the Central Valley. Los Angeles is the most favored destination in the United States for Mexicans, Filipinos, and Koreans. The San Francisco Bay area is the second most common destination for Chinese, Vietnamese, and Filipinos (Portes and Rumbaut, 1996). As a result, 33 percent of Los Angeles County residents and 20 percent of San Francisco Bay area residents are foreign born. The foreign born in Los Angeles totaled about 1.5 million in 1990, with over half arriving since 1980 (Vernez, 1992). The growing presence of Latino and Asian immigrants, the higher birth rates of Latinos relative to whites, and an exodus of whites from Los Angeles have all combined to account for the steep decline in the percentage of the white population (Morrison and Lowry, 1994). The popularity of the San Francisco Bay area is evident in the fact that about 20 percent of immigrants to California name that region as the place where they intend to settle (Clark, 1998). Asians, in particular, favor the region, as indicated by the rapid growth of the Asian population relative to the Latino population. However, the effect of immigration on Orange County and the Inland Empire should not be discounted. Orange County has one of the largest shares of immigrants of all counties in the state—one in four residents is foreign born, and one in three speaks a language other than English (Baldassare, 1996; Clark, 1998).

The role of these four regions in the changing demographics of the state is evident in the countywide trends in immigration. There were 1.2 million legal immigrants to California between 1990 and 1995 (California Department of Finance, 1997). Of these individuals, 38 percent, or 475,577, settled in Los Angeles; 25 percent, or 308,661, settled in the San Francisco Bay area; 14 percent, or 164,010, settled in Orange County and the Inland Empire; and 11 percent, or 131,000, settled in the Central Valley. Together, these four regions were the destinations of almost nine in ten legal immigrants to California. The racial and ethnic change in the state that is now under way is largely the product of immigration to Los Angeles, Orange County, and the San Francisco Bay area.

ECONOMIC AND SOCIAL DISTINCTIONS

There are also major economic differences between the four regions. The Central Valley is the agricultural heartland of California. The transition it is making from farmlands to tract homes, office parks, and shopping malls places its growth in the unique context of a rural-to-urban-transformation. Orange County and the Inland Empire is also distinct. This region consists of industrialized suburban counties that some describe as the engine that powers economic growth in the state.

It is very telling to compare the Central Valley with the mature metropolises of Los Angeles County and the San Francisco Bay area. Eight percent of the Central Valley workforce is employed in farms and agriculture, 17 percent in manufacturing, and 26 percent in service employment. The Central Valley leads the coastal regions in farm and agricultural employment, while it has lower manufacturing employment. The San Francisco Bay area and Los Angeles are considerably ahead of the Central Valley in service employment, an indication of their more advanced postindustrial economies. Per-capita income is considerably lower in the Central Valley than in the coastal regions. Income growth has been strong in the San Francisco Bay area and relatively weak in the Central Valley (Dardia, 1995). Moreover, eleven of the fifteen counties with the highest unemployment rates in California are located in the Central Valley, as are many of the counties with the lowest household incomes (Lichtblau, 1998). In contrast, many of the counties with the highest household incomes are in the San Francisco Bay area. Both manufacturing and service wages are high in this region, as are educational levels, reflecting the presence of high-tech and computer industries. The large and relatively new immigrant population in Los Angeles has lowered the wage, income, and educational levels in that region. Housing is more expensive in the San Francisco region than anywhere else in the nation. By comparison, home prices are relatively modest, by California standards, in the Central Valley (Dardia and Luk, 1999).

The Orange County and Inland Empire region has experienced very strong industrial and commercial development in recent decades. By 1990, there were nearly 2.5 million jobs in the three-county area, as a result of employment growth actually outpacing population growth (Baldassare, 1998). This region is no longer a bedroom community to Los Angeles; most of the residents who live in this mega-suburb also work there (see Kotkin, 1998; U.S. Census, 1994). From 1990 to 1997, one-quarter of a million jobs were created in Orange County and the Inland Empire, even as the state was in a deep recession and Los Angeles suffered severe reductions in employment (Dardia and Luk, 1999; Hahn, 1998).

The four regions also have distinct socioeconomic profiles, as evident from the responses to our statewide surveys, which included more than 10,000 interviews.

- **Education and income.** The San Francisco Bay area has the most adults who are college graduates (49%), followed by Orange County and the Inland Empire (37%), Los Angeles (33%), and the Central Valley (29%). San Francisco Bay area residents are more likely to earn $60,000 or more (46%) compared with the residents of Orange County and the Inland Empire (32%), Los Angeles (25%), or the Central Valley (25%). As another sign of the impact of the high-technology industry in the region, San Francisco Bay area employees are more likely to use a computer at work (71%) than are employees in Orange County and the Inland Empire (61%), Los Angeles (55%), or the Central Valley (56%).

- **Age.** Los Angeles residents are the youngest, with 42 percent under 35 years old, compared with 30 percent in the San Francisco Bay area, 30 percent in Orange County and the Inland Empire, and 29 percent in the Central Valley. The more youthful population is a product of the higher immigration rates.

- **Home ownership.** Central Valley residents (71%) and Orange County and Inland Empire residents (69%) are more likely to be homeowners than San Francisco Bay area (66%) and Los Angeles (53%) residents. The high level of home ownership in the Central Valley, despite the lower income levels, indicates that housing is by far the least expensive in this region.

While these four regions are quite distinct from one another, each also has considerable internal variety. Los Angeles County covers a very large area with eighty-eight cities, ranging from the large and diverse city of Los Angeles to nearly all-white suburbs and small cities in the Antelope Valley (Sonenshein, 1993). The San Francisco Bay area consists of ninety-eight cities within nine counties. The region includes the racially diverse city of San Francisco; the no-growth, white suburbs of Marin; the small towns in the Napa Valley wine country; the growing, white suburbs of Contra Costa County; and Silicon Valley, which is the high-tech capital of the world (Dowall, 1984; Joint Venture, 1998). The Central Valley is 400 miles long, with ninety-five cities within eighteen counties, stretching from Bakersfield to Redding. Some researchers have subdivided the Central Valley into the Sacramento Valley to the north and the San Joaquin Valley to the south (Umbach, 1998). Orange County has thirty-one and the Inland Empire forty-eight cities, ranging from larger cities such as Santa Ana, Riverside, and San Bernardino to job centers such as the Ontario Airport and the Irvine Spectrum to smaller, upper-middle-class bedroom suburbs. Even within Orange County, there are great differences in income and race and ethnicity between the older northern cities and the developing southern communities (Baldassare and Katz, 1997, 1998).

DIFFERENT POLITICAL PROFILES

The four regions have become enormously important in California politics and elections. Millions of dollars are spent on television commercials directed to the voters in these major media markets. The regional newspapers, such as the *Sacramento Bee, Los Angeles Times, San Francisco Chronicle, San Jose Mercury News, Orange County Register, San Bernardino Sun,* and *Riverside Press-Enterprise,* are highly courted for endorsements. The attention corresponds to the number of votes the regions represent. Eighty percent of the state's voters reside within these regions—27 percent in Los Angeles, 22 percent in the San Francisco Bay area, 16 percent in the Central Valley, and 16 percent in Orange County and the Inland Empire. The regional turnout in elections typically reflects a similar 80 percent of state voters (Field Institute, 1999).

Table 5-3 shows the numbers of registered voters and the percentages of party affiliation in the regions. The party registration statistics indicate some striking similarities between Los Angeles County and the San Francisco Bay area. Both regions have a majority of Democrats and fewer than 30 percent Republicans, making them more heavily Democratic than the state as a whole. In Orange County and the Inland Empire, the Republicans lead the Democrats by 47 percent to 37 percent. In statewide elections, it is crucial that the Republicans win big in Orange County and the Inland Empire, given the large number of Democrats in Los Angeles and the San Francisco Bay area. The Central Valley has a voter profile that is quite different from the other regions in that it is nearly evenly divided between Democrats and Republicans (45% to 41%).

The Central Valley has about one-quarter of the voters among all four of the regions. However, it attracts more interest from the parties and the candidates than that percentage would suggest, for two reasons. First, it is one of the fastest-growing regions in the state. Moreover, the politics of the region are in flux. This was a rural Democratic stronghold as recently as 1970, but every county in the region has seen a large drop in Democratic registration over the past 30 years. A combination of factors is at work. Many of the Central Valley Democrats had conservative values and became "Reagan Democrats."

TABLE 5-3   VOTER REGISTRATION BY REGION

	Los Angeles	San Francisco Bay	Central Valley	Orange/ Inland
Democrats	54%	53%	45%	37%
Republicans	29	27	41	47
Independents	13	15	10	11
Other parties	4	5	4	5
Registered voters (millions)	3.77	3.26	2.37	2.37

SOURCE: California Secretary of State (1998a).

Additionally, many of the white middle-class residents migrating from the urban coastal areas arrived with conservative ideas about government spending and taxes. The Central Valley could thus be in the midst of a political realignment similar to the "New South" in the eastern United States (Barabak, 1998). Whatever the cause, the political professionals believe that the "New Central Valley" voters may be forming their voting habits. Both parties would like their future support.

The Central Valley has also become the focus of the search for "swing voters." The Central Valley is considered a "swing" region because it is large enough to determine the election outcome and is not strongly allied with either of the major parties. "You can predict how L.A. will vote. You know what the Bay Area will do . . . but you can't be certain what will happen in the Valley," said Great Valley Center President Carol Whiteside (Barabak, 1998).

The 1998 election showed that the Central Valley vote is indeed unpredictable. Orange County and the Inland Empire are also becoming less dependable for Republicans. In the governor's race, Davis won over Lungren by more than a 2-to-1 margin in Los Angeles (66% to 31%) and the San Francisco Bay area (68% to 28%), while Davis took the Central Valley by only a 5-point margin (51% to 46%) and Lungren won by the narrowest of margins in Orange County and the Inland Empire (49% to 48%). In the U.S. Senate race, Boxer won easily over Fong in Los Angeles (61% to 36%) and the San Francisco Bay area (63% to 24%), but Fong actually won in the Central Valley (50% to 45%), despite the fact that the region gave Davis an edge and has more registered Democrats than registered Republicans (Field Institute, 1999). Fong won over Boxer in Orange County and the Inland Empire (52% to 43%), but by a small margin for the state's Republican stronghold. The voting outcomes in the Central Valley are a testament to the varied reactions of the swing voters to the candidates. The recent trends in Orange County and the Inland Empire also suggest a growing suburban independence from party politics.

The Central Valley also voted differently from the coastal regions in earlier state elections. In the 1990 governor's race, Wilson won over Feinstein by a large margin in the Central Valley (57% to 38%), lost narrowly in Los Angeles (47% to 49%), and lost by a large margin in the San Francisco Bay area (60% to 39%). Four years later, Wilson won by a large margin over Brown in the Central Valley (62% to 34%), won by a close margin in Los Angeles (50% to 46%), and lost in the San Francisco Bay area (52% to 44%). In the 1992 presidential race, Clinton tied Bush in the Central Valley (40% to 39%) while winning in Los Angeles (53% to 29%) and the San Francisco Bay area (56% to 25%). Four years later, Clinton lost narrowly to Dole in the Central Valley (44% to 47%) while winning by large margins in Los Angeles (63% to 33%) and the San Francisco Bay area (62% to 27%). The coastal regions are predictably Democratic. The Central Valley plays a pivotal "swing" role (California Secretary of State, 1990, 1992, 1994, 1996; Lubenow, 1995; Skelton, 1990).

In the meantime, the lock that Republicans seemed to have had on Orange County and the Inland Empire in the 1980s became less of a certainty in the 1990s. Reagan and Bush won in these regions by better than a 2-to-1 margin in the 1980, 1984, and 1988 presidential elections. Republican gubernatorial candidate George Deukmejian polled over 60 percent of the votes in the two gubernatorial races of 1982 and 1986. In many cases, the large margins of victory in Orange County and the Inland Empire offset the Democratic advantages in the San Francisco Bay area and Los Angeles, allowing these Republican candidates to win in a mostly Democratic state (California Secretary of State, 1980, 1982, 1984, 1986, 1988; Quinn, 1988). The results in the mega-suburbs have been more mixed for the Republicans in the major statewide races of the 1990s. Wilson received over 60 percent of the vote in two gubernatorial elections. In two presidential races, however, the Republican candidates won by narrow margins and fell short of majority support. The appeal of the Republicans to the suburban swing voters who were Democrats and independents seems to have faded fast, especially as indicated by the most recent election (California Secretary of State, 1990, 1992, 1994, 1996, 1998b).

The state's major regions have also differed in their support for the controversial citizens' initiatives in recent elections (see California

TABLE 5-4   POLITICAL ORIENTATION BY REGION

	Los Angeles	San Francisco Bay	Central Valley	Orange/ Inland
Liberal	35%	36%	22%	24%
Middle of-the-road	34	33	36	36
Conservative	31	31	42	40

SOURCE: PPIC Statewide Survey, 1998, all adults.

Secretary of State, 1994, 1996, 1998a). In 1994, Proposition 187, the anti–illegal immigrant initiative, barely passed in the San Francisco Bay area (51% to 49%), while it won by a larger margin in Los Angeles (56% to 44%), and by a 2-to-1 edge in the Central Valley (66% to 34%) and in Orange County and the Inland Empire (68% to 32%). In 1996, Proposition 209, the anti–affirmative action measure, lost in the San Francisco Bay area (46% to 54%) and Los Angeles (46% to 54%), while it won overwhelmingly in the Central Valley (63% to 37%) and Orange County and the Inland Empire (63% to 37%). In 1998, Proposition 227 won narrowly in the San Francisco Bay area (52% to 48%), while it passed by a wider margin in Los Angeles (56% to 44%) and overwhelmingly in the Central Valley (64% to 36%) and in Orange County and the Inland Empire (69% to 31%). These results indicate how differently the voters in these regions have responded to these controversial ballot measures. They also point to a strong conservative streak in the Central Valley and the Southern California mega-suburbs that has affected the outcomes of state initiatives.

That streak is borne out by the percentages shown in Table 5-4. When asked to describe their political philosophy, one-third of both the Los Angeles and San Francisco Bay area residents said they were liberals, one-third said they were middle-of-the-road, and one-third said they were conservatives. In both the Central Valley and Orange County and the Inland Empire, less than one-quarter called themselves liberal while about 40 percent described themselves as conservative. This is despite the fact that the Central Valley has a higher proportion of Democrats than Orange County and the Inland Empire. Mark Barabak (1998) observed the following about the Central Valley: "Valley Democrats were always a distinct breed, more like their conservative Southern brethren than, say, urban counterparts in Los Angeles or San Francisco."

It is important to note that conservatism has its limits even in the Central Valley and the Orange County–Inland Empire region. About two-thirds of residents in the two regions call themselves middle-of-the-road to somewhat conservative in their politics. Only about one-eighth of residents say they are very conservative. Los Angeles (56%) and San Francisco Bay area (57%) residents are less likely to say they are in the center or somewhat right of center politically. This moderately conservative position explains the preponderance of "swing" voting in the Central Valley and mega-suburbs. There is a great reservoir of support for candidates from either party who position themselves in the center or somewhat to the right on many issues. Even in a bastion of conservatism such as Orange County, few voters are responding to an ultra-conservative message today (see Baldassare and Katz, 1997, 1998). Indeed, many suburban voters find themselves at odds with the strong ideological positions taken by the major-party candidates.

REGIONAL STATES OF MIND

The region of residence has a dramatic effect on how residents perceive the state of the state. To some extent, the differences in perceptions throughout the state can be explained by the composition of the populations—that is, by variations in their social, economic, and political profiles. To some degree, these differences can also be traced to the context of each region—that is, to its unique geography, land use, history, and culture. Whatever the causes, this phenomenon has profound implications for both public policy and elections in California.[4] The fact that Los Angeles, the San Francisco Bay area, the Central Valley, and

---

4. The fact is that both context and composition account for the regional differences reported in this chapter, as is evident in the mixed results from multiple regressions including region, age, income, gender, race and ethnicity, and voter registration. The following B's and significance levels from the final equations including all variables illustrate the significant effects of region (i.e., Central Valley versus others) on state and regional perceptions, political attitudes, and trust in government: crime in the state = .12 (.001); traffic in the region = −.44 (.001); jobs in the region = −.06 (.001); support for abortion rights = −.09 (.05); support for gay rights = −.10 (.003); support for environmental regulations = −.11 (.001); trust government to do what is right = −.12 (.001); government wastes money = −.9 (.05). However, region had an insignificant effect after other variables were controlled for for the following survey questions, also concerned with state and regional perceptions, political attitudes, political interest, and trust in government; right direction versus wrong direction for the state, ratings of the state economy, support for tax increases, support for government regulations, perceptions that the government is run by special interests, perception that the government is crooked, and all the questions concerning interest in politics and media attentiveness. As noted in the text, regional diversity in attitudes is important to policy, whether it is derived from the geographic context or population composition. It is highly unlikely that the respective compositions of these four regions will undergo major changes any time soon.

TABLE 5-5   STATE PERCEPTIONS BY REGION

	Los Angeles	San Francisco Bay	Central Valley	Orange/ Inland
State Conditions				
Right track	64%	53%	48%	62%
Wrong track	29	38	43	32
Don't know	7	9	9	6
California Economy				
Excellent or good	52%	70%	48%	59%
Fair	38	23	38	33
Poor	10	7	14	8
Crime in California				
Big problem	69%	53%	78%	74%
Somewhat of a problem	26	42	20	24
Not a problem	5	5	2	2

SOURCE: PPIC Statewide Survey, April, May, and September 1998, all adults.

Orange County and the Inland Empire can see the same state so differently presents enormous challenges for political campaigns and state lawmakers seeking consensus.

DIVERSE PERCEPTIONS OF THE STATE'S DIRECTION

Most Californians felt upbeat about California during 1998, but at times substantial differences surfaced across the state's four major regions. When asked, "Do you think things in California are generally going in the right direction or the wrong direction?" 54 percent overall thought that things were going in the right direction and 34 percent in the wrong direction, with 9 percent unsure. However, Table 5-5 shows how different the state can look from different regions. In Los Angeles and in Orange County and the Inland Empire, optimists outnumbered pessimists by a wide margin. In the San Francisco Bay area, those who thought things were going in the right direction led by a 15-point margin. In the Central Valley, almost equal numbers said the state was on the right track or the wrong track. This is intuitively consistent with the fact that economic conditions are not as robust in the Central Valley as in the other regions. That connection is clarified in residents' perceptions of the state's economic conditions. In 1998, 57 percent of California residents believed that the state's economy was in excellent or good condition, one-third said it was in fair shape, and 10 percent considered it to be in poor condition. But regional responses were quite different. In the San Francisco Bay area, 70 percent thought that the state's economy was in excellent or good shape, and 60 percent in the Southern California mega-suburbs echoed that perception. In contrast, 52 percent in Los Angeles rated the state's economy as excellent or good. Fewer than half of those in the Central Valley gave the state economy a high rating, and more in this region than elsewhere rated it as poor. Evidently, the same, booming economy can look very different depending on where you are standing in the state.

Californians' perceptions of economic threats to the state also differ on a regional basis. In the fall of 1998, we asked residents if they thought the current financial situation in Asia would hurt the California economy in the next year or so. Statewide, two in three residents said they thought the Asian financial crisis would hurt California either a great deal (22%) or somewhat (44%). San Francisco residents (75%) were the most convinced that the Asian financial crisis would have at least some impact on the state's economy. Sixty-five percent of residents in both Los Angeles and Orange County and the Inland Empire were worried about the Asian crisis. Only 59 percent of residents in the Central Valley thought that the Asian problems would affect California. Here the varying views about the state's economy appear to be a result of regional dependence on technology exports.

We saw more evidence that the structure of the regional economy can affect the outlook on the state. Late in 1998, we asked residents if they thought that economic conditions in California would get better, get worse, or stay the same in the next 12 months. Recall that people in the San Francisco Bay area have higher incomes and are more likely than people in other regions to give high ratings to the state's economy. Yet people in that same area were more likely to say that economic conditions would get worse rather than better (30% to 22%). This is another indication of the fears generated in that region by the Asian financial crisis. Those in the Los Angeles area (31% to 21%) and in Orange County and the Inland Empire (27% to 21%) were more likely to say that the economy would get better than worse. Central Valley residents were evenly divided between optimism and pessimism (24% to 23%).

Residents' views about noneconomic conditions in the state can also vary dramatically from region to region. Crime perceptions offer a good example. As Table 5-5 shows, when asked how much of a problem crime was in California, two-thirds of the respondents answered that crime was a big problem. However, three in four residents in the Central Valley and in Orange County and the Inland Empire believed that crime was a big problem, compared with about two in three residents in Los Angeles and about half of the residents in the San Francisco Bay area. What makes people see the state's crime conditions differently may have more to do with the local media and demographic trends than actual crime statistics. Los Angeles and the San Francisco Bay area have, respectively, the highest and lowest overall crime rates of the four regions. The Central Valley and the Inland Empire and Orange County have similar crime rates, falling between those two extremes (U.S. Census, 1994), and yet people in the Central Valley are more worried than Los Angeles residents about crime. Another question in the same survey also revealed an elevated concern about crime in the Central Valley. The question asked residents if they thought that the crime rate in California had increased, had decreased, or had stayed about the same in the past few years. Government statistics reported rather frequently by the media indicate that the state's crime rate has gone down in recent years. Nevertheless, nearly half of Californians (46%) believed that the crime rate had increased, 28 percent said that it had stayed the same, and only 24 percent thought that it had actually declined. Central Valley residents were the most likely to say that the state's crime rate had increased (53%), followed by those living in Orange County and the Inland Empire (49%), the San Francisco Bay area (45%), and the Los Angeles area (40%).

We also observed differences in the perceptions of the state's public school system. We asked in one survey, "How much of a problem is the quality of education in kindergarten through twelfth-grade public schools?" Altogether, 46 percent of Californians thought it was a big problem. In the San Francisco Bay area, 53 percent thought that the quality of the state's schools was a big problem, compared with a little under half of the residents in Los Angeles (49%) and in Orange County and the Inland Empire (46%). On the other hand, only 39 percent of those living in the Central Valley thought that the public school system represented a "big problem" for the state.

Clearly, differing state perceptions can result in varying priorities for state action. Many Central Valley residents were concerned about the direction of the state, while in the Southern California regions there was a sunny optimism about the way things were going. San Francisco Bay area residents were worried about the economic implications of a financial meltdown in Asia, while many other state residents saw it as a distant news story that did not affect them. Central Valley residents and those living in the mega-suburbs see crime as a big and escalating problem in the state, while those in the more urban coastal regions feel less threatened. The issue of public schools also registered different levels of concern across the major regions of the state. It seems to be difficult for Californians to reach basic agreement on what is taking place in the state.

DIVERSE CONDITIONS IN THE REGIONS

It seems reasonable to assume that the differing views of the state result largely from different conditions in the regions where the respondents live. Certainly, the economic conditions were different in the four regions during the 1990s. High wages were the rule in the booming high-technology industries of the San Francisco Bay area. Jobless rates were low in Orange County and the Inland Empire. The economy improved markedly in Los Angeles after tanking in the early 1990s. Some observers have referred to the Central Valley as the place the recovery has left behind. In the late 1990s, housing prices were escalating in Los Angeles and the mega-suburbs, and homes for sale in the San Francisco Bay area were routinely receiving multiple offers. At the same time, home prices were declining in some parts of the Central Valley. The coastal regions are among the most expensive areas in the nation in which to live; Orange County and the Inland Empire have many new areas that are more affordable, but the cost of living is considerably lower in the Central Valley. To what extent are these economic conditions reflected in residents' perceptions of their regions?

In the focus groups, respondents offered different views about jobs and housing. Their perceptions were highly dependent on their region. Coastal residents were predictably worried about housing and the cost of living, while this was less of a concern elsewhere. "With rents as high as they are, a lot of people can't afford to live here," said a San Francisco resident. "If you want to get into a decent area, you almost have to work two jobs to survive," complained a Los Angeles resident. "Housing is very affordable," said a Sacramento resident. "There's plenty of housing," observed a Fresno resident.

Table 5-6 shows the regional differences in satisfaction with jobs and housing. Seventy-six percent of Californians are satisfied with the job opportunities in their region, with 26 percent saying they are very satisfied. About half of the San Francisco Bay area residents are very satisfied with the job opportunities, compared with one-fourth in the Southern California regions and even fewer in the Central Valley. As for the avail-

TABLE 5-6   REGIONAL PERCEPTIONS BY REGION

	Los Angeles	San Francisco Bay	Central Valley	Orange/ Inland
Job Opportunities				
Very satisfied	22%	46%	18%	23%
Somewhat satisfied	54	42	45	51
Not satisfied	24	12	37	26
Housing Availability				
Very satisfied	23%	11%	31%	29%
Somewhat satisfied	44	31	49	49
Not satisfied	33	58	20	22
Traffic Conditions				
Big problem	36%	54%	15%	31%
Somewhat of a problem	38	29	34	41
Not a problem	26	17	51	28
Population Growth				
Big problem	27%	38%	15%	28%
Somewhat of a problem	38	40	42	37
Not a problem	35	22	43	35

SOURCE: PPIC Statewide Survey, April and May, 1998, all adults.

ability of affordable housing, the regional trends are again very strong. Throughout the state, about one-third are not satisfied with the housing choices in their region. More than half in the San Francisco Bay area are not satisfied with the selection of affordable housing available to them in their region, compared with one-third in Los Angeles, and one-fifth in the Central Valley and in Orange County and the Inland Empire region.

When asked about the most pressing issues facing the state, Californians put education and crime at the top of the list in the statewide surveys. However, traffic, growth, and sprawl emerged in the focus groups when we asked people about the issues that are creating big problems for the regions they live in. These issues were more prominent in the coastal areas. The salient issue for the Central Valley was rural-to-urban change generated by recent growth. "Since I moved here five years ago, my commute has doubled," said a San Francisco resident. "We have too many people in too small an area," lamented a Los

Angeles resident. "Growth . . . it's going to get worse," predicted an Orange County resident. "This is the San Joaquin Valley and a lot of our trees are being cut down . . . and we are supposed to feed the world," said a Fresno resident of the changes under way. "We probably will have lovely freeways to get from one end of the sprawl to another," a Fresno resident predicted for the region's future.

One in three Californians in the statewide survey considered traffic congestion a big problem in their region. As Table 5-6 shows, San Francisco Bay area residents were the most likely to complain about this issue, with more than half seeing traffic congestion as a big problem. In Los Angeles and in Orange County and the Inland Empire, about one-third said that traffic congestion was a big problem. Central Valley residents were by far the least likely to complain about traffic.

Since traffic congestion and population growth usually go hand in hand, one would expect a correlation between people's concern about these phenomena. About 25 percent of Californians rate population growth and development as a big problem in their region. As Table 5-6 shows, San Francisco Bay area residents were, once again, the most likely to complain, with 38 percent saying that growth was a big problem in their region. Slightly more than one-quarter of Los Angeles and Orange County and Inland Empire residents saw growth as a major problem. The fewest complaints were, once again, voiced in the Central Valley, where 15 percent said growth was a big problem for their region.

DIFFERENCES IN LOCAL PUBLIC SERVICES

It is important to know if the ratings of the local public services provided to residents by their governments vary across the four regions. Drastic differences could shift public priorities and thus affect policy preferences and election choices. On the one hand, differences in local service ratings may be expected because of the different contexts of the regions. The coastal regions of Los Angeles and the San Francisco Bay area are heavily populated, congested, and urban in character. The Central Valley still has a strong agricultural presence and a rural-community ambience. Orange County and the Inland Empire are being transformed from a residential to a more industrial region but remain heavily suburban in character. On the other hand, differences in local services within a region—as a result, for instance, of the respective income levels and ages of the communities—may be more significant than the differences across regions. We explored this important issue in the statewide survey.

TABLE 5-7   LOCAL SERVICE RATINGS BY REGION

	Los Angeles	San Francisco Bay	Central Valley	Orange/ Inland
Police Protection				
Excellent or good	69%	67%	62%	71%
Fair	23	28	29	21
Poor	8	5	9	8
Parks and Recreation				
Excellent or good	69%	71%	61%	68%
Fair	23	23	29	24
Poor	8	6	10	8
Streets and Roads				
Excellent or good	50%	38%	43%	49%
Fair	36	38	38	33
Poor	14	24	19	18
Schools				
Excellent or good	46%	43%	50%	53%
Fair	34	36	36	35
Poor	20	21	14	12

SOURCE: PPIC Statewide Survey, May 1998, all adults.

Table 5-7 shows how people rated the local public services they are receiving. Each of the regions seems to have unique strengths and weaknesses. Two in three Californians give excellent or good ratings to police protection and the parks and other public recreational facilities in their areas. Central Valley residents give somewhat lower ratings to both police and parks compared with residents of other regions. As for the highest and lowest scores across regions, there is a 9-point difference in the ratings of the police (71% to 62%) and a 10-point difference in the ratings of parks (71% to 61%).

Two other public services received mixed reviews from state residents. Less than half of Californians say their local streets and roads (46%) and local public schools (48%) are excellent or good. San Francisco Bay area residents give the lowest ratings to their local streets (38%). Los Angeles (50%) and Orange County and the Inland Empire (49%) give higher ratings to their local streets. The trend is similar for public school ratings. San Francisco Bay area residents (43%) are the least likely to give excellent or good ratings. The school

ratings for Orange County and the Inland Empire are 10 points higher
(53% to 43%).

There are also subtle differences in the "quality of life" among the
different regions that can affect people's attitudes toward policy and
government. One San Franciscan defined the quality of life in her region
as "the ability to get on my mountain bike and ride over the Golden
Gate Bridge and go up to open space." A Fresno resident said, "Fresno
is a large city that is trying to keep hold of the small town idea." A Los
Angeles resident focused on an ever-present fear of crime: "The gangs
are causing problems. At night I hear the helicopters flying over." An
Orange County resident worried about the growing presence of ethnic
gangs: "I see where I live a lot of graffiti. It's getting worse."

When asked about the separate "quality of life" domains, most
Californians reported that they are pretty satisfied. However, there are
major differences between the regions with respect to leisure and housing. One-half of Californians are very satisfied with their houses or
apartments. Residents of the Central Valley (60%) and Orange County
and the Inland Empire (60%) are much more likely to say they are very
satisfied with their housing than either San Francisco Bay area (52%)
or Los Angeles (45%) residents. Slightly less than half of Californians
(47%) say they are satisfied with their leisure activities. Those living in
Orange County and the Inland Empire (51%) and the San Francisco
Bay area (48%) report higher satisfaction than those in the Central
Valley (44%) or Los Angeles (42%).

Many people define their quality of life in terms of financial com-
fort. Here regional differences in socioeconomic status result in sharp
variations. About one-third of Californians say that their income is
more than adequate so that they can save money and buy extras.
Despite having higher housing costs, San Francisco Bay area residents
(40%) are more likely to say they have more than enough income to
meet their current needs compared with Los Angeles (29%), Orange
County and the Inland Empire (31%), and Central Valley (31%) residents. Three out of four Californians are satisfied with their current finances. San Francisco Bay area residents (81%) were the most likely
to say they were satisfied with their finances; Los Angeles, Orange
County and the Inland Empire, and Central Valley residents reported
equal levels of satisfaction (72%). Eighty-seven percent of
Californians described their current standard of living as comfortable.
Once again, San Francisco Bay area residents (91%) are more likely
than Los Angeles (85%), Orange County and the Inland Empire

(86%), and Central Valley (86%) residents to say that their current financial status is comfortable.

The local public service ratings do vary by region. Satisfaction with the quality of life also differs across the state. These variations partly reflect real differences in wealth and community conditions between the San Francisco Bay area, the Central Valley, Orange County and the Inland Empire, and Los Angeles. The regional diversity in personal attitudes makes it all the more difficult to reach statewide consensus about the public policy issues that need attention. Candidates running election campaigns have to face the fact that residents' moods vary by region.

DIVERSE OPINIONS ON RACE AND IMMIGRATION

The four regions have all experienced a substantial amount of immigration and undergone a significant degree of racial and ethnic change. These demographic changes have been very dramatic in Los Angeles, significant in the San Francisco Bay area and in Orange County and the Inland Empire, and least evident in the Central Valley. The regions have also had varied experiences with racial problems. In 1992, Los Angeles suffered the most destructive outburst of racial violence in the United States in the twentieth century, with the participants including Latinos, blacks, Koreans, and whites. Next we examine the ways in which residents of these regions differ in their feelings about race and immigration issues.[5]

Our survey shows surprisingly little variation across regions in perceptions of immigration and of racial change. Three in four residents in all four regions think that California has been experiencing an increase in the immigrant population. Across all regions, at least two in three residents believe that the racial and ethnic makeup of their region has been changing.

In the focus groups, participants also said that they were highly aware of immigration and racial change. However, in both the focus groups and the surveys we found regional variations in opinions about the effects of these changes. "Demographics are changing. A lot of businesses are catering to different ethnic groups," said a San Francisco resident. "There's a lot of new arrivals from out of the country into our

5. Many have written about racial and ethnic tensions in Los Angeles (see Baldassare, 1994; Dear, Schockman, and Hise, 1996; Fulton, 1997; Keil, 1998; Rieff, 1991; Scott and Sonja, 1998; Sonenshein, 1993; and Steinberg, Lyon, and Vaiana, 1996). See Neiman (1997), Fernandez and Neiman (1997), and Neiman and Fernandez (1998) for findings and analysis of anti-immigrant attitudes in the Inland Empire.

area and it's impacting things," remarked a Los Angeles resident. "Most of the communities are multimixed, and people seem to be getting along pretty good," said a Sacramento resident. "It seems like we've got our pockets where everyone keeps themselves segregated and separated," observed an Orange County resident. "Fresno is such a culturally diverse community. There are so many misunderstandings and misconceptions about each other's races," said a Fresno resident. "No matter where you are, there's that racial tension, discrimination," said another Fresno resident.

Perceptions about the effects of immigration differ markedly between the more liberal coastal regions and the more conservative Central Valley and the Orange County and Inland Empire regions. As Table 5-8 shows, San Francisco Bay area residents by a 20-point margin (53% to 33%), and Los Angeles residents by a 12-point margin (50% to 38%) believe immigration is a benefit rather than a burden to the state. By contrast, Central Valley residents are divided in perceiving immigration as a benefit versus a burden (45% to 42%), while a majority in Orange County and the Inland Empire see immigration as more of a burden than a benefit (52% to 37%).[6] San Francisco Bay area residents by an 8-point margin (26% to 18%) and Los Angeles residents by a 6-point margin (27% to 21%) say that racial and ethnic change has had a good effect rather than a bad effect on their region. By contrast, Central Valley residents are as likely to say that racial and ethnic change has had a bad effect as a good effect (22% to 20%), while in Orange County and the Inland Empire more residents say that racial and ethnic change has been bad rather than good for their region (25% to 19%).

A more conservative outlook of Central Valley and of Orange County and Inland Empire residents is clearly evident in other attitudes toward immigration. The residents of Orange County and the Inland Empire (55%) and the Central Valley (49%) are more likely than San Francisco Bay area (41%) and Los Angeles (40%) residents to say that illegal immigration from Mexico to California has been a big problem in recent years. Residents in Orange County and the Inland Empire (27%) and the Central Valley (24%) are more likely than residents in the San Francisco Bay area (19%) and Los Angeles (17%) to say that children

6. In the December 1998 survey, we asked if Mexican immigrants were a benefit or a burden to California. The findings were consistent with responses to the general immigration questions, with "benefit" leading "burden" by a bigger margin in the San Francisco Bay area (53% to 31%) and Los Angeles (57% to 30%), than in the Central Valley (48% to 39%) and Orange County and the Inland Empire (47% to 43%).

TABLE 5-8   IMMIGRATION AND RACIAL ATTITUDES
BY REGION

	Los Angeles	San Francisco Bay	Central Valley	Orange/ Inland
Effect of Immigrants				
Benefit	50%	53%	45%	37%
Burden	38	33	42	52
Neither	12	14	13	11
Effect of Racial Change				
Good	27%	26%	20%	19%
Bad	21	18	22	25
No difference	52	56	58	56

SOURCE: PPIC Statewide Survey, April, and October 1998, all adults.

who are illegal immigrants should be prevented from attending public schools. Many people continue to be swayed by the arguments that led to the passage of Proposition 187, and the message is especially powerful in the more conservative regions, where the initiative passed overwhelmingly.

The coastal region's more liberal politics is most evident in attitudes toward affirmative action and other policies aimed at improving the economic opportunities for racial and ethnic groups. The higher proportion of Latinos and nonwhites in Los Angeles also contributes to support for affirmative action. Many residents of Los Angeles (47%) and the San Francisco Bay area (40%) want affirmative action programs to continue, with fewer in the Central Valley (33%) and Orange County and the Inland Empire (35%) in favor. Two in three people in Los Angeles (66%) and the San Francisco Bay area (65%) favor having employers and colleges use outreach programs to hire minority workers and attract minority students, compared with about half of the people in the Central Valley (51%) and Orange County and the Inland Empire (55%). Similarly, residents in Los Angeles (72%) and the San Francisco Bay area (66%) are strongly in favor of high schools and colleges providing special educational programs to assist minorities in competing for college admissions. Once again, public support is weaker in the Central Valley and Orange County and the Inland Empire.

In sum, there is a very high level of public recognition that the state and its major regions are undergoing racial and ethnic change as a result of immigration. The attitudinal differences seem to be largely explained by the conservative politics in the Central Valley and in Orange County and the Inland Empire versus the more liberal political orientations in the coastal regions. The more conservative views in the most rapidly growing regions of the state—the Central Valley and the mega-suburbs of Southern California—will have an increasing effect on elections and public policy. There is already evidence of this in the success of the three race and immigration initiatives.

REGIONAL VARIATION IN DISTRUST OF GOVERNMENT

Given the growing political influence of the Central Valley, it is interesting to note how this region differs from the others in opinions of the government and elected officials. Central Valley residents tend to behave like "swing voters," switching party allegiance from election to election. This points to a certain political independence, perhaps tinged with cynicism about politics and government. Our surveys show that Central Valley residents are indeed more distrustful of their government than those living in the more liberal coastal regions.

The four-question "Trust in Government Index" provides the most consistent evidence of regional differences in overall confidence in government. Only one-third of Californians trust the federal government to do what is right either always or most of the time. Table 5-9 presents the regional differences. The Central Valley (24%) is much less trusting than Los Angeles (41%), the San Francisco Bay area (34%), or Orange County and the Inland Empire (34%). Two in three state residents think the federal government wastes a lot of the taxpayer's money. The Central Valley (72%) is more likely than the San Francisco Bay area (61%), Los Angeles (59%), or Orange County and the Inland Empire (66%) to say that a lot of tax money is wasted. Seven in ten Californians believe that the federal government is pretty much run by a few big interests. The Central Valley (78%) is more likely than the San Francisco Bay area (74%), Los Angeles (62%), and Orange County and the Inland Empire (69%) to say that a few big interests run the government. Four in ten Californians say that quite a few of the people running the government are crooked. This perception is higher in the Central Valley (42%) than in the San Francisco Bay area (37%), Los Angeles (38%), or Orange County and the Inland Empire (39%).

We also saw regional differences in the survey concerning government responsiveness. About one-third of Californians believe that the

TABLE 5-9   GOVERNMENT DISTRUST BY REGION

	Los Angeles	San Francisco Bay	Central Valley	Orange/ Inland
Trust Federal Government				
Always or most of the time	41%	34%	24%	34%
Only sometimes	56	61	71	62
Never	3	4	4	4
Don't know	0	1	1	0
Government Wastes Money				
Wastes a lot	59%	61%	72%	66%
Wastes some	34	32	25	30
Doesn't waste much	6	5	3	4
Don't know	1	2	0	0
How Government Is Run				
Few big interests	62%	74%	78%	69%
Benefit of all people	32	20	15	28
Don't know	6	6	7	3

SOURCE: PPIC Statewide Survey, September 1998, all adults.

government does not pay much attention to what the people think when it decides what to do. The government is seen as less responsive by residents in the Central Valley (34%) and Los Angeles (34%) than by residents in Orange County and the Inland Empire (30%) and the San Francisco Bay area (26%). One in five Californians say that having elections does not do much in terms of making the government pay attention to what the people think. The assertion that the government pays "not much" attention to elections was heard more often in the Central Valley (24%) than in Los Angeles (20%), the mega-suburbs (18%), or the San Francisco Bay area (16%).

There is also a tendency for residents in the Central Valley and in Orange County and the Inland Empire to express more political alienation, which is perhaps tied to their conservatism. About half of Californians agree that "people like me don't have any say about what the government does." Those in the Central Valley (50%) and Orange County and the Inland Empire (50%) are more likely than those in Los Angeles (45%) and the San Francisco Bay area (44%) to say they have no influence. Half of Californians believe that "most elected officials don't care what people like me think." Residents in Orange County and the Inland Empire (58%) and in the Central Valley (57%) are more likely than those in Los Angeles (54%) and the San Francisco Bay area (50%) to feel this way.

The regional differences in trust in state government are small but consistent. Only about one-third of Californians say that you can usually trust the state government to do what is right, half say the state government wastes a lot of the taxpayer's money, and two in three say the state government is pretty much run by a few big interests. Central Valley residents (59%) are a little more likely than Los Angeles (52%), Orange County and the Inland Empire (52%), and San Francisco (51%) residents to say that state government wastes tax money. Los Angeles residents (41%) are more likely than those in the Central Valley (35%), Orange County and the Inland Empire (34%), and the San Francisco Bay area (33%) to say that they always or usually trust the state government to do what is right. Perhaps as a result of a mix of their more conservative leanings, political independence, and history of "swing voting," Central Valley and Orange County and Inland Empire residents are more interested in shaking up the status quo. Residents in Orange County and the Inland Empire (71%) and the Central Valley (66%) are a little more likely to say that term limits have been a good thing for California than residents in Los Angeles (58%) or the San Francisco Bay area (63%).

The performance ratings of specific elected officials point to additional differences between the Central Valley and other regions. Late in 1998, about six in ten Californians said that Clinton was doing an excellent or good job in office. Yet the Democratic president's positive ratings were lower in the Central Valley (51%) and in Orange County and the Inland Empire (54%) than in the San Francisco Bay area (63%) and Los Angeles (72%). In the fall just before Pete Wilson left office, about four in ten Californians gave him either excellent or good ratings for the job he was doing. In this case, the Republican governor's positive ratings were somewhat higher in Orange County and the Inland Empire (48%) and in the Central Valley (45%) than in the San Francisco Bay area (38%) or Los Angeles (39%). The regions did not differ much in their evaluations of the U.S. Congress officeholders or the state legislature.

Another respect in which the regions vary is the level of government they trust the most. We asked Californians in the statewide survey, "What level of government do you trust the most to spend your tax money wisely?" Central Valley residents (6%) were the least likely to say they trusted the federal government the most, followed by San Francisco Bay area (9%), Orange County and Inland Empire (11%), and Los Angeles (14%) residents. Central Valley residents (24%) were also the least likely to say they trusted their city governments the most, followed by residents in the San Francisco Bay area (30%), Orange County and the Inland Empire (33%), and Los Angeles (37%). A financial scandal in Fresno had soured Central Valley residents on their city governments, and consequently about half said they trusted their county and state governments the most with their money—a much higher proportion than in the coastal regions.[7]

Central Valley residents also voiced pessimistic sentiments about government in the focus groups. The Fresno residents were especially appalled by a city government scandal involving developers and a mayoral recall. One resident said, "This is an extraordinarily corrupt city as far as development goes. The upshot of the whole thing is that it's going to cost the taxpayer." Another added, "I think it's basically the structure of our city government. The whole structure is bad because this is allowed to happen." Sacramento residents were the most keenly aware and unflattering of state government because the local media covered the state capitol. "I think political action committees have changed politics. Whoever has the biggest war chest wins," said one resident. "When they get in there it's just, are the Republicans going to win or are the Democrats going to win? They forget the ones in the middle, which is us," added another. "When you go to vote you say, which one is the lesser crook? The name 'politician' is synonymous with 'crook,'" said an especially cynical Sacramento resident.

There is a reservoir of political discontent throughout California, but especially in the Central Valley. These feelings make it easier for politicians to tap into the antigovernment sentiments in the Central Valley than in the coastal areas. This is evident in the responses to most of the trust-in-government items. In fact, the presence of a growing number of "angry white voters" in the Central Valley has helped Republican candidates and conservative initiatives overcome the Democratic and liberal strongholds of the San Francisco Bay area and Los Angeles. As evidenced by the large numbers of disenchanted voters in the Central

7. In the April 1998 survey we found similar results. When respondents were asked what level of government they trusted the most to solve problems, city government was mentioned by 20 percent of Central Valley residents compared with 29 percent in the coastal regions. More than half of Central Valley residents (53%) trusted their county and state governments the most, as opposed to four in ten residents from the coastal regions.

Valley, the extent of political distrust is larger than the Republican base. Democrats and independents must also be included.

Voter distrust is also a powerful force in Orange County and the Inland Empire, although to a lesser degree than in the Central Valley. What is interesting to note, however, is that the conservative, antigovernment reputation of this suburban region is somewhat overstated. In Los Angeles, voter distrust is diminished within the population as a whole as a result of the growing presence of Latinos. As noted earlier, Latinos tend to hold less negative views of the federal government and elected officials. The San Francisco Bay area shows more confidence in government than the other regions—undoubtedly a reflection of the higher proportion of liberal and Democratic residents who hold a progressive vision of a government that can be trusted to be more involved in solving problems.

DIFFERENT ROLES FOR GOVERNMENT

There are many reasons to expect the four regions to differ in their preferences for government involvement. The coastal regions are more Democratic, while the Central Valley and Orange County and the Inland Empire are more Republican. The policy preferences of the various regions presumably should simply reflect party membership. However, other important factors may contribute to regional differences. Residents of the Central Valley fit the profile of "swing voters" who distrust politicians and political parties, which could limit their interest in government activism. Los Angeles has a high concentration of Latino residents. As noted earlier, many immigrants in this group have conservative tendencies when it comes to social issues, despite their Democratic leanings. San Francisco Bay area residents have a traditionally liberal perspective. This should incline them toward favoring more government intervention. Orange County and the Inland Empire are suburban regions with the demographic profile of the "New Political Culture." This should push this region to the left on personal freedom and environmental issues and to the right on fiscal issues. Most significantly, we found evidence of strong regional differences in perceptions of state conditions and regional problems that could influence policy preferences. What people want from government may vary according to what they think is most needed to solve the problems in their region. We next examine how the regions of the state view government intervention in a number of major policy areas.

Table 5-10 shows how the regions differ in attitudes about abortion. Three in four residents in the San Francisco Bay area think the

TABLE 5-10 PREFERRED ROLES FOR GOVERNMENT
BY REGION

	Los Angeles	San Francisco Bay	Central Valley	Orange/ Inland
Abortion				
Choice up to woman	58%	74%	57%	57%
Illegal in some cases	27	19	29	29
Illegal in all circumstances	14	6	14	14
Don't know	1	1	0	0
Environmental Regulations				
Cost too many jobs	33%	30%	45%	37%
Worth the cost	61	67	48	57
Don't know	6	3	7	6
Government Regulation of Business				
Needed to protect the public	59%	56%	49%	50%
Does more harm than good	37	41	48	47
Don't know	4	3	3	3

SOURCE: PPIC Statewide Survey, May 1998, all adults.

choice on abortion should be left up to the woman and her doctor. Despite the fact that Los Angeles is as Democratic as the San Francisco Bay area, four in ten residents there think abortions should be illegal in all or some circumstances. This regional difference in abortion attitudes reflects the influence of the Latino population in Los Angeles. Nearly six in ten residents in the Central Valley and in Orange County and the Inland Empire think that the choice on abortion should be left up to the woman and her doctor. The fact that these two regions do not hold a strong anti-abortion position indicates that there are many conservative voters who have libertarian views on social issues, placing them at odds with some of the recent Republican candidates.

Some regional differences are also found on the issue of gay rights. Sixty-five percent of the people in the San Francisco Bay area think that homosexuality is a way of life that should be accepted by society. Los Angeles (60%) and Orange County and Inland Empire (55%) residents also strongly believe that homosexuality should be accepted by society. In the Central Valley, residents are equally divided between thinking that homosexuality should be encouraged and discouraged by society (46% to 48%). The ambivalence points to some strength of conservative and religious beliefs. The Central Valley does have residents who fit the traditional or "family values" profile.

As shown in the table, large differences emerge in attitudes toward the environment. In the San Francisco Bay area, 67 percent say that stricter environmental laws and regulations are worth the cost, while only 30 percent believe that stricter environmental laws and regulations would cost too many jobs and hurt the economy. The pro-environment stand in this region is somewhat stronger than in Los Angeles (61%). Despite its conservatism, Orange County and the Inland Empire (57%) want more environmental controls as well. This is perhaps because this suburban region includes a highly educated and affluent population that fits the profile of the "New Political Culture," which, among other things, is concerned about environmental issues (Clark and Inglehart, 1998). In the Central Valley, residents are divided over the issue of stricter environmental regulations, with half saying they are worth the cost and half saying they are not. This indicates a skepticism about government in a region where independent-minded people are distrustful of government.

The regions are also divided in their attitudes toward government regulation of business. Los Angeles residents are the most likely to say that government regulation of business is necessary to protect the public interest and the least likely to say that government regulation does more harm than good (59% to 37%). There is a 15-point margin in the San Francisco Bay area between those who think government regulation of business is needed and those who believe it does more harm than good (56% to 41%). Once again, the Central Valley is evenly divided on the issue of government regulation, which indicates a large degree of skepticism about the benefits of government activism. In this instance, Orange County and Inland Empire residents express similar ambivalence.

Attitudes toward government assistance for the poor also vary in a predictable liberal/conservative pattern across the regions. When asked if poor people have become too dependent on government assistance programs, those in the Central Valley (84%) and in Orange County and the Inland Empire (79%) are more likely to agree than are residents of Los Angeles (75%) and the San Francisco Bay area (71%). About half of

Central Valley (48%) and Orange County and Inland Empire (46%) residents think the government is spending too much money on programs to help the poor, compared with about four in ten in the San Francisco Bay area (42%) and Los Angeles (40%). Six in ten residents across all four regions, however, agree that it is the responsibility of government to take care of people who can't take care of themselves. Thus, there is a basic belief in a safety net for the poor that crosses regional boundaries.

There are also differing attitudes across the state toward income inequality and the government's role in addressing the income gap between the wealthy and the poor. We asked residents if they perceived California as divided into economic groups—the haves and have-nots. The perception of haves and have-nots led by a 20-point margin in Los Angeles and the San Francisco Bay area. Residents in the Central Valley and in Orange County and the Inland Empire did not hold such strong views on this subject. About half of Los Angeles (52%) and San Francisco Bay area (47%) residents said that the government should do more to make sure that all Californians have an equal opportunity to succeed. In stark contrast, most Central Valley (60%) and Orange County and Inland Empire (57%) residents believed that people have an equal opportunity to succeed, and there is no need for government intervention. These regional trends point to the powerful differences in government distrust, political ideology, and fiscal conservatism across the regions.

We found general consensus on tax and spending issues across the regions. However, there are important variations in levels of support. We asked residents what priorities they would give to each of the major categories of spending in the state budget. Central Valley residents were not as likely as others to give a high priority to state spending in any of the categories, which fits in with their general reluctance to have the government involved in solving problems. Los Angeles residents were most likely to give a high priority to spending for public colleges and universities (62%), followed by Orange County and the Inland Empire (56%), the San Francisco Bay area (54%), and, in last place, the Central Valley (48%)—despite the fact that a new University of California campus in the Central Valley was awaiting state funding. A similar pattern emerged for public health and welfare, with residents in Los Angeles (57%), Orange County and the Inland Empire (57%), and the San Francisco Bay area (56%) showing a little more support for state funding than Central Valley residents (51%). Even in the highly popular arena of K-12 public school funding, with about eight in ten residents saying this was a high priority, the Central Valley lagged a little behind the other regions. It was only with respect to prison funding that the Central Valley's spending priorities were close to the other three regions. The emphasis that the Central Valley residents placed on prison funding points to their heightened concerns about crime and suggests that perceptions of regional problems can overcome negative views of government intervention.

The reduction in the state vehicle license fee and other state tax cuts recently approved by the governor and state legislature were highly popular in all four regions. However, as might be expected, more residents in the Central Valley (86%) said that the tax cut was important to them, compared with 81 percent of the residents in Los Angeles, 81 percent in Orange County and the Inland Empire, and 70 percent in the San Francisco Bay area. Moreover, nearly half of Central Valley residents described the tax cut as "very important" to them.

There is not much enthusiasm anywhere in the state for tax increases. However, in the San Francisco Bay area, a narrow majority (52%) are in favor of allowing local school districts to raise local taxes with a simple majority instead of a two-thirds vote. About two-thirds are opposed to allowing a simple majority in the other three regions of the state. In this case, we can attribute the differences in tax policy preferences to the heightened concerns about the quality of schools that we observed in the San Francisco Bay area. This is because all four regions are opposed to lowering the supermajority threshold for passing local tax increases by a similar margin of 60 percent to 40 percent. Once again, we have consistent evidence that regional perceptions of problems do matter in shaping specific preferences for government intervention.

What role the government does and should play is a highly charged issue, as was borne out time and again in our focus groups. The Orange County focus groups were particularly emphatic on this topic. Welfare was very unpopular, and most participants talked about it as if they were unaware of the 1996 welfare reform legislation. "I think that so many people abuse the welfare system," said one Orange County resident. "They get housing, they get medical, they get everything and I don't see them getting off of it," said another. Another common theme was that there are too many regulations interfering with people's lives. "There's constantly more restrictions and it just feels very repressive," said one Orange County resident. "I feel sorry for children because there's so many rules," said another. Many also expressed concerns about taxes and spending. "It would be nice if we could vote on the budget, prioritize a list," said one Orange County resident. "Small government, small taxation, a lot of freedom. I would almost be a Libertarian but I don't agree with everything they do," said another participant.

The four regions do reflect different ideas about the extent to which the government should be involved in people's lives. Some but not all of the differences can be explained by the concentrations of Republicans and Democrats in certain areas. Other differences are the result of demographics, such as the large Latino population in Los Angeles and the presence of affluent and highly educated "New Political Culture" residents in Orange County and the Inland Empire. Some differences are a function of a political climate of distrust, as in the Central Valley. Others point to policy preferences that are driven by regional conditions in need of attention, such as traffic congestion in the San Francisco Bay area. Whatever the reasons, the regional differences evident today are certain to have a major effect on future public policy debates and elections.

REGIONAL DIVERSITY AND ELECTION CHOICES

State elections in California are not set on a single stage; they take place on regional platforms. Each contains its own television stations and newspapers. Each requires a separate campaign strategy. As we have seen, the regions' voters have distinct profiles and issues, and they react differently to different campaign messages. To win, candidates need at least a respectable showing in each of the four major regions. Republicans have to run strong in Orange County and the Inland Empire to compensate for the Democratic advantages in Los Angeles and the San Francisco Bay area. Democrats and Republicans both have to keep the margin close in the "swing region" of the Central Valley. To demonstrate the regional nature of state politics, we use the 1998 statewide surveys to look at the governor's race and the U.S. Senate race over time in each of the four regions.

The regions share one important characteristic: a high degree of political inattentiveness. Throughout the 1998 election cycle, fewer than one in five people claimed to have a great deal of interest in politics. About one-third of the residents in the four regions said that they followed government and public affairs most of the time. The level of disinterest in politics was the same across the state's four major regions.

The elections themselves do not seem to generate any more attentiveness to political news in one region than in another. In all four regions throughout the 1998 election cycle, more than half said they did not closely follow the state's political news. Nor did the numerous debates in the governor's race and U.S. Senate race have much of an effect on residents throughout the state. Less than one in ten said the debates had a major effect on how they voted. There were no differences between Los Angeles, the San Francisco Bay area, Orange County and the Inland Empire, and the Central Valley.

While all residents were similarly inattentive, there were regional differences in the sources they relied on for political information. Television has a more significant impact in Los Angeles and the Central Valley. When asked where they received most of their information about what's going on in politics today, Los Angeles residents named television over newspapers (42% to 33%) as did Central Valley residents (45% to 30%) by fairly wide margins. San Francisco Bay area residents gave newspapers a slight edge over television (37% to 32%), and Orange County and Inland Empire residents mentioned television and newspapers equally (37% to 38%). San Francisco Bay area and Orange County and Inland Empire residents are also the most likely to say they frequently read a newspaper. Their greater reliance on newspapers reflects the higher overall education and income levels in these regions. Still, when it comes to general news, it is important to note that television dominates in all of the regions. Six in ten Californians watch television news daily.

The issue of mixing religion and politics is a complicated one in California, and one that was put to the test in the 1998 elections. The ambivalent reactions of voters statewide are partly the result of differences in religious attitudes across the major regions, as shown in Table 5-11. The San Francisco Bay area lags behind all other regions in terms of religious interest. The greater emphasis placed on religion in Los Angeles points to the higher proportion of Latinos and immigrants. A majority of Central Valley (56%) and Orange County and Inland Empire (53%) residents said that religion is a very important part of their lives, reflecting their conservative outlook and traditional values. San Francisco Bay area residents were the least likely to say they regularly attend religious services.

Central Valley (45%) and Orange County and Inland Empire (46%) residents were more likely than residents of the major coastal regions to approve of political candidates talking about religious values when campaigning for office. This might be a reflection of the fact that there are more Republicans in these two regions and that they had accepted the interjection of religion into politics by their candidate Dan Lungren. However, few in any of the regions said that the clergy in their place of

TABLE 5-11   RELIGIOUS ATTITUDES BY REGION

	Los Angeles	San Francisco Bay	Central Valley	Orange/ Inland
Religion in Daily Life				
Very important	53%	41%	56%	53%
Somewhat important	31	33	30	29
Not important	16	26	14	18
Attend Religious Services				
Weekly	34%	32%	37%	39%
Monthly or				
a few times	40	36	36	33
Seldom or never	26	32	27	28
Politicians Discussing Religion				
Approve	36%	32%	45%	46%
Disapprove	60	62	49	47
Don't know	4	6	6	7
Clergy Urged How to Vote				
Yes	13%	10%	9%	11%
No	87	90	91	89

SOURCE: PPIC Statewide Survey, September 1998, all adults.

worship had urged them how to vote. All things considered, we should not assume that the Central Valley or Orange County and the Inland Empire have the strongly conservative politics of the southern Bible Belt. For instance, we know that many people in these regions are pro-choice when it comes to abortion and are in favor of gay rights. Moreover, Central Valley residents are no more likely than those living in Los Angeles or the San Francisco Bay area to say that their clergy have urged them to vote in a particular way. It would appear that Central Valley residents are simply more interested in talking about religion and politics, while others are less tolerant about mixing these topics.

We first looked at the governor's race and the U.S. Senate race in April 1998.[8] Scarcely anyone was paying attention to the election, with two in three residents in every one of the four regions saying they were not following the news about California politics. However, television

8. The percentages from the statewide surveys reported in this section are based on the total sample of all adults, rather than registered voters or likely voters.

commercials for the governor's race were being noticed, with most people saying they recalled the commercials by Democratic businessman Al Checchi. The television ads by all of the gubernatorial candidates were recalled more in the San Francisco Bay area and Los Angeles (75% each)—perhaps reflecting the targeting of Democratic voters—than they were in the Central Valley (69%) and in Orange County and the Inland Empire (70%).

In the U.S. Senate race, fewer than one-sixth of residents recalled the political advertising, with Republican businessman Darrell Issa receiving the most mentions. The commercials by all of the U.S. Senate candidates were remembered least in the heavily Democratic San Francisco Bay area, perhaps reflecting the fact that more money was spent on television ads targeting independents and Republicans in the Central Valley and Southern California mega-suburbs. At this early stage, Central Valley and Orange County and Inland Empire residents appeared to be more interested than others in candidates who were political outsiders, such as Issa and Checchi. Residents in these two regions were less likely than those in other regions to say they were bothered by the idea of wealthy candidates spending their own money to run for office. Although Checchi and Issa showed strength in the Central Valley and the mega-suburbs, about one-third of the voters in all four regions had not yet chosen a favorite candidate.

Californians were still fairly oblivious to the upcoming June primary when this major political event was only one month away. Six in ten in each region said they were not paying attention to the news about the state election. In the governor's race, the television commercials were once again most often noticed in the San Francisco Bay area (76%) and Los Angeles (72%), and less often recalled in the Central Valley (67%) and Orange County and the Inland Empire (68%). In the U.S. Senate race, Central Valley residents (24%) remembered the advertisements more than the Los Angeles (16%), Orange County and Inland Empire (16%), and San Francisco Bay area (4%) residents. Issa and Checchi ran the commercials most remembered in these races. There was a sharp distinction in the candidate qualities favored in each region. Los Angeles and San Francisco Bay area residents strongly preferred candidates with political experience, while Central Valley and Orange County and Inland Empire residents were divided between favoring political experience and business experience. As a result, Issa and Checchi continued to lead in these regions.

In the end, the coastal preferences for political experience won out in the June primary. Republicans selected Attorney General Dan Lungren and Democrats chose Lieutenant Governor Gray Davis as their candidates in the governor's race. Democrats selected incumbent Barbara Boxer and Republicans chose State Treasurer Matt Fong to be the candidates in the U.S. Senate race. The strong preference for political outsiders in the Central Valley and in Orange County and the Inland Empire had been overcome by the more conventional leanings of voters in the populous coastal regions.

When we next visited the governor's race and U.S. Senate race in the fall, there were already very sharp divisions between the regions. Davis was leading Lungren by a 2-to-1 margin in Los Angeles and the San Francisco Bay area, while the two were tied in the Central Valley and in Orange County and the Inland Empire. The latter situation was an ominous sign for a Republican candidate. Boxer enjoyed big leads over Fong in Los Angeles and the San Francisco Bay area, while Fong was ahead of Boxer in the Central Valley and the two were tied in Orange County and the Inland Empire. At this point, about six in ten residents were not highly focused on the election news in each of the four regions. The television commercials in the U.S. Senate race were noticed by roughly one in five people in each of the regions. The regional differences in the recall of television commercials for the governor's race are interesting. Nearly six in ten residents in the Central Valley remembered seeing television advertising by the gubernatorial candidates, compared with only one-quarter of the residents in the other three regions. This difference indicates that both campaigns had decided that this "swing" area was critical to winning the election. In all four regions, residents said that in deciding whom to vote for in the election, they were more concerned with the candidates' stands on the issues than with their experience, character, or political party.

A month before the November general election, the regions remained distinct in their candidate choices for both of the major statewide races. About half of Californians, with similar numbers from the respective regions, were still not making much of an effort to follow the election. Davis was ahead of Lungren by a wide margin in the San Francisco Bay area and Los Angeles. The two gubernatorial candidates were tied in the Central Valley and in Orange County and the Inland Empire. About six in ten had seen the television advertisements in each of the four regions, indicating similar amounts of time and effort spent trying to reach the voters in each of the crucial regions. A similar geographic pattern was evident in preferences in the U.S. Senate race. Boxer was well ahead of Fong in Los Angeles and the San Francisco Bay area, and the two candidates were tied in the Central Valley and in Orange County and the Inland Empire. There were very different patterns in recollection of the television ads for the U.S. Senate race across the four regions. About half recalled the commercials in the San Francisco Bay area (56%), Orange County and the Inland Empire (52%), and Los Angeles (45%), compared with only about one-third of the residents in the Central Valley (36%). A majority in all regions said that the candidates' stands on the issues mattered more than character, experience, or party. Nor did the Clinton-Lewinsky scandal seem to have more effect in one region than another. Seven in ten across all regions said that the scandal would not affect their likelihood of voting. Three in four said it would not affect the party they supported in the state races.

In the November election, Davis won the governor's race by 20 points statewide, collecting overwhelming margins of support in the major coastal regions and even a 5-point win in the Central Valley. Davis and Lungren tied in the Republican stronghold of Orange County and the Inland Empire. Boxer won the U.S. Senate race by 10 points statewide, with large margins in Los Angeles and the San Francisco Bay area, while losing the Central Valley to Fong by a 5-point margin. Fong won over Boxer by an even larger margin in Orange County and the Inland Empire. Once again, the regions behaved very differently in a statewide election. The state had elected officials who did not enjoy a similar level of support across regions. This time, the coastal regions had prevailed.

CONCLUSIONS AND IMPLICATIONS

One of the major challenges facing California in the new century is how to make a whole out of the sum of its parts. A sense of togetherness has never been a strong suit for this state. The vast and diverse geography and water wars have, since long ago, led to calls for dividing California into two or more states. Today, the variations in growth experiences and a lack of appreciation about what Californians have in common has taken its toll. The major regions are drifting further apart at a time when there is a great need to reach a statewide consensus on social, environmental, land use, and infrastructure issues. The ongoing regional population changes add further complications, shaping how the political power in the future will be shared by the urban coastal, vast inland,

and mega-suburban regions. Los Angeles has experienced the most rapid ethnic and racial change due to immigration, and it is already a "majority-minority" region. The San Francisco Bay area has enjoyed the explosive growth of the high-technology industry and has also experienced a large amount of racial and ethnic change as a result of immigration from Asia and Latin America. The Central Valley has been undergoing a rural-to-urban transformation. Orange County and the Inland Empire have been experiencing some of the fastest employment and population growth in the state.

The coastal regions have a very different political profile from the Central Valley and Orange County and the Inland Empire. Los Angeles and the San Francisco Bay area both have high concentrations of Democratic voters and a fairly liberal political profile. The Central Valley has roughly equal numbers of Republicans and Democrats and a more conservative political orientation. Orange County and the Inland Empire have more Republicans than Democrats. The coastal regions tend to vote Democratic in statewide elections, the Central Valley is a "swing" region, and Orange County and the Inland Empire more often than not overwhelmingly support the Republican tickets. The Central Valley is the most unpredictable of all of the major regions: either Democrats or Republicans can win if they appeal to the many independent-minded voters who say they are moderate to somewhat conservative in their politics.

There are major differences among the regions in perceptions and evaluations of the state's economy and local community conditions. Across regions, residents differ even in their ratings of local public services and satisfaction with the quality of their lives. These differences are a result of the varying economic, growth, racial and ethnic, and community conditions in the regions.

There are also significant differences in political attitudes. Central Valley residents are less trusting of government than others. San Francisco Bay area residents are more in favor of environmental regulations and more opposed to abortion restrictions. Los Angeles and San Francisco Bay area residents are more likely to favor an active role for government in assisting the poor and reducing inequality. Orange County and Inland Empire residents are more conservative on fiscal issues, such as spending, tax cuts, and tax increases. The political differences reflect regional variations in party affiliation, race and ethnicity, income, and local problems. The four regions responded very differently to the candidates and issues in the statewide races in 1998. There is also evidence that the campaigns were specifically geared toward the voters in the separate regions. The 1998 election was yet another example of how regional diversity is having an impact on California politics, elections, and public policy. State campaigns are focusing on regional distinctions rather than statewide similarities, forgoing the much-needed public dialogue about California's future.

CHAPTER 6

The Future
of the Golden State

The California of the mid-twenty-first century is going to be a very different state from the California of today. There is every reason to expect the state's population to exceed 50 million in the next 30 years or so.[1] The proportion of Californians who are white will steadily decline, while Latinos become the dominant racial and ethnic group. Uneven growth will tip the regional balance of the state away from Los Angeles and the San Francisco Bay area toward the Central Valley and Southern California's mega-suburbs. Aging Baby Boomers and new immigrants will add dramatically to the old and young populations. Manufacturing jobs will continue to disappear while service employment increases its share of the labor force, raising questions about whether the "new economy" will bring about widespread prosperity or a two-tier economic system.[2]

Californians know they are living in the midst of historic growth and change, and they are clearly worried about it. More than 80 percent of residents said in the surveys that they expect their regions to grow ei-

1. See California Department of Finance (1998a) for a description of the methodology that was used to make projections of the California population. These predictions tend to be more modest than others (see Bouvier, 1991; Center for the Continuing Study of the California Economy, 1999).

2. Kimball and Richardson (1997, p. 10) predict that from 1996 to 2020, the percentage of California nonfarm jobs in manufacturing will decline from 14 percent to 9 percent, while service jobs will increase from 30 percent to 40 percent of the total share.

ther rapidly or modestly in population over the next 10 years. Most believe that the basic infrastructure in their regions today will be inadequate for the growth that lies ahead, including the transportation system and water supply. Californians emphatically say that they want their government to start planning for the future today. Nearly everyone said it was important to get ready for the future by building more schools and colleges, expanding water storage facilities, and building more roads.

How California copes with its challenges is of great importance, and not only to residents of the state. Americans are accustomed to looking to California as the trendsetter for the nation, the harbinger of things to come, and the symbol of what is right and wrong with the nation. Indeed, the world itself is influenced by the economic currents in the Golden State, as California—the seventh largest economy in the world—has become a major exporter and importer in the global marketplace.

As of this writing, there is a great deal of talk about what the state needs to do to prepare for its future.[3] In the 1950s and 1960s, California took a giant leap forward by investing in infrastructure, including freeways and highways, dams and aqueducts, parks and beaches, and public colleges and universities that were second to none. Today, the state seems to have lost the will and the way to get things done. In the 1990s, when it was time to go from planning to actions, policy gridlock often ruled the day.[4] "Uncontrolled growth, unplanned growth. No long-term planning for the problems involving growth," was the summation of a San Francisco resident.

The preceding chapters have argued that there are three powerful forces at work in shaping California political life and policy debates. This chapter looks beyond 2000 and offers some general ideas about how these forces—political distrust, racial and ethnic change, and regional diversity—are likely to play out in the state's political and policy process. Some recommendations are then offered that, hopefully, will

3. See discussions on suburban sprawl, proposals for statewide land use initiatives, and the implementation of "smart growth" (California Futures Network, 1999; California State Treasurer, 1999; Center for the Continuing Study of the California Economy, 1998; Chawkins, 1999; Egan, 1998; King, 1999; Purdum, 1999b).

4. The state government did make efforts to study the issue of state growth management in the early 1990s. The issue was studied by the governor and state legislature, but no actions were taken (Baldassare et al., 1996; California Economic Development Corporation, 1990).

help the state find better ways to cope with the many challenges looming before it.

BEYOND 2000

There is every reason to believe that the three forces discussed in this book will affect California politics and elections for many decades to come. This is evident from the information provided in the public opinion surveys and the focus groups, and from recent demographic and voting trends. The power of these phenomena was also evident in our early surveys of the 2000 elections, in which we found continuing evidence of political disengagement and distrust, a unique pattern of Latino voting, and a regional division in ballot preferences.[5] No doubt, there are other important trends that will define the future—for instance, the gender gap in voting and the low level of voting interest among young adults. So what are some of the likely effects?

1. In general, reaching public consensus on policy issues in the state will become more difficult as a result of a continuation of current trends.
There are a number of reasons why the current trends of regional diversity, racial and ethnic change, and political distrust will make it more difficult to gain public agreement on policy issues in the future. Regional diversity is creating conflicting views about the state's economic conditions and the local problems that are most in need of government action. It is becoming more difficult to find unifying perceptions that will bring together the residents of the large coastal metropolises, the growing megasuburbs, and the Central Valley. The state is also showing signs of divisive attitudes along racial and ethnic lines. For instance, blacks and whites are concerned about the negative effects of increased immigration, while Asians and Latinos tend to see this demographic trend in positive

5. The December 1998 survey included questions on the 2000 presidential election, which are included in the appendices. The findings indicate that politics remained very fluid in the state. Despite speculation after the 1998 elections, there is little evidence of a "permanent realignment" of the California electorate that favors the Democrats and liberal causes. With regard to possible presidential matchups, independents split their support between Republican and Democratic contenders, support for major party candidates varied sharply across the regions, and Latinos showed less than overwhelming support for the Democratic ticket. The conservative undercurrents were evident in support for a possible ballot measure that would create a voucher system for public schools and a "definition of marriage" initiative that would recognize only a marriage between a man and a woman as valid.

terms. Blacks and Latinos favor affirmative action programs, while Asians and whites are less sympathetic toward government involvement in helping minorities succeed in education and employment. The climate of political distrust will, of course, make these policy disputes more difficult to resolve. Many people have a tendency to discount the policy reactions of the governor and state legislature, since they lack any faith in this process working. One possibility is that battles over the state's public policy directions will be settled at the ballot box with dueling citizens' initiatives.

2. *California elections will continue to be dominated by political distrust, affecting voter turnout, advertising messages, and ballot choices.* The surveys provided substantial documentation of a climate of political distrust in California that has broad implications for politics. Residents have little confidence in their state and federal governments. They hold politicians and elected leaders in low esteem, citing their inability to get the job done, their lack of responsiveness, and their poor record in fiscal management. Some voters even question their honesty and integrity. Against this backdrop, many Californians show little or no interest in politics. Relatively few closely follow political and government news. Many are simply not watching when the television news and newspapers turn their attention to the California election. Until this changes, and there are no signs that it will any time soon, it will remain a very difficult task for candidates for statewide offices to engage the attention of Californians.

Political candidates are becoming ever more reliant on the strategy of spending millions of dollars on 30-second commercials to win statewide elected offices. It seems to be the only way they know to reach disinterested voters. The last two governor's races each set records for spending. It will likely cost more in future elections to motivate the same, or even a lower, number of voters. Campaign financing raises some questions about the promises that politicians make when they take so much money from special interests to pay for their political commercials. It also leaves many residents feeling even more dubious about the campaign process and elected officials. A large number of Californians are not registering to vote. Only about half of those who are eligible to vote are showing up at the polls for presidential elections, and even fewer show up to vote for other state and local elections. There is no reason to believe there are forces at work that will stop the cycle of political distrust, political disengagement, and low voter turnout.

One other consequence of political distrust is that it breeds a cynical brand of political activism. Proposition 13 and the more recent initiatives limiting government spending and taxes are but one example. Term limits to ensure that elected officials are removed from office on a regular basis is another example. Candidates and initiatives carrying antigovernment themes will continue to have popular appeal in California.

3. Citizens' initiatives will continue to play a major role in elections and will be the leading force in shaping the public policy directions of the state.

State propositions have been appearing on the ballot in increasing numbers for the past two decades. In the 1998 primary and general elections, there were as many state propositions on the ballot as there were in all of the state elections in the 20-year period between 1950 and 1969. Their success rate is also increasing. Throughout the 1990s, sixty-nine state propositions were placed on the ballot, and thirty-two of them passed.

There is every reason to believe that the trend of relying on initiatives to shape public policy will continue. Voters are inclined to think that the initiative process is better suited than the governor or state legislature for tackling the difficult problems facing California. The political distrust they feel toward elected leaders ensures that they will use initiatives frequently in the future, sometimes with the goal of limiting the powers of elected officials. In their turn, the governor and legislators have incentives to leave the controversial decisions up to the voters and thereby avoid any political fallout.

Many citizens' groups and special interests believe that it is worth the cost to try to create policy, or thwart it, at the ballot box rather than in the halls of government. A sophisticated initiative industry has evolved for gathering signatures, raising funds, creating advertising, and getting out the vote for and against initiatives. The implication is that consequential state policies will be made at the ballot box. Moreover, statewide candidates will continue to run campaigns based on themes derived from the popular initiatives on the ballot.

4. An increasing proportion of independent voters will participate in California elections, giving the major parties less political control.

About one in eight voters today is registered as "decline to state" or nonpartisan. The number of independent voters in California has been increasing more rapidly than Democratic or Republican registration. This is a political trend at least partly fueled by political distrust. In an era when Californians have proclaimed that they have little faith in their elected leaders, they have increasingly turned away from the major political parties that have been running their governments.

The "open primary" initiative that passed in 1996 is an indication of the extent to which there is a lack of respect for political parties and a yearning on the part of many voters to be free from partisanship. The open primary has also opened the door to an even greater increase in the number of independent voters. The fact that voters can participate in primaries and choose the local and state party candidates to run for offices without belonging to a major political party removes one of the remaining incentives for registering as a Republican or a Democrat. As Californians become more aware of the full range of options that the open primary has provided for them, new voters and currently registered voters alike will find little reason not to register as independents.

The major implication of a growing base of independent voters is that California elections will become a much more volatile arena. We have seen evidence that independent voters can switch their allegiances from party to party, even within the same election. Independent voters are more demanding that candidate stands be based on issues that matter to them, rather than on political ideology, partisanship, or strength of moral character. Independent voters have a tendency to view government involvement with more skepticism than others, so they will tend to support candidates and policies that keep government out of their private lives.

5. Latinos will play an increasingly important role in state elections, although their political impact is far from certain.
Latinos have been one of the fastest-growing racial and ethnic groups in California since the 1980s. Sometime in the twenty-first century, there will be more Latinos than whites living in California. Exit polls show a steady increase in the proportion of the electorate who are Latino, but this proportion is still far short of their overall representation in the California population. As the Latino population ages and citizenship rates increase, more and more Latinos will be eligible to vote in every election for several decades to come. However, the extent to which Latinos become full participants in the electoral process is an open question. Latinos in the surveys lagged other groups in the amount of political information they sought, in their level of interest in elections, and in their intentions to vote. Whether these attitudes change depends on many unknown factors. Will race and immigration

initiatives appear on future ballots? Will these "wedge issues" politically mobilize the Latino population, as has been the case in the 1990s? Will Latinos awaken to their growing political strength? If not, the only effect of having more Latinos in the voting-eligible population could be to further reduce an already low voter turnout rate in California.

There is, at any rate, the possibility of a larger Latino vote that could shift the policy debates and election outcomes. Latinos have provided overwhelming support for Democratic candidates in recent statewide elections. If this partisan trend continues as the Latino vote grows, this will be an advantage to the Democrats. Some have argued, however, that this particular trend is a short-term phenomenon, perhaps a response to the GOP support for Proposition 187 in 1994. It may be too early to assume that Latino partisan patterns have emerged. The effect of a growing number of Latinos on public policy debates is already being felt and could be more profound in the future. Latino participation has caused statewide candidates to avoid supporting "wedge issues," such as the anti–bilingual education initiative in 1998, that could alienate this large and growing block of voters. Even though their political orientations are similar, a decline in white voting and an increase in Latino voting, if it occurs, could affect the policy landscape of the state. Latinos have a different pattern of liberal/conservative interests than whites, for instance, showing more support for social spending and less support for abortion rights. Another important trend is that Latinos are now being elected to statewide offices and are holding more powerful legislative positions, ensuring that a Latino perspective will enter into state policy decisions.

6. Older voters will have an increasing presence in California elections, affecting voter turnout, issue salience, and ballot choices.
Another powerful demographic trend is under way in the state, but so much attention has been paid to immigration and racial and ethnic change that this one is sometimes forgotten: the aging of the Baby Boom generation and the growing population of older Californians. This trend can barely be seen now because it is in its beginning stages. It will become very evident in 20 or 30 years. The growth of the older population will have a powerful influence on elections. Voting is highly correlated with older age. This is because older voters have the time to participate in elections. They are also more residentially stable than younger adults and are thus more likely to be registered to vote. For these and other reasons, the proportion of voters who are 60 and older is always higher

than the proportion of the state population that is 60 and older. This imbalance is likely to increase in the future. Thus, older voters, who are already carefully courted by prudent politicians, will become an even more dominant force in state politics in the years to come.

The growing population of older voters is a demographic trend that could help the Republicans and conservative causes. In the 1998 elections, for instance, Fong was virtually tied with Boxer (48% to 50%) in the U.S. Senate race and Davis won only narrowly over Lungren in the governor's race (51% to 46%) among the voters who were 60 and older and who constituted more than one-quarter of the state's voters. Both of the Democrats won by very large margins among the younger voters. Some observers believe that the Baby Boomers, as they age, will establish a more Democratic and liberal voting record than the current group of older voters. But consider the fact that many of the older voters today were once the "Roosevelt Democrats" who supported an era of big government.

There is one aspect of the aging trend that tends to favor the Democrats: the "gender gap" in California voting. Women are more inclined than men to register as Democrats and to vote for Democratic candidates. For instance, in the 1998 election, women supported Davis over Lungren (60% to 35%) by a much wider margin than men (54% to 43%), and while women overwhelmingly favored Boxer over Fong (57% to 39%), men were evenly divided between the Democrat and the Republican (48% each). Since women live longer than men, a much higher proportion of older Californians are women. Thus, the aging of the population will place more power in the hands of women voters and raise the possibility of an advantage for the Democrats.

It is also very likely that the large block of older voters will influence the public policy debates in the state. The quality of public schools is an issue that holds special appeal to parents of young children, not the old. Freeway traffic is a big problem for working people, not the old. Issues such as health care costs and access to mass transit may be more pressing concerns for older Californians, and it is likely that the concerns of these Californians will become the concerns of politicians as they seek the support of older voters.

7. *The Central Valley vote will increase in the state's elections, creating a regional shift in policy issues and in the balance of political power.*
In recent decades, the Central Valley has been one of the fastest-growing regions in the state. It is also expected to have a larger share of the state's

population in the next few decades, as it grows faster than the coastal regions. The Central Valley has already become one of the few areas where politicians for statewide office go seeking large numbers of "swing voters." Over the past few decades, Central Valley voters have swung back and forth between Democrats and Republicans. This is a region that is well known for its political independence. Republicans can overcome the large Democratic advantages in the coastal regions if they can do very well in the Central Valley, while Democrats have to worry about losing by overwhelming margins in this vast area. A lot of time, attention, and money is dedicated to attracting the Central Valley voter. These efforts will only increase as the Central Valley grows in political importance relative to the heavily populated, but more slowly growing, urban coastal regions.

On the whole, the growth of the Central Valley is a trend that helps Republicans more than Democrats. Republicans are significantly outnumbered by Democrats in the San Francisco Bay area and Los Angeles, but Central Valley voters are about evenly split in their party registration. Moreover, many of the Democrats and independents in the Central Valley are conservatives. In the 1998 election, for instance, Davis just barely beat Lungren and Boxer lost to Fong in the Central Valley, even as the Democrats went on to win by large margins in the state.

It is likely that the growth in size and importance of the Central Valley will exert a conservative influence on public policy. Central Valley voters are more conservative than coastal voters in general and hold more conservative positions on a range of specific policy issues, including environmental regulations and government intervention in social and economic problems. There will be greater representation from the Central Valley as its seats in the state legislature continue to grow, and this, too, will affect policy debates.

8. The Orange County–Inland Empire vote will increase in state elections, but racial and ethnic change makes the impact of this regional shift uncertain.
California is a suburban state becoming more suburban all the time. The largest and most concentrated suburban area is Orange County and the Inland Empire. It has been growing at a rapid pace for many decades and is expected to be among the fastest-growing areas in California for the next 30 to 40 years. The political importance of this suburban region cannot be overstated. There are as many voters in the three-county region as in the Central Valley, accounting for about one-sixth of the

state's voters. In the future, the proportion of state voters who live in Orange County and the Inland Empire will be even greater. With the expected rapid growth of this region and other large suburban regions, such as northern San Diego County and Ventura County, we can anticipate an even greater suburban emphasis in California politics than we see today.

The growth of suburban regions is a trend that should help the Republicans and conservative causes. The strength that Republican candidates have had in Orange County and the Inland Empire has often helped to offset Democratic advantages elsewhere in the state, leading to Republican victories. As Orange County and the Inland Empire grows, one would think that the number of Republican voters will increase. Because this area is growing faster than the rest of the state, Republicans should have even more of an advantage in the future. However, the countertrend for the suburban areas is that the Latino population is increasing, limiting the advantages of Republicans and contributing to the support of the Democrats. One example is the victory of Democrat Loretta Sanchez over Republican Bob Dornan in a congressional race in central Orange County. Another is the fact that Republican candidates who ran for statewide office in the 1990s did not fare as well in these increasingly diverse suburbs as they did in the 1980s. The growth of suburban areas will also have an effect on policy debates. White suburban residents, for instance, are concerned about immigration and the racial and ethnic change occurring in their midst. Suburban sprawl may also become a pressing issue for voters as freeways become more congested and travel times increase.

POLICY RECOMMENDATIONS
FOR THE FUTURE CALIFORNIA

According to all of the predictions about California's future, the first half of the twenty-first century will be filled with growth and change. How government and the people will respond to the challenges accompanying these changes is less certain. Although change may be inevitable, we need not face the future with fatalistic pessimism. Efforts can be made today that will help to reduce some of the public's distrust of government and prepare for the racial and ethnic transformation and increasing regional diversity that lie ahead. The following ten policy recommendations outline some of those efforts. Six deal with the issue of voter distrust, two tackle the challenges involving racial and ethnic change, and two are concerned with regional diversity.

1. State and local government reforms should be implemented with the goal of increasing government efficiency, responsiveness, and accountability.

A "C–" grade for the state government just will not do for a California that is confronted with so many social challenges and economic opportunities. The residents of the state are deeply distrustful of government and politicians. Few expect their governments to do what is right. Many fret that the people they have elected to office are wasting their tax money. Californians do not believe that their government represents average people like themselves, and they see their politicians as more inclined to bend to the wishes of special interests. Some of these sentiments are drawn from negative reports in the media, but many times these perceptions are based on real experiences. Some even say that the system of state and local government today is dysfunctional.

With the state expected to grow by leaps and bounds, it is time for a top-to-bottom assessment of how to improve the quality of state and local government. There is no shortage of good proposals for reform, including the solid recommendations of the California Constitution Revision Commission (1996), which calls for the following changes:

· Allow the governor and lieutenant governor to run on the same ticket, to work as a team, and to appoint certain constitutional officeholders who are now elected.

· Require that the governor and state legislature set long-term goals and performance measures for the state budget.

· Establish an accountability system for local public schools.

· Give local communities the power to supplement revenue to local schools.

· Require each county to develop a community charter that allocates local services and provides methods for reducing the number and cost of local governments.

The ideas for government are well developed. What has been lacking thus far is the political will to change the status quo. Political distrust, and the growth and increasing diversity of the state, call for meaningful change.

2. Public, private, and nonprofit groups in the state need to stimulate civic dialogue and public engagement to prepare for the growth and change ahead.

One of the keys to a successful future for California is having an informed and involved citizenry. Today, California has neither. Many longtime residents are too cynical to participate, while many new immigrants are too intimidated to try. Californians are not that knowledgeable about public affairs. Many residents have little or no interest in state politics. Voters have become as out of touch with government and with state and local issues as they claim the politicians and public institutions are with them. Those who are voting are often asked to make difficult and complicated decisions that will have implications for years to come on issues they know little about.

It is healthy in a democracy for citizens to have a say in public policy decisions, and for that reason many Californians treasure the initiative process. But it takes work to stay on top of the issues and motivation to get involved in politics and state and local affairs, and those elements are currently in short supply. There are occasional efforts by state organizations to "get out the vote," but they have not succeeded in improving turnout. Neither has a series of gubernatorial debates that were sparsely covered by the media and dismissed as canned events by the public. A more sustained effort of education and outreach that connects the public with its government is needed. Too often, the political professionals are focusing on targeting messages to narrow constituencies. Campaigns are rarely designed to stimulate higher voter turnout. This is a political strategy with short-term gains and long-term repercussions. Californians have to be reminded that they are a part of the solution to the state's problems.

Everyone would seem to have a great stake in encouraging a civic dialogue and public engagement in state and local policy issues. In greatest need of discussion is the topic of growth and change in the state. Our surveys indicate that residents are keenly aware that rapid growth is already occurring. They are worried about what they see as a lack of planning for the future. Their concerns about growth and change offer an excellent opportunity for government, the private sector, and nonprofit leaders to work together with local and regional groups to engage the California public in a civic dialogue on the future. These public policy conversations need to deal with people's real concerns about their everyday lives. The topics of sprawl, traffic, housing, and schools need to be connected with state and local governance issues. The state issues must also be brought to people's doorsteps. Local associations and regional organizations should be called upon to host the dialogue. Government officials and state leaders have become so cynical about the public that many have stopped trying to actively engage the citizens they serve. This has increased the public's cynicism toward government. Average residents in our focus groups told us that they want to hear more in person from their elected officials. They also want a voice in the decisions that affect their lives. The public named town halls and forums as their preferred format for listening and being listened to. Preparation for the growth and change that will occur in the state makes a civic dialogue not only imperative, but a real possibility.

3. The state government should remove barriers and create more programs to encourage voter registration and higher participation rates in elections.

Many Californians today are not registering to vote. About half of eligible adults are not participating in presidential elections, and six in ten are not involved in the selection of their governor and U.S. senator in off-year state elections. The primaries and local elections are reflecting the preferences of only a small proportion of the voters. Many reasons are given for not voting. Some say they are too busy to register to vote, don't have time to vote on election day, or find the whole process too overwhelming. More and more people are turning in absentee ballots, as even the most committed voters cannot be sure of their whereabouts on election day. As California becomes a "majority-minority" state, it will become all the more important for voting to become a more inclusive process. Many elections today are decided by older, white, affluent residents. If that trend continues into the future, then elections are sure to create feelings of alienation and resentment among the younger, nonwhite, and less affluent residents.

Voter registration has too often relied on a chance meeting of eligible adults and party officials in shopping malls and on street corners. The places where people can register should be expanded to the places they most frequent in today's society, such as grocery stores and gas stations. The recent efforts to stimulate voting, including the "motor voter," the open primary, and extending the registration period, are good starts but not sufficient to reverse the trend. The technology exists for people to vote electronically at home, through cable television and the Internet. California could and should lead the nation in innovative efforts to increase voter registration and election turnout.

4. The state government should encourage television to expand its election role from advertising to town hall meetings, call-ins, and live debates.

Californians are tired of the way campaigns are run today, largely because they know they have become overly dependent on television advertising. Voters are introduced to statewide candidates through 30-second commercials that offer much in the way of image and little in the way of policy substance. They are exposed to a steady diet of commercials for months, followed by a barrage in the final weeks of the campaign. People know they are seeing the candidates in artificial and contrived situations, and they resent it. They know that these commercials are slanted and are not intended to provide the whole truth, and they dislike much of what they see. Californians are aware that the negative commercials or "hit" pieces can be filled with inaccuracies, and they despise this political gamesmanship. But this is the television era, and more and more voters are relying on commercials in making their decisions in the statewide elections. This trend is likely to accelerate, as fast-growing voter groups such as young adults and Latinos let television become their primary source of political information.

Television needs to branch out from paid commercials. Focus group participants told us about some of the different formats they would prefer:

· Candidates interacting in live televised debates
· Candidates being asked questions by average voters in town hall meetings
· Candidates responding to one-on-one television interviews and answering questions that are called in by the television audience

In a democracy, television has a responsibility to do more than simply broadcast paid commercials.

5. State government should reform campaign financing, as money and its sources threaten to further undermine the credibility of elected officials.

The costs of statewide campaigns have been skyrocketing while efforts to reform campaign financing have stalled. The candidates and initiative campaigns spent $500 million in the 1998 California election—much more than the $297 million spent in the 1996 state election and the $262 million spent in 1994 (Morain, 1999b). The candidates for governor are spending between $20 million and $30 million on the primary and general election. Senate candidates are spending similar amounts. Most of their expenses go to pay for television commercials in the major media markets.

Expensive campaigns have several consequences. Some qualified candidates are not running for statewide office, because they do not think they can raise large enough sums of money. Third-party candidates and independents have virtually no chance of succeeding, as they have in other states, because they do not have access to the big donors. The candidates who do run for statewide office have to collect enormous sums of money from individuals and groups with a political agenda, such as big corporations, labor unions, developers, and the special interests. By taking money from big donors with deep pockets, candidates have made voters even more cynical by raising questions about the promises they are making to get elected to office. Many Californians are therefore saying they prefer political outsiders who spend their own money to get elected, but millionaire status should not be a qualification for running for statewide office.

There is no shortage of ideas for reforming campaign finances. The biggest roadblock to reform has been partisan bickering among political candidates and a lack of interest on the part of the professionals who profit from expensive initiative campaigns. Other states and nations have found workable solutions, and California needs to do so if it hopes to break the cycle of public cynicism and political disengagement. Reforms that are needed include spending limits on individual, special interest, and corporate donations. The need for eliminating "soft money" contributions that are used for television advertising has often been discussed as a crucial reform. A variety of public incentives, including tax credits, have been suggested to encourage a return to funding campaigns from average voters who give small amounts to their favorite candidates and causes. For the time being, candidates and initiative proponents would be well served to agree to spending limits on campaigns, dollar limits on contributions, and disclosure of the names of their campaign donors on a timely basis. The benefits they would see include less costly campaigns for themselves and more public respect for the election process.

6. The citizens' initiative process should include review and legal testing by the state legislature before initiatives become state propositions on the ballot.
Californians are becoming very frustrated by what they see as the prospect of long or permanent delays in implementing initiatives once

they pass. The voters supported automobile insurance reforms in 1988, but it was years before their costs were reduced. They voted in favor of Proposition 187 in 1994, but the restrictions on illegal immigrants became tied up in the courts. They wanted to legalize marijuana use for medicinal purposes in 1996, but this was blocked by state and federal law authorities. There are obviously many problems with the ways initiatives are being used in the state, but little hope of passing sweeping initiative reforms. Citizens are simply too distrustful of elected officials and suspicious of their motives to allow them to tamper with the initiative process.

One important reform, which received an overwhelming public endorsement in the surveys, would be to have a thorough legislative review of the wording and legality of initiatives before they reach the ballot box. People do not want to find out later that poor wording misled them, and that a "yes" really meant a "no" vote on an initiative. They don't want to learn afterward that an initiative they enthusiastically supported cannot become law because it is illegal or unconstitutional. Voters would be well served by their elected lawmakers to have the legislators play a major role in reviewing proposed initiatives. The state legislature could hold hearings, obtain legal advice, and make recommendations to proponents about initiative wording before it is too late in the process to be helpful.

7. *The state has to make a major investment in a public education system that will improve the socioeconomic standing of the large immigrant population.*

Most Californians today think that the state is divided into haves and have-nots. A surprising number of people place themselves in the have-not category. A trend of rising inequality, with the rich getting richer and the poor getting poorer, has persisted through the boom and bust cycles of the 1980s and 1990s. The fact that inequality appears to be worse in California than elsewhere in the nation has been largely attributed to the growth of the immigrant population. But the real culprit is the public school system, which has failed to raise the educational levels of immigrant children so that they can escape the life of low wages and poor living conditions in which their parents have struggled. Without a better-performing public school system, a large number of Latinos in the state will not be able to receive the college education they need to rise to better-paying jobs and a comfortable middle-class existence. This means that the population group that will be the largest in the state is at risk of having a substantial underclass. The social and economic ramifications of this possibility are enormous.

The future of California thus depends, in large measure, on how successful education reforms are in improving student learning and raising educational achievement. The state will have to invest tremendous resources in elementary, secondary, and higher education in order to make real and lasting improvements in the life circumstances of the large numbers of immigrants. Not all of the school funding that is needed can be expected from a state government that is hard-pressed for cash to build more roads, prisons, and water storage systems. Local voters will have to become convinced that improving schools is worth the cost, a political challenge made all the more difficult by the two-thirds threshold for passing local taxes.

8. Public, private, and nonprofit groups should have an ongoing commitment to programs that will improve racial and ethnic harmony.
California is in the midst of a historic change in its demographic composition. Whites have been the majority since the settlers arrived from the East in large numbers more than a century and a half ago. However, the Asian and Latino populations have been growing faster than the white and black populations since the 1980s as a result of immigration and birth rates. Whites will soon lose their majority status, as the state takes on the character of a "majority-minority" population. In a few decades, Latinos will be the largest group in the state, while the Asian population continues to grow and the white and black populations remain stable.

There are many signs that California is not prepared for this demographic transition. White voters have supported initiatives seeking to deny public services to illegal immigrants, end affirmative action programs, and restrict bilingual education in the public schools. Our surveys indicate that whites, blacks, Asians, and Latinos have very different views about race and immigration in the state. The likelihood for political conflict is very high. The possibility of a recurrence of the 1992 Los Angeles riots, in which blacks, whites, Asians, and Latinos were victims or participants, is present so long as race and ethnic relations remain in their current troubled state.

Californians need to have an open and ongoing dialogue about racial and ethnic change in government arenas, workplaces, communities, and places of worship. Cultural insensitivity, racial misunderstanding, prejudice, and discrimination cannot be allowed to fester in the new multiethnic society. Government, business, and nonprofits must make it a priority to improve race relations. Politics will have to adjust to the need for representation by different ethnic and racial groups, starting with the redistricting after the 2000 census. If the racial and ethnic groups do not feel they have the representation they need, political alienation and distrust of government will reach new heights in the twenty-first century. This could have repercussions beyond politics, as the social and economic well-being of the state will depend on the success of the ongoing multiethnic experiment in California.

9. *The state and local governments, collaborating with the private sector, should invest in regional infrastructure and encourage "smart" regional growth.*
California's population is expected to grow, on average, by 6 million residents per decade between 2000 and 2040. This growth will put enormous strains on the land, water, and resources of a state that is already by far the most populous in the nation. The cost of providing transportation, schools, and other infrastructure will be enormous. The likelihood is that the already chronic problems of air, water, and environmental pollution will intensify, threatening the health and quality of life for most residents. Population growth will occur in several places in the state, though less so in its big cities. The large metropolitan regions in the coastal areas, notably Los Angeles, San Diego, and the San Francisco Bay area, will experience growth on their outer boundaries. The suburban sprawl in Orange County and the Inland Empire will continue to spread out in all directions, filling whatever spaces are yet undeveloped. The Central Valley will see growth through the transformation of agricultural lands to suburban communities.

Today, planning for growth is very decentralized. Local communities make the call about how to use their land without much attention to what their neighbors are doing. The local tax structure has encouraged cities to compete with one another for the sales tax dollars that can be generated by commercial growth and retail development. A new approach of "smart growth" or compact development is needed throughout California. The land has to be developed more intensively from the outset, with more careful planning in all of the regions. Otherwise, it will be much more costly for state and local governments to extend the roads and infrastructure through highly spread-out suburban areas. The state government will have to play a more active role in directing the local governments to make the right land use choices for coping with growth in their regions.

10. *Public, private, and nonprofit groups should make a commitment to policy efforts and programs that will encourage regional cooperation in the state.*

There have always been strong regional divisions in California. The north and the south have struggled over political power and economic development. The coastal and inland areas have fought over the rights to the water that flows out of the Sierra mountains. Today, each of the state's major regions—Los Angeles, the San Francisco Bay area, the Central Valley, the mega-suburbs of Orange County and the Inland Empire, and San Diego—has sufficient population and economic activity to constitute a state unto itself. The regions struggle over political power in the state legislature. The structure of media and communications are not helping to bring the state together. There are no newspapers or television stations that cover the entire state, so political discourse is fractured. Policy discussions are often fragmented and incomplete, focusing on what's best for the region as opposed to what's right for the state.

More recently, the regions have been doing a better job of creating a regional dialogue on public policy and economic development issues. With the help of government, business, and foundations, there has been a proliferation of nonprofit organizations such as the Bay Area Council, the Los Angeles Metropolitan Forum, San Diego Dialogue, the Great Valley Center, and Joint Venture: Silicon Valley Network. Cities and counties within a region are communicating about their common needs. Now, a concerted effort needs to be made by the same parties to bring together regions across the state to coordinate their common goals and aspirations. One starting point would be to plan for the infrastructure within and between the state's regions as the population expands in the twenty-first century. California will not be able to cope with growth and change unless the regions and the state government can work together.

In sum, California is at a critical juncture. The social and political landscape is shifting even as growth is beginning to put incredible pressure on its resources and radically challenge the state's will to respond. This is also a time full of opportunities, when thoughtful, tough-minded planning and careful preparation can make a difference.

It will require a new resolve to bridge the gap that is increasingly evident between the people and their government, between the racial and ethnic groups who share a common destiny, and between the regions that make up this diverse state. How the state responds will irrevocably decide its future. But California has the talent and resources within its grasp to meet the challenges—and a history of resilience and resolve, which it will need to redefine itself.

Focus Group Summary

The Changing Social and Political
Landscape of California,
January and February 1998

INTRODUCTION

The purpose of the focus groups was to gather detailed information from residents living in different regions of the state. This study was designed to test themes and generate new ideas for the PPIC surveys in 1998. The topics we asked about were identification of the state's most important policy problems; perceptions of social, economic, and political changes; attitudes toward state government; preferences for state policies; voting interest; and the 1998 elections. This is a qualitative study, and the information gathered was not intended to be generalizable to the California adult population. The summary provided here is abstracted from the final report submitted by Kay Lavish, who organized the focus groups and co-moderated them with Mark Baldassare. This summary was edited and revised by Mark Baldassare.

METHODS

A total of twelve focus groups including 142 adult respondents were conducted in six areas: Irvine, Los Angeles, San Diego, San Francisco, Fresno, and Sacramento. The two-hour sessions were organized by Kay Lavish and co-moderated with Mark Baldassare on January 27, 28, and 29 and February 2, 3, and 4. The respondents were selected to include a mix of registered voters and nonvoters and different age, income, and ethnic and racial backgrounds.

IMPORTANT POLICY ISSUES

The most pressing policy issues facing California today are crime, education, immigration, overpopulation, the cost of living, and the children.

CRIME

Crime and crime-related issues—gangs, drugs, and violence—are uppermost on the minds of Californians today. There is fear for personal, family, and neighborhood safety. People are afraid to walk outside their areas, they worry about their children walking to school, and drivers are wary of random shootings. There are also concerns about nonviolent crimes, such as vandalism and graffiti, which are caused by a lack of respect for property.

EDUCATION

The concern over the quality of education is universal. California, one of the leaders in education in the past, has fallen behind in test scores. Children are not learning the basics, including reading, writing, and math. They are being passed on to the next grade level even though they are not ready or qualified. People feel that all children deserve a quality education, which is perceived as a solution to poverty, unemployment, welfare, and crime.

OVERPOPULATION

Overpopulation and growth is a concern in all areas of the state. Growth is uncontrolled, and there is no long-term planning to address the problem. The personal impacts of growth include overcrowded schools; lack of affordable housing; traffic and the need for more freeways, roads, and public transportation; and the depletion of natural resources. The major cause of overpopulation is seen as foreign immigration.

IMMIGRATION

People see the pros and cons of foreign immigration. California needs the immigrant labor for the economy. However, immigrants are draining government resources because of their health, welfare, and education needs. Many blame the immigration problems on employers who hire and underpay the workers. Others feel that Hispanics have been made the scapegoats for the problem, since there are many other immigrants moving into the state.

COST OF LIVING

Taxes and the cost of housing are having an impact on many Californians. The costs for child care, transportation, and insurance are concerns for all people. Wages have not kept up with the cost of living in the state. Unemployment is not seen as a problem at this time. There are plenty of jobs. The problem is that new jobs require technical skills or offer low wages.

THE CHILDREN

Even respondents who weren't parents felt that there is a great need for child care, a good education system, and health care for children. Most households require two incomes to survive, and many are single-parent families. Some parents do not have the skills and resources needed to raise their children. There is a perception that many children are being neglected because parents are working and do not have quality time to spend with them.

SOCIAL AND ECONOMIC CHANGES

The perception that emerged in every area of the state was that California's social structure is changing. There is a great divergence of the classes; the middle class is getting crunched, leaving the haves and have-nots. The impacts of this change are manifested in fewer mid-level jobs available.

RACE AND ETHNIC RELATIONS

There is widespread recognition that immigration is having a major impact on the ethnic and racial composition of the state. Many feel that race and ethnic relations have improved in recent years. Still, some described the tensions and resentment toward immigrants in their regions. San Franciscans feel they are more racially tolerant than those in other areas of the state.

QUALITY OF LIFE

The quality of life in California is viewed as pretty good. The state has a lot to offer—good weather, a variety of job opportunities, state-supported higher education, and outdoor sports and recreation. The perception we had is that people can find in California pretty much whatever quality of life means to them individually.

THE ECONOMY

People are very positive and optimistic about the economy in California—locally and statewide. They feel that the economy is on an upswing, rebounding and recovering. They also feel very positive about the nation's economy and its effect on California.

BUSINESS CLIMATE

The most negative economic change seen for the state is that businesses are leaving California for less-expensive locations. Government is perceived to be unfriendly to business. Taxes are very high, and there are too many restrictions and regulations imposed on business. This migration of businesses out of the state is limiting job opportunities for residents.

RIGHT VERSUS WRONG TRACK

Overall, people think that California is on the right track. The economy is good, unemployment is down, some social issues are being addressed, and it is generally a good place to live. Some people felt that California is on the wrong track because there are too many laws and regulations, too much government intrusion, and out-of-touch politicians.

POLITICAL CHANGES

People were mostly positive about the political changes that have come about as a result of the state initiatives passed in recent years.

PROPOSITION 13: TAX LIMITATIONS

Some people didn't know about Proposition 13. Many indicated that they thought Proposition 13 was unfair—even those who benefited from the tax ceiling. However, most agreed that Proposition 13 was needed. If it had not passed, taxes would have continued to rise, and people would probably be worse off today.

PROPOSITION 187: ILLEGAL IMMIGRANTS

The issue about Proposition 187 that generated the strongest opinions was the frustration over the fact that the law passed, and then nothing happened as it was held up in court. Many felt that Proposition 187 was controversial, hypocritical, and discriminating against immigrants generally and Hispanics specifically. Again, many people were able to see both sides of the issue: Immigrants are providing useful labor, which no one else will do; on the other hand, they may be draining health and welfare services.

PROPOSITION 209: ANTI–AFFIRMATIVE ACTION

While opinions were mixed about Proposition 209 and ending affirmative action, most people, again, could see both sides. Quotas were discriminatory, and it is not possible to legislate equality. Some of the people felt that the state was not ready for the proposition in totality—there should have been a transition or preparation period. Some worried about the signal that California was sending to the rest of the nation by ending affirmative action in the state.

PROPOSITION 198: OPEN PRIMARY

Most people understood what an open primary is; however, few were aware that California would have one this June. Many people could see a positive impact for all voters; however, several felt that it opens the door to sabotaging their own candidates. Instead of voting for their own party's strong candidate, some could instead vote for the other party's weakest candidate.

PROPOSITION 140: TERM LIMITS

People were mostly positive about term limits—the strengths being that "dead-wood" would have to move on, and the perception that it would be a motivation for elected officials to get things done sooner.

STATE GOVERNMENT

There is a lack of confidence in elected officials at all levels. Politicians are viewed as not trustworthy; they are too ambitious and serve only themselves and special interests. They make promises, get elected, start out doing a good job, and then cave in to special interests or other influences. While there was little confidence in elected officials at any level, people had the perception that they personally have more control at the local level than at the state or federal level because of proximity and accessibility to local officials.

ELECTION OF STATE OFFICIALS

People are jaded about the election of state officials. They believe that the candidates with the most money win because they have the money to advertise and get the name recognition necessary to win. Many people think that elections are out of their control: they have already been decided by political action groups or special interests.

CONFIDENCE IN STATE OFFICIALS

Opinions were mixed about confidence in the current governor, Pete Wilson. Many felt that he had done a good job and accomplished a lot; others felt that he had started out on the right track but had lost his focus and become too politically ambitious. People, other than Sacramento residents, are not as knowledgeable about the state legislature and its functions as they are about other elected officials. Legislators are perceived as not wanting to do their job, and that is a reason why there are so many propositions on the ballot. Legislators pass their work on to the voters.

STATE INITIATIVES

Propositions provide a challenging aspect of voting. Voters and nonvoters alike feel that there are too many propositions, they are too confusing, and it takes too much time to study all of them. People said that they want the propositions to be short and the wording to be simple and easy to understand. On the other hand, they want the propositions to answer a lot of their questions and to clarify the exact outcome. They expressed frustration that, even with diligent research, propositions are so ambiguous that it is still difficult to determine if your vote means yes or no. This confusion increases voter apathy. For many people, the propositions are just too overwhelming. Many people also said they are disenchanted with the proposition process. Propositions are passed and then not enforced or are held up in the courts.

STATE POLICIES

When people were asked what should be done about the major issues facing the state, many found it difficult to describe their favored solutions.

IMMIGRATION REFORM

People feel that statewide solutions to immigration are limited because the federal government mandates the policies. Many people feel that the federal government should give more financial support to reduce the state's costs.

GROWTH CONTROLS

People indicated that you can't legislate controls or restrictions on U.S. citizens to keep them from locating someplace in California. Again, most feel that there should be stricter federal policies regarding immigration.

K-12 EDUCATION REFORM

Children in public schools need smaller classes, qualified teachers, and adequate facilities. Children should be educated so that they can read, write, and do math. They should not be passed on to the next grade until they are ready.

WELFARE REFORM

People generally are in favor of welfare reform and feel that it's a step in the right direction. However, many people feel that there should be a transition period in which people receive some type of assistance before they become completely independent. People on welfare are viewed as having to take lower-paying jobs because of their lack of skills and training. Most people feel that working welfare parents need financial assistance to alleviate the costs of working—specifically, the cost of child care.

ENVIRONMENTAL REGULATIONS

Although most people feel that pollution in the state has decreased, many expressed concerns about the future: California needs long-term planning and more stringent laws to protect the air, water, and land.

CRIME CONTROL

People feel that the "three strikes" law has helped to keep crime off the streets. However, the result has been overcrowded prisons. People say that they want the state to be tough on crime, but they are not sure this new law is always fair: the third strike may not be for a serious crime.

VOTING INTEREST

Registered voters cited these reasons for voting every time: It is a responsibility and a duty, it is a privilege and a right, and each person's vote counts and makes a difference. Some said that their racial or ethnic group could not vote in the past, and this reinforced their determination to vote now. Latino immigrants and African Americans are enthusiastic about the right to vote.

Registered voters who don't always vote gave these reasons: They are less concerned about local elections for minor offices, the election outcome does not have a perceived impact on their families, and they do not know enough to make an intelligent choice.

Voter apathy is prevalent even among registered voters. People talked about having no control: They vote, laws are passed, but nothing is done about it. People are less likely to vote in the national elections if the outcome has already been projected before they get to the polls.

Reasons for not registering to vote were (1) people do not feel that voting is important, (2) their single vote does not make a difference, (3) they are not citizens at this time, and (4) their religion prohibits them.

CREDIBLE INFORMATION SOURCES

Most people said the news media is their most credible source of information about elections. However, some were negative about the news media's role in campaigns. The news media does not check out stories because they want to be first with the story and they are more interested in ratings than facts. Some also feel that the media is biased and does too much editorializing. Civic groups, the League of Women Voters, friends, and family are also favored information sources. Some were helped by discussions in their place of worship. The voting pamphlet is seen as a useful document.

PRIMARY NEWS SOURCE

Most people indicated that television is their primary source for the news. Newspapers were chosen as a good news source because their reporting is more in-depth, with more details and facts. Radio is a good source because people can listen while commuting, and talk radio often debates the pros and cons.

INTEREST IN THE 1998 ELECTION

While most voters indicated that they will vote in the 1998 election, their interest level and awareness about the candidates and issues were low at this point in time. They feel that they will get more involved closer to the election.

CAMPAIGN ADVERTISING

People almost unanimously said that they do not like campaign advertising. It is described as "mudslinging" and negative in tone. However, people do watch campaign ads and had good recall of some of the ads currently airing. People feel that campaign advertising is not fair to candidates who do not have the war chests to compete in the exposure battle. They think that spending should be regulated or limited. Many indicated that they don't always know who is on the ballot and they may not be aware of well-qualified candidates who have not advertised. Some people long to go back to the town hall–type meetings or debates to hear candidates, because the candidates might be more honest and accountable in person.

1998 ELECTIONS

On all of the ballots presented, many people had difficulty voting because of the lack of information at this time about the candidates and propositions.

GOVERNOR'S RACE

In the decision about voting for governor, the most important factors cited for consideration were honesty, integrity, and a proven track record. People want the candidates to state their platforms, tell how they plan to accomplish their goals, and show that they have the courage to follow through and not cave in to special interests. While people say that they do not want a "career politician," they do believe that political experience is an advantage because it means the candidate already knows his or her way around in state government. Many people said that they thought a businessperson would do a good job because he or she would run the state like a business.

In the ballot for governor, the votes were very close among Lungren, Davis, and Checchi (Harman was not an active candidate). The primary reasons given for choosing Checchi were name recognition from campaign advertising on television, his stand on education, and the fact that he is a businessman rather than a career politician. The reasons for voting for Davis were his experience in state government, reputation, and name recognition. People chose Lungren because of his party affiliation, name recognition, track record, tough stand on crime, and experience in office.

U.S. SENATE RACE

In the choice for the U.S. Senate, the important factors mentioned were the candidate's knowledge and concern for the state, the belief that he or she would not sell out in Washington, a good voting record and experience, and representation of the whole population in California. Most had heard of U.S. Senator Barbara Boxer. A lot of people felt that she had done a good job, she was a hard worker, and she had held her own in Washington. Others felt that she had not done anything or been effective. A few said they had negative impressions, but they could not remember why.

Boxer received the most votes for U.S. senator, followed by Fong and Issa, who received equal support. Boxer's support was due to her track record, her party affiliation, her name recognition, her incumbency, the fact that she is female, and a lack of familiarity with other candidates. The reasons given for voting for Fong were name recognition, his ethnic background, his party affiliation, and the job he had done as treasurer. People voted for Issa because he is a businessman rather than a career politician and based on his campaign advertising.

PROPOSITION 227: "ENGLISH FOR THE CHILDREN" INITIATIVE

The overwhelming majority of people indicated that they supported Proposition 227 because English is the native language of this country, and everyone who chooses to live here should accept the language. They also believe that speaking English is necessary to mainstream children into this society so that they can become productive, tax-paying citizens. Although they support the concept of teaching English to children, people are not sure whether a great deal of money should be spent on it or how the proposed English immersion programs would affect other programs in the schools. Many feel that the children will learn English on their own.

PROPOSITION 226: CAMPAIGN REFORM INITIATIVE

Proposition 226 received almost unanimous support among those who voted. They believe that the person who pays the union dues should have a say about where the money goes, and individuals should have the right to make their own decisions about campaign contributions. Many who supported the change, however, do not feel that the initiative attacks the problem globally. They feel that corporations should be held to similar restrictions. People are curious about and a little concerned over the addition of the "foreign contribution" section of the initiative. However, most people do not approve of foreign contributions to political campaigns.

SCHOOL BOND MEASURE

A proposed $2 billion bond measure for school construction received strong support from most voters. They said that education is important, the state needs new schools to address overcrowding, repairs are needed for existing schools to create an environment conducive to learning, and funds are required so that better teachers can be hired. Again, many people feel that there is enough money already for education and that the money simply needs to be managed better.

April Survey

Methods

The PPIC Statewide Survey findings are based on a telephone survey of 2,002 California adult residents interviewed from April 1 to April 8, 1998. Interviewing took place on weekend days and weekday nights, using a computer-generated random sample of telephone numbers to ensure that both listed and unlisted telephone numbers were called. All telephone exchanges in California were eligible for calling. Telephone numbers in the survey sample were each called up to four times to increase the likelihood of reaching eligible households. Once a household was reached, an adult respondent (18 or older) was randomly chosen for interviewing using the "last birthday" method to avoid biases in age and gender. Each interview took an average of 20 minutes to complete. Interviewing was conducted in English and Spanish, as needed.

We used recent U.S. Census and state figures to compare the demographic characteristics of the survey sample with characteristics of California's adult population. The survey sample was closely comparable with U.S. Census and state figures. The survey data in this report were statistically weighted to account for any demographic differences.

The sampling error for the total sample of 2,002 adults is ±2 percent at the 95 percent confidence level. This means that 95 times out of 100, the results will be within 2 percentage points of what they would be if all adults in California had been interviewed. The sampling error for subgroups is larger. The sampling error for the 1,623 voters is ±2.5 percent and for the 993 likely voters is ±3.2 percent. Sampling error is just one type of error to which surveys are subject. Results may also be affected by factors such as question wording, question order, and survey timing.

In the PPIC Statewide Survey in April, questions were repeated from the national surveys conducted in 1996, 1997, and 1998 by the Pew Research Center (questions 24, 32, 33, 34, 37, 38, 40) in order to compare California with the nation. We also repeated questions that were asked in surveys of California voters conducted during the 1994 election cycle by Mark Baldassare for KCAL-TV News in Los Angeles (questions 16, 17, 18, 41, 42) for time trends.

APPENDIX B APRIL SURVEY:
QUESTIONS AND RESPONSES

April 1–8, 1998; 2,002 California Adult Residents; English and Spanish
Margin of Error ±2% at 95% Confidence Level for Total Sample
(Responses recorded for first fifteen questions are from likely voters only.
All other responses are from all adults.)

First, I have a few questions about the June 2 primary. California is holding an open primary this year. That means voters are now able to vote for anyone they choose, regardless of the candidate's party.

1. If the June primary election for governor were being held today, who would you vote for? (*Rotate names, then ask* "or someone else?")

   19% Al Checchi
   12   Gray Davis
   18   Jane Harman
   23   Dan Lungren
   3   or someone else
   25   don't know

2. In the past month, have you seen any television advertisements by the candidates for governor? (*If yes:* Whose ads have you seen the *most?*)

   56% yes, Al Checchi
   1   yes, Gray Davis
   22   yes, Jane Harman
   0   yes, Dan Lungren
   0   yes, other answer
   21   no

3. Next, if the June primary election for the U.S. Senate were being held today, who would you vote for? (*Rotate names, then ask,* "or someone else?")

   43% Barbara Boxer
   9   Matt Fong
   14   Darrell Issa
   5   Frank Riggs
        or someone else
   29   don't know

4. In the past month, have you seen any television advertisements by the candidates for the U.S. Senate? (*If yes:* Whose ads have you seen the *most?*)

   0%   yes, Barbara Boxer
   1   yes, Matt Fong
   15   yes, Darrell Issa
   0   yes, Frank Riggs
   1   yes, other answer
   83   no

5. People have different ideas about the qualifications they want when they vote for candidates for statewide office, such as governor or U.S. senator. Which of these is *most important* to you? (*Rotate a and* b.) (a) The candidate has experience in elected office. (b) The candidate has experience running a business.

   43% experience in elected office
   40   experience running a business
   6   neither
   7   both
   4   don't know, it depends

6. How do you feel about a candidate for statewide office using *mostly* his or her *own* money to pay for political campaigning? Are you more inclined or less inclined to vote for such a candidate, or does this make no difference to you?

   25% more inclined
   17   less inclined
   58   no difference

7. How do you feel about a candidate for statewide office who uses his or her private wealth to spend *millions of dollars* for political campaigning? Are you more inclined or less inclined to vote for such a candidate, or does this make no difference to you?

   11% more inclined
   33   less inclined
   56   no difference

8. On another topic, Proposition 227, the "English for the Children" initiative on the June ballot, requires that all public school instruction be conducted in English. It provides short-term placement, usually for not more than one year, in English immersion programs for children not fluent in English. If the election were being held today, would you vote yes or no on Proposition 227?

75% yes
21 no
4 don't know

9. How much do you know about current bilingual education programs in California's public schools?

20% great deal
47 fair amount
33 only a little or nothing

10. Do you approve or disapprove of allowing local school districts to decide whether or not to keep their bilingual education programs?

55% approve
41 disapprove
4 don't know

11. Proposition 226, the "Campaign Reform" initiative on the June ballot, requires public and private employers and labor organizations to obtain permission from employees and members before withholding pay or using union dues or fees for political contributions. It also prohibits contributions to state and local candidates by foreign residents, governments, or entities. If the election were held today, would you vote yes or no on Proposition 226?

67% yes
25 no
8 don't know

12. Do you approve or disapprove of placing restrictions on the ability of labor unions to contribute to political candidates and ballot initiatives?

50% approve
43 disapprove
7 don't know

13. Do you approve or disapprove of requiring corporations to obtain permission from their stockholders before using corporate funds for political contributions?

77% approve
20 disapprove
3 don't know

14. On another topic—so far, how closely have you been following the news stories about the upcoming 1998 California elections?

9% very closely
43 fairly closely
39 not too closely
9 not at all closely

15. And how would you rate the job that news organizations are doing in reporting about the upcoming 1998 California elections?

3% excellent
22 good
46 fair
24 poor
5 don't know

16. Next, some questions about the state. Thinking about the public policy issues in California, what do you think is the *most* serious problem today? (*Code, don't read.*)

28% crime, gangs
20 schools, education
7 immigration, illegal immigration
5 jobs, economy
4 drugs
4 growth
4 poverty
3 state government
2 taxes
2 values
10 other
11 don't know

17. And do you think things in California are generally going in the right direction or the wrong direction?

    55%   right direction
    36   wrong direction
    9   don't know

18. How would you rate the economy in California today? Is it . . .

    11%   excellent
    46   good
    33   fair
    10   poor

19. Do you think the current financial situation in Asia will hurt the California economy in the next year or so? (*If yes*: Do you think it will hurt the California economy a great deal or only somewhat?)

    14%   yes, great deal
    36   yes, somewhat
    31   no
    19   don't know

20. On another issue, in the past few years, do you think that the overall immigrant population in California has been increasing, decreasing, or staying about the same?

    73%   increasing
    2   decreasing
    21   staying about the same
    4   don't know

21. And which of these two views is closest to yours? (*Rotate* a *and* b.) (a) Immigrants today are a benefit to California because of their hard work and job skills. (b) Immigrants today are a burden to California because they use public services.

    46%   immigrants are a benefit
    42   immigrants are a burden
    12   neither, don't know

22. Now, we have some questions about kindergarten through twelfth-grade public schools in California. Where do you think California ranks in *spending per pupil*? Compared to other states, is California's spending . . .

    5%   near the top
    9   above average
    28   average
    27   below average
    20   near the bottom
    11   don't know

23. And where do you think California ranks in *student test scores*? Compared to the other states, are California's student test scores . . .

    2%   near the top
    8   above average
    32   average
    39   below average
    14   near the bottom
    5   don't know

24. On another topic, how much of the time do you think you can trust the government in *Washington* to do what is right?

    3%   just about always
    23   most of the time
    62   only sometimes
    12   never
    0   don't know

25. How much trust and confidence do you have at this time in *President Bill Clinton*, when it comes to handling national problems?

    30%   a great deal
    43   fair amount
    16   not very much
    11   none at all
    0   don't know

26. And how much trust and confidence do you have at this time in *the legislative branch of the federal government*, including the U.S. Senate and House of Representatives, when it comes to handling national problems?

    9%   a great deal
    55   fair amount
    29   not very much
    6   none at all
    1   don't know

27. How much trust and confidence do you have at this time in *California Governor Pete Wilson*, when it comes to handling state problems?

    11% a great deal
    42 fair amount
    28 not very much
    17 none at all
    2 don't know

28. And how much trust and confidence do you have at this time in *the California legislature*, including the state senate and assembly, when it comes to handling state problems?

    4% a great deal
    58 fair amount
    29 not very much
    6 none at all
    3 don't know

29. How much trust and confidence do you have at this time in your *County Board of Supervisors*, when it comes to handling county problems?

    8% a great deal
    54 fair amount
    27 not very much
    7 none at all
    4 don't know

30. How much trust and confidence do you have at this time in your *mayor and city council*, when it comes to handling city problems?

    16% a great deal
    50 fair amount
    20 not very much
    8 none at all
    6 don't know

31. What level of government do you trust the *most* to solve problems of concern to you? (*Rotate.*)

    20% federal government
    26 state government
    18 county government
    27 city government
    5 none
    4 don't know

Now, I'm going to read you a few statements that will help us understand how people feel about a number of things. For each statement, please tell me if you completely agree, somewhat agree, somewhat disagree, or completely disagree. First:

32. Most elected officials are trustworthy. Do you . . .

    55% agree
    44 disagree
    1 don't know

33. Most elected officials care what people like me think. Do you . . .

    51% agree
    48 disagree
    1 don't know

34. When something is run by the government, it is usually wasteful and inefficient. Do you . . .

    62% agree
    37 disagree
    1 don't know

35. On another topic, are you currently registered to vote as a Democrat, a Republican, another party or independent, or are you not registered to vote?

    39% Democrat
    33 Republican
    12 independent or other party
    16 not registered

36. Would you consider yourself to be politically:

    8% very liberal
    20 somewhat liberal
    36 middle-of-the-road
    24 somewhat conservative
    11 very conservative
    1 don't know

37. Generally speaking, how much interest would you say you have in politics?

    16% a great deal
    47 fair amount
    31 only a little
    6 none

38. Would you say you follow what's going on in government and public affairs . . .
    - 36% most of the time
    - 38 some of the time
    - 19 only now and then
    - 7 hardly, never

39. Where do you get *most* of your information about what's going on in politics today? From . . . (*Rotate.*)
    - 35% newspapers
    - 40 television
    - 10 radio
    - 4 magazines
    - 6 talking to people
    - 3 the Internet or online services
    - 2 other

40. How often would you say you vote?
    - 48% always
    - 25 nearly always
    - 12 part of the time
    - 5 seldom
    - 10 never

41. On another topic, as far as your own situation, would you say you (and your family) are financially better off or worse off or just about the same as you were a year ago?
    - 37% better off
    - 12 worse off
    - 51 same

42. Now, looking ahead, do you think that a year from now you (and your family) will be financially better off or worse off or just about the same as now?
    - 44% better off
    - 6 worse off
    - 48 same
    - 2 don't know

43. Thinking about your household income, would you say that it is more than enough so that you can save money or buy some extras, just enough to meet your bills and obligations, or is it not enough to meet your bills and obligations?
    - 33% more than enough
    - 53 just enough
    - 13 not enough
    - 1 don't know

44. Next, a few questions about your *region.* How do you feel about the job opportunities that are available in the *region* you live in? Are you . . .
    - 26% very satisfied
    - 49 somewhat satisfied
    - 25 not satisfied

45. And how do you feel about the availability of housing that you can afford in the *region* you live in? Are you . . .
    - 22% very satisfied
    - 43 somewhat satisfied
    - 35 not satisfied

46. And how do you feel about the overall cost of living in the *region* you live in? Are you . . .
    - 15% very satisfied
    - 53 somewhat satisfied
    - 32 not satisfied

Now, I'd like to ask you how you would rate some of the public services you receive in your local area.

47. Police protection. Would you say this is . . .
    - 21% excellent
    - 46 good
    - 25 fair
    - 7 poor
    - 1 don't know

48. Parks, beaches, or other public recreational facilities.
    - 24% excellent
    - 43 good
    - 24 fair
    - 8 poor
    - 1 don't know

49. Local freeways, streets, and roads.

9%	excellent	10%	excellent
37	good	34	good
35	fair	32	fair
19	poor	15	poor
0	don't know	9	don't know

50. How would you rate your local   (51–60: demographic questions)
    public schools?

May Survey

Methods

The PPIC Statewide Survey findings are based on a telephone survey of 2,008 California adult residents interviewed from May 1 to May 6, 1998. Interviewing took place on weekend days and weekday nights, using a computer-generated random sample of telephone numbers to ensure that both listed and unlisted telephone numbers were called. All telephone exchanges in California were eligible for calling. Telephone numbers in the survey sample were each called up to four times to increase the likelihood of reaching eligible households. Once a household was reached, an adult respondent (18 or older) was randomly chosen for interviewing using the "last birthday" method to avoid biases in age and gender. Each interview took an average of 20 minutes to complete. Interviewing was conducted in English and Spanish

We used recent U.S. Census and state figures to compare the demographic characteristics of the survey sample with characteristics of California's adult population. The survey sample was closely comparable with U.S. Census and state figures. The survey data in this report were statistically weighted to account for any demographic differences.

The sampling error for the total sample of 2,008 adults is ±2 percent at the 95 percent confidence level. This means that 95 times out of 100, the results will be within 2 percentage points of what they would be if all adults in California had been interviewed. The sampling error for subgroups is larger. The sampling error for the 1,557 voters is ±2.5 percent and for the 960 likely voters is ±3 percent. Sampling error is just one type of error to which surveys are subject. Results may also be affected by factors such as question wording, question order, and survey timing.

In the PPIC Statewide Survey in May, questions were repeated from the national surveys conducted in 1996, 1997, and 1998 by the Pew Research Center (questions 30, 31, 32, 37, 38, 40) the National Opinion Research Center (question 33), and the *Wall Street Journal* and NBC News (question 34) in order to compare California with the nation. We also repeated questions that were asked in surveys of California voters conducted during the 1994 election cycle by Mark Baldassare for KCAL-TV News in Los Angeles and the California Business Roundtable (questions 16, 17, 20, 41, 43) for time trends.

APPENDIX C   MAY SURVEY:
QUESTIONS AND RESPONSES

May 1–6, 1998; 2,008 California Adult Residents; English and Spanish
Margin of Error ±2% at 95% Confidence Level for Total Sample

*(Responses recorded for first fifteen questions are from likely voters.
All other responses are from all adults.)*

First, I have a few questions about the June 2 primary. California is holding an open primary this year. That means voters are now able to vote for anyone they choose, regardless of the candidate's party.

1. If the June primary election for governor were being held today, who would you vote for? (*Rotate names, then ask, "or someone else?"*)

19%	Al Checchi, a Democrat
23	Gray Davis, a Democrat
8	Jane Harman, a Democrat
23	Dan Lungren, a Republican
2	or someone else (specify)
25	don't know

2. In the past month, have you seen any television advertisements by the candidates for governor? (*If yes:* In the past month, whose ads have you seen the *most*?)

52%	yes, Al Checchi
4	yes, Gray Davis
19	yes, Jane Harman
2	yes, Dan Lungren
0	yes, other answer
23	no

3. Next, if the June primary election for the U.S. Senate were being held today, who would you vote for? (*Rotate names, then ask, "or someone else?"*)

39%	Barbara Boxer, a Democrat
10	Matt Fong, a Republican
22	Darrell Issa, a Republican
2	or someone else (specify)
27	don't know

4. In the past month, have you seen any television advertisements by the candidates for the U.S. Senate? (*If yes:* In the past month, whose ads have you seen the *most*?)

0%	yes, Barbara Boxer
1	yes, Matt Fong
19	yes, Darrell Issa
1	yes, other answer
79	no

5. People have different ideas about the qualifications they want when they vote for candidates for statewide office, such as governor or U.S. senator. Which of these is *most important* to you? (*Rotate a and b.*) (a) The candidate has experience in elected office. (b) The candidate has experience running a business.

46%	experience in elected office
36	experience running a business
6	neither
7	both
5	don't know, it depends

6. People have different opinions on how candidates for statewide office should pay for their political campaigns. Which of these do you view *most* positively? (*Rotate a and b.*) (a) A candidate using mostly his or her *own money* to pay for political campaigning. (b) A candidate using mostly money collected from his or her *supporters* to pay for political campaigning.

34%	own money
52	money from supporters

8   makes no difference
6   don't know

7. In deciding who to vote for in the June primary election for governor, how important to you are the candidates' performances in a public debate?

37%   very important
48   somewhat important
13   not important
2   don't know

8. On another topic, Proposition 227, the "English Language in Public Schools" initiative on the June ballot, requires that all public school instruction be conducted in English. It provides short-term placement, usually for not more than one year, in English immersion programs for children not fluent in English. The measure would also provide $50 million per year for 10 years for English tutoring. If the election were being held today, would you vote yes or no on Proposition 227?

67%   yes
28   no
5   don't know

9. How much do you know about current bilingual education programs in California's public schools?

24%   great deal
47   fair amount
24   only a little
5   nothing

10. Do you approve or disapprove of allowing local school districts to decide whether or not to keep their bilingual education programs?

52%   approve
42   disapprove
6   don't know

11. Proposition 226, the "Political Contributions by Employees, Union Members, and Foreign Entities" initiative on the June ballot, requires public and private employers and labor organizations to obtain permission from employees and members before withholding pay or using union dues or fees for political contributions. It also prohibits contributions to state and local candidates by foreign residents, governments, or entities. If the election were held today, would you vote yes or no on Proposition 226?

59%   yes
33   no
8   don't know

12. Do you approve or disapprove of placing restrictions on the ability of *labor unions* to contribute to political candidates and ballot initiatives?

50%   approve
44   disapprove
6   don't know

13. Do you approve or disapprove of placing restrictions on the ability of *business corporations* to contribute to political candidates and ballot initiatives?

55%   approve
39   disapprove
6   don't know

14. On another topic—so far, how closely have you been following the news stories about the 1998 California elections?

13%   very closely
48   fairly closely
32   not too closely
7   not at all closely

15. And how would you rate the job that news organizations are doing in reporting about the upcoming 1998 California elections?

4%   excellent
31   good
42   fair
18   poor
5   don't know

16. Next, some questions about the state. Do you think things in California are generally going in the right direction or the wrong direction?

    56% right direction
    34 wrong direction
    10 don't know

17. Overall, thinking about the quality of life in California today, do you think things are going . . .

    13% very well
    57 somewhat well
    21 somewhat badly
    9   very badly

18. On another issue—in your opinion, how much of a problem is *crime* in California today? Is it a . . .

    66% big problem
    28 somewhat of a problem
    4   not much of a problem
    2   don't know

19. In the past few years, do you think the crime rate in California has increased, decreased, or stayed about the same?

    46% increased
    24 decreased
    28 stayed about the same
    2   don't know

20. And how safe do you feel walking alone in your neighborhood at night?

    33% very safe
    33 somewhat safe
    17 somewhat unsafe
    16 very unsafe
    1   don't know

21. Turning to another issue, how much of a problem is the *quality of education* in kindergarten through twelfth-grade public schools in California today? Is it a . . .

    46% big problem
    33 somewhat of a problem
    14 not much of a problem
    7   don't know

22. Please tell me whether you favor or oppose these school reform proposals. Do you favor or oppose allowing local school districts to raise local taxes with a simple majority instead of two-thirds vote?

    38% favor
    56 oppose
    6   don't know

23. Do you favor or oppose providing parents with tax-funded vouchers to send their children to any public, private, or parochial school they choose?

    58% favor
    37 oppose
    5   don't know

24. On another topic, how much of the time do you think you can trust the government in *Washington* to do what is right?

    3% just about always
    21 most of the time
    59 only sometimes
    16 never
    1   don't know

25. How do you rate the job performance of *President Bill Clinton* at this time?

    21% excellent
    37 good
    25 fair
    16 poor
    1   don't know

26. How do you rate the job performance of the *legislative branch of the federal government* at this time, including the U.S. Senate and House of Representatives?

    3% excellent
    30 good
    49 fair
    15 poor
    3   don't know

27. How do you rate the job performance of *California Governor Pete Wilson* at this time?

    6% excellent
    28 good
    34 fair

29   poor
3   don't know

28. And how do you rate the job
performance of the *California
legislature* at this time, including
the state senate and assembly?
    2%   excellent
    28   good
    52   fair
    13   poor
    5   don't know

29. What level of government do
you trust the *most* to spend your
tax money wisely? (*Rotate.*)
    10%   federal government
    17   state government
    22   county government
    31   city government
    15   none of the above
    0   other answer
    5   don't know

Now, I'm going to read you some
pairs of statements. As I read each
pair, please tell me whether the first
statement or the second statement
comes closer to your own views—
even if neither is exactly right. The
first pair is . . . (*Read and rotate.*)

30. (a) Government regulation of
business is necessary to protect
the public interest. (b) Government regulation of business usually does more harm than good.
    54%   government regulation
           necessary
    43   government regulation
           more harm
    3   neither, don't know

31. (a) Stricter environmental laws
and regulations cost too many
jobs and hurt the economy. (b)
Stricter environmental laws and
regulations are worth the cost.
    37%   cost jobs
    58   worth the cost
    5   neither, don't know

32. (a) Homosexuality is a way of
life that should be accepted by
society. (b) Homosexuality is a
way of life that should be
discouraged by society.

55%   should be accepted
40   should be discouraged
5   neither, don't know

33. If the government had a choice
between reducing taxes or spending more on social programs like
health care, social security, and
unemployment benefits, which do
you think it should do? (*Rotate.*)
(a) Reduce taxes, even if this
means spending less on social
programs. (b) Spend more on
social programs, even if this
means higher taxes.
    44%   reduce taxes, spend less
    51   spend more, raise taxes
    5   don't know

34. And which of the following best
represents your views about abortion? The choice on abortion
should be left up to the woman
and her doctor; abortion should
be legal only in cases where preg-
nancy results from rape or incest
or when the life of the mother is
at risk; or abortion should be illegal in all circumstances.
    61%   up to woman and doc
           tor
    26   legal in some cases
    12   illegal in all
           circumstances
    1   don't know

35. On another topic, are you
currently registered to vote as a
Democrat, a Republican, another
party or independent, or are you
not registered to vote?
    37%   Democrat
    29   Republican
    14   other party, indepen
           dent
    20   not registered

36. Would you consider yourself to
be politically:
    8%   very liberal
    21   somewhat liberal
    34   middle-of-the-road
    25   somewhat conservative
    10   very conservative
    2   don't know

37. Generally speaking, how much interest would you say you have in politics?

    15% a great deal
    47 fair amount
    31 only a little
    7   none
    0   don't know

38. Would you say you follow what's going on in government and public affairs . . .

    34% most of the time
    39 some of the time
    19 only now and then
    6   hardly at all
    2   never
    0   don't know

39. Where do you get *most* of your information about what's going on in politics today? From . . . (*Rotate.*)

    33% newspapers
    41 television
    10 radio
    3   magazines
    8   talking to people
    3   the Internet or online services
    1   other
    1   don't know

40. How often would you say you vote?

    47% always
    24 nearly always
    10 part of the time
    6   seldom
    13 never
    0   other
    0   don't know

41. On another topic—as far as your own situation, would you say you (and your family) are financially better off or worse off or just about the same as you were a year ago?

    36% better off
    13 worse off
    51 same

42. How would you describe your current standard of living? Would you say it is . . .

    14% more than comfortable
    73 comfortable
    13 not comfortable

43. Are you concerned that you or someone in your family will lose their job in the next year, or not? (*If yes:* Are you very concerned or somewhat concerned?)

    14% yes, very concerned
    12 yes, somewhat concerned
    73 no
    1   already lost job

44. Next, a few questions about your region. How much of a problem is *transportation and traffic congestion* in your region? Is it a. . .

    33% big problem
    35 somewhat of a problem
    31 not a problem
    1   don't know

45. How much of a problem is *population growth and development* in your region?

    27% big problem
    38 somewhat of a problem
    34 not a problem
    1   don't know

46. And how much of a problem is *air pollution, water pollution, and other forms of environmental pollution* in your region?

    27% big problem
    46 somewhat of a problem
    26 not a problem
    1   don't know

How satisfied are you with each of the following? (*Rotate.*)

47. The house or apartment in which you live?

    53% very satisfied
    38 somewhat satisfied
    9   not satisfied

48. Your job (excludes those not working)?

    52% very satisfied
    38 somewhat satisfied
    10 not satisfied

49. Your leisure activities?
    47%   very satisfied
    41   somewhat satisfied
    12   not satisfied

50. Taken all together, how would you say things are these days? Would you say you are. . .
    28%   very happy
    59   pretty happy
    13   not too happy

(51–60: demographic questions)

September Survey

Methods

The PPIC Statewide Survey findings are based on a telephone survey of 2,008 California adult residents interviewed from September 1 to September 7, 1998. Interviewing took place on weekend days and weekday nights, using a computer-generated random sample of telephone numbers to ensure that both listed and unlisted telephone numbers were called. All telephone exchanges in California were eligible for calling. Telephone numbers in the survey sample were each called up to four times to increase the likelihood of reaching eligible households. Once a household was reached, an adult respondent (18 or older) was randomly chosen for interviewing using the "last birthday" method to avoid biases in age and gender. Each interview took an average of 20 minutes to complete. Interviewing was conducted in English or Spanish.

We used recent U.S. Census and state figures to compare the demographic characteristics of the survey sample with characteristics of California's adult population. The survey sample was closely comparable with U.S. Census and state figures. The survey data in this report were statistically weighted to account for any demographic differences.

The sampling error for the total sample of 2,008 adults is ±2 percent at the 95 percent confidence level. This means that 95 times out of 100, the results will be within 2 percentage points of what they would be if all adults in California had been interviewed. The sampling error for subgroups is larger. The sampling error for the 1,557 voters is ±2.5 percent and for the 960 likely voters is ±3 percent. Sampling error is just one type of error to which surveys are subject. Results may also be affected by factors such as question wording, question order, and survey timing.

In the PPIC Statewide Survey in September, questions were repeated from national surveys conducted by the Pew Research Center in 1997 and 1998 (questions 28, 32, 33, 37, 38, 39, 47, 48), by Gallup in 1996 (questions 30, 34), and by the University of Michigan's National Elections Studies in 1996 (questions 29, 31) in order to compare California with the nation. We also repeated questions that were asked in surveys of California voters conducted during the 1994 election cycle by Mark Baldassare for KCAL-TV News in Los Angeles and the California Business Roundtable (questions 16, 41, 42) for time trends.

APPENDIX D   SEPTEMBER SURVEY:
QUESTIONS AND RESPONSES

September 1–7, 1998; 2,000 California Adult Residents; English and Spanish
Margin of Error ±2% at 95% Confidence Level for Total Sample

*(Responses recorded for first fifteen questions are from likely voters.
All other responses are from all adults.)*

First, I have a few questions about the November 3 general election.

1. If the election for governor were being held today, who would you vote for? (*Rotate names, then ask,* "or someone else?")

   47%   Gray Davis, a Democrat
   38   Dan Lungren, a Republican
   2   or someone else (specify)
   13   don't know

2. In the past month, have you seen any television advertisements by the candidates for governor? (*If yes*: Whose ads have you seen the most?)

   18%   yes, Gray Davis
   14   yes, Dan Lungren
   6   yes, other answer
   62   no

3. The Democratic and Republican candidates for governor are having a series of debates. Some people learn about debates from news reports as well as seeing or hearing them. So far, have the debates helped you a great deal, somewhat, very little, or not at all in deciding who to vote for in the governor's race?

   7%   great deal
   22   somewhat
   19   very little
   37   not at all
   15   don't know/haven't seen, read, or heard debates

4. Next, if the election for the U.S. Senate were being held today, who

would you vote for? (*Rotate names, then ask,* "or someone else?")

   45%   Barbara Boxer, a Democrat
   43   Matt Fong, a Republican
   1   or someone else (specify)
   11   don't know

5. In the past month, have you seen any television advertisements by the candidates for the U.S. Senate? (*If yes*: Whose ads have you seen the most?)

   11%   yes, Barbara Boxer
   7   yes, Matt Fong
   2   yes, other answer
   80   no

6. The Democratic and Republican candidates for the U.S. Senate also had a debate. Some people learn about debates from news reports as well as seeing or hearing them. Has the debate helped you a great deal, somewhat, very little, or not at all in deciding who to vote for in the U.S. Senate race?

   6%   great deal
   16   somewhat
   14   very little
   45   not at all
   19   don't know/haven't seen, read, or heard debate

7. On another topic, people have different ideas about the qualifications they want when they vote for candidates for statewide office, such as governor or U.S. senator. Which of these is most important to you? Would it be . . . (*Rotate.*)

14% the candidate's experience
18 the candidate's character
5 the candidate's political party
61 the candidate's stands on the issues
2 don't know, it depends

8. On another topic, Proposition 1A on the November ballot is a $9.2 billion bond issue to finance construction of new buildings and to repair older buildings over the next four years for California's kindergarten through twelfth-grade public schools, community colleges, and public universities. If the election were held today, would you vote yes or no on Proposition 1A?
70% yes
21 no
9 don't know

9. Proposition 1A would impose limits on local government fees charged to housing developers to pay for building new schools. Do you favor or oppose this feature of Proposition 1A?
48% favor
32 oppose
20 don't know

10. Do you think that the current level of state funding for California's kindergarten through twelfth-grade public schools is more than enough, just enough, or not enough?
10% more than enough
21 just enough
63 not enough
6 don't know

11. Proposition 8, the public schools initiative on the November ballot, would authorize state funds to ensure that public school classes in kindergarten through the third grade have no more than twenty students per class. It would also establish school-site governing councils of parents and teachers, provide for teacher evaluations based on student performances, impose a new credential requirement for teachers, authorize a principal to expel a student for possessing illegal drugs, and create a statewide Chief Inspector of Public Schools. If the election were held today, would you vote yes or no on Proposition 8?
72% yes
19 no
9 don't know

12. Class sizes in California public schools are now being reduced to a maximum of twenty students in most kindergarten to third-grade classes. Do you think the smaller classes will make a big difference, a moderate difference, or no difference in helping children learn reading, writing, and arithmetic?
65% big difference
26 moderate difference
7 no difference
2 don't know

13. Do you think that Proposition 8's efforts to improve teacher quality, that is, establishing stricter credential requirements and basing teacher evaluations on student performances, would make a big difference, a moderate difference, or no difference in helping children learn reading, writing, and arithmetic?
48% big difference
38 moderate difference
11 no difference
3 don't know

14. On another topic, so far, how closely have you been following the news stories about the 1998 California elections?
9% very closely
45 fairly closely

36   not too closely
10   not at all closely

15. How would you rate the job
    that news organizations are
    doing in reporting about the
    1998 California elections?
    4%   excellent
    31   good
    43   fair
    17   poor
    5   don't know

16. Next, some questions about the
    state. Thinking about the public
    policy issues in California, what
    do you think is the most serious
    problem today? (*Code, don't
    read.*)
    30%   crime, gangs
    20   schools, education
    7   drugs
    5   immigration, illegal
          immigration
    4   jobs, the economy
    3   state government, gover-
          nor, legislature
    3   poverty, the poor,
          homeless, welfare
    3   morality, values
    2   environment, pollution
    2   growth, overpopulation
    2   traffic and transportation
    2   taxes
    8   other
    9   don't know

17. Do you think things in California
    are generally going in the right
    direction or the wrong direction?
    57%   right direction
    34   wrong direction
    9   don't know

18. Do you think the current financial
    situation in Asia will hurt the
    California economy in the next
    year or so? (*If yes:* Do you think it
    will hurt the California economy a
    great deal or only somewhat?)
    22%   yes, a great deal
    44   yes, only somewhat
    22   no
    12   don't know

On another topic, we have a few
questions about Proposition 13, the
citizen's initiative that reformed the
property tax system in California.
Proposition 13 was passed by the
voters in 1978.

19. Proposition 13 limits the tax
    rate to 1 percent of the sales
    price of the property when it is
    purchased and also limits the
    growth of property tax increases
    to 2 percent annually until the
    property is sold. Overall, do you
    think the property tax limita-
    tions imposed by Proposition 13
    have had a good effect or a bad
    effect or no effect on local gov-
    ernment services provided to res-
    idents in the state of California?
    38%   good effect
    23   bad effect
    27   no effect
    12   don't know

20. Under Proposition 13, property
    taxes are collected at the local
    level, and the state legislature
    and governor are responsible for
    dividing the property tax money
    among the local governments
    that provide services to residents.
    Do you favor or oppose this fea-
    ture of Proposition 13?
    55%   favor
    34   oppose
    11   don't know

21. As a result of Proposition 13
    and increases in home prices in
    California, a homeowner who
    recently purchased a home will
    pay much higher property taxes
    than a homeowner who pur-
    chased a similar home several
    years ago in the same neighbor-
    hood. Do you favor or oppose
    this feature of Proposition 13?
    35%   favor
    59   oppose
    6   don't know

22. Under Proposition 13, a two-
    thirds vote at the ballot box is re-

quired to pass any new local special taxes. Overall, do you think the supermajority vote requirement imposed by Proposition 13 has had a good effect or a bad effect or no effect on local government services provided to residents in the state of California?

38% good effect
22 bad effect
28 no effect
12 don't know

23. Do you favor or oppose allowing local special taxes to pass with a simple majority instead of a two-thirds vote?

38% favor
58 oppose
4 don't know

24. On another topic, how do you rate the job performance of President Bill Clinton at this time?

22% excellent
36 good
21 fair
20 poor
1 don't know

25. How do you rate the job performance of California Governor Pete Wilson at this time?

7% excellent
35 good
30 fair
26 poor
2 don't know

26. How do you rate the job performance of the California legislature at this time, including the state senate and assembly?

3% excellent
33 good
46 fair
12 poor
6 don't know

27. The governor and the state legislature recently approved a $1.4 billion tax cut for the 1998–1999 fiscal year, including a reduction in the state vehicle license fee. How important is this state tax cut to you? Is it . . .

41% very important
37 somewhat important
20 not important
2 don't know

28. On another topic, people have different ideas about the government in Washington. These ideas don't refer to Democrats or Republicans in particular, but just to government in general. We want to see how you feel about these ideas. How much of the time do you think you can trust the government in Washington to do what is right—just about always, most of the time, or only some of the time?

5% just about always
28 most of the time
63 some of the time
4 none of the time
(*Code, don't read.*)

29. Do you think that the people in government waste a lot of the money we pay in taxes, waste some of it, or don't waste very much of it?

65% a lot
31 some
3 don't waste very much
1 don't know

30. Would you say the government is pretty much run by a few big interests looking out for themselves or that it is run for the benefit of all the people?

70% few big interests
25 benefit of all the people
5 don't know

31. Would you say that quite a few of the people running the government are crooked, not very many are, or do you think hardly any of them are crooked?

39% quite a few
45 not many

14   hardly any
2   don't know

Now, I'm going to read to you a few statements that will help us understand how people feel about a number of things. For each statement, please tell me if you completely agree, mostly agree, mostly disagree, or completely disagree.

32. Poor people have become too dependent on government assistance programs. Do you . . .

    29%   completely agree
    48   mostly agree
    18   mostly disagree
    4   completely disagree
    1   don't know

33. It is the responsibility of government to take care of people who can't take care of themselves. Do you . . .

    21%   completely agree
    42   mostly agree
    24   mostly disagree
    12   completely disagree
    1   don't know

34. The government is spending too much money on programs to help the poor. Do you . . .

    13%   completely agree
    31   mostly agree
    37   mostly disagree
    17   completely disagree
    2   don't know

35. On another topic, are you currently registered to vote as a Democrat, a Republican, another party or independent, or are you not registered to vote?

    37%   Democrat
    31   Republican
    13   independent or other party
    19   not registered

36. Would you consider yourself to be politically . . .

    8%   very liberal
    20   somewhat liberal
    34   middle-of-the-road

26   somewhat conservative
10   very conservative
2   don't know

37. Generally speaking, how much interest would you say you have in politics?

    18%   a great deal
    48   fair amount
    29   only a little
    5   none

38. Would you say you follow what's going on in government and public affairs . . .

    39%   most of the time
    37   some of the time
    17   only now and then
    5   hardly at all
    2   never

39. How often would you say you vote?

    51%   always (skip question 40)
    22   nearly always
    11   part of the time
    5   seldom
    11   never
    0   other

40. Here are some reasons people give for not always voting. Which of these is the main reason you do not always vote? (Rotate.)

    16%   voting doesn't change things
    9   I'm not interested in politics
    3   there are fewer major problems today
    24   I'm too busy to vote
    36   I don't know enough about the choices
    9   other answer
    3   don't know

41. On another topic, as far as your own situation, would you say you and your family are financially better off or worse off or just about the same as you were a year ago?

    33%   better off
    12   worse off

54   same
1   don't know

42. Now, looking ahead, do you think that a year from now you and your family will be financially better off or worse off or just about the same as now?
40%   better off
7   worse off
51   same
2   don't know

43. How satisfied are you with your current financial situation? Are you . . .
21%   very satisfied
54   somewhat satisfied
25   not satisfied

Next, a few questions about population trends in your region.

44. In the next 10 years, do you think that the population in your region will grow rapidly, grow slowly, stay about the same, or decline?
62%   grow rapidly
20   grow slowly
15   stay about the same
2   decline
1   don't know

45. Do you think that the water supply that is available for your region today will be adequate or inadequate for your region's needs 10 years from now? (*If inadequate:* Is that somewhat or very?)
41%   adequate
30   somewhat inadequate
23   very inadequate
6   don't know

46. Do you think that the freeways, roads, and transportation system in your region today will be adequate or inadequate for your region's needs 10 years from now? (*If inadequate:* Is that somewhat or very?)
28%   adequate
25   somewhat inadequate
45   very inadequate
2   don't know

Now, I'd like to ask you some questions about religion.

47. How important would you say religion is in your own life? Would you say it is very important, fairly important, or not important?
49%   very important
32   fairly important
19   not important

48. Aside from weddings and funerals, how often do you attend religious services?
11%   more than once a week
23   once a week
18   once or twice a month
18   a few times a year
16   seldom
14   never

49. Thinking back to recent elections, have the clergy at your place of worship or any other religious groups urged you to vote in a particular way?
11%   yes
89   no

50. And what is your opinion about political candidates who talk about religious values when they are campaigning for office? Do you approve or disapprove?
39%   approve
56   disapprove
5   don't know

(51–61: demographic questions)

October Survey

Methods

The PPIC Statewide Survey findings are based on a telephone survey of 2,005 California adult residents interviewed from October 1 to October 6, 1998. Interviewing took place on weekend days and weekday nights, using a computer-generated random sample of telephone numbers to ensure that both listed and unlisted telephone numbers were called. All telephone exchanges in California were eligible for calling. Telephone numbers in the survey sample were each called up to four times to increase the likelihood of reaching eligible households. Once a household was reached, an adult respondent (18 or older) was randomly chosen for interviewing using the "last birthday" method to avoid biases in age and gender. Each interview took an average of 20 minutes to complete. Interviewing was conducted in English or Spanish.

We used recent U.S. Census and state figures to compare the demographic characteristics of the survey sample with characteristics of California's adult population. The survey sample was closely comparable with U.S. Census and state figures. The survey data in this report were statistically weighted to account for any demographic differences.

The sampling error for the total sample of 2,005 adults is ±2 percent at the 95 percent confidence level. This means that 95 times out of 100, the results will be within 2 percentage points of what they would be if all adults in California had been interviewed. The sampling error for subgroups is larger. The sampling error for the 1,574 voters is ±2.5 percent and for the 793 likely voters is ±3.5 percent. Sampling error is just one type of error to which surveys are subject. Results may also be affected by factors such as question wording or order, and survey timing.

In the PPIC Statewide Survey in October, questions were repeated from the national surveys conducted by the Pew Research Center in 1998 (questions 36, 37, 40), by CBS/*New York Times* in 1997 (questions 32, 33, 34), by the University of Michigan's National Election Studies in 1996 (questions 28, 29, 30, 31), and by the University of Virginia for the American Association of Retired Persons in 1996 (questions 38, 39, 47, 48, 49, 50) in order to compare California with the nation. We also repeated questions that were asked in surveys of California voters conducted during the 1994 election cycle by Mark Baldassare for KCAL-TV News in Los Angeles and the California Business Roundtable (questions 17, 41, 42) for time trends.

APPENDIX E OCTOBER SURVEY: QUESTIONS AND RESPONSES

October 1–6, 1998; 2,005 California Adult Residents; English and Spanish
Margin of Error ±2% at 95% Confidence Level for Total Sample

*(Responses recorded for first fifteen questions are from likely voters only.
All other responses are from all adults.)*

First, I have a few questions about the November 3 general election.

1. If the election for governor were being held today, who would you vote for? (*Rotate names, then ask, "or someone else?"*)
   - 49% Gray Davis, a Democrat
   - 41 Dan Lungren, a Republican
   - 1 or someone else (specify)
   - 9 don't know

2. In the past month, have you seen any television advertisements by the candidates for governor? (*If yes:* Whose ads have you seen the most?)
   - 29% yes, Gray Davis
   - 19 yes, Dan Lungren
   - 16 yes, other answer
   - 36 don't know

3. The Democratic and Republican candidates for governor are having a series of debates. Some people learn about the debates from news reports as well as seeing or hearing them. So far, have the debates helped you a great deal, somewhat, very little, or not at all in deciding who to vote for in the governor's race?
   - 6% great deal
   - 20 somewhat
   - 19 very little
   - 40 not at all
   - 15 haven't seen, read, or heard debates
   - 0 don't know

4. Next, if the election for the U.S. Senate were being held today, who would you vote for? (*Rotate names, then ask, "or someone else?"*)

   - 47% Barbara Boxer, a Democrat
   - 44 Matt Fong, a Republican
   - 1 or someone else (specify)
   - 8 don't know

5. In the past month, have you seen any television advertisements by the candidates for the U.S. Senate? (*If yes:* Whose ads have you seen the most?)
   - 37% yes, Barbara Boxer
   - 10 yes, Matt Fong
   - 6 yes, other answer
   - 47 no
   - 0 don't know

6. On another topic, people have different ideas about the qualifications they want when they vote for candidates for statewide office, such as governor or U.S. senator. Which of these is most important to you? Would it be . . . (*Rotate.*)
   - 13% candidate's experience
   - 22 candidate's character
   - 5 candidate's political party
   - 58 candidate's stands on the issues
   - 0 other
   - 2 don't know, it depends

7. Do you think that the scandal involving President Clinton, and the ongoing congressional investigation of his actions, will make you more inclined to vote or less inclined to vote, or won't they affect your likelihood to vote in November?
   - 29% more inclined to vote
   - 1 less inclined to vote
   - 69 won't affect voting
   - 1 don't know, it depends

8. How do you think that the scandal involving President Clinton, and

the ongoing congressional investigation of his actions, will affect
your voting for candidates for
statewide office, such as governor
or U.S. senator? Will these events
make you more inclined to vote
for Democratic candidates or more
inclined to vote for Republican
candidates, or won't they affect
your decision on which candidates
to vote for in November?

18% more inclined to vote
     Republican
14   more inclined to vote
     Democrat
67   no difference
1   don't know, it depends

9. On another topic, Proposition
1A on the November ballot is a
$9.2 billion bond issue that will
provide funding for necessary education facilities for at least 4
years for class size reduction, to
relieve overcrowding and accommodate student enrollment
growth, to repair older schools,
and for wiring and cabling for
education technology. Funds
will also be used to upgrade and
build new classrooms in community colleges and public universities. If the election were held
today, would you vote yes or no
on proposition 1A?

66% yes
22   no
12   don't know

10. Do you think that the current
level of funding for California's
community colleges and public
universities is more than enough,
just enough, or not enough?

9%   more than enough
27   just enough
51   not enough
13   don't know

11. On another topic, Proposition 8,
the Public Schools initiative on
the November ballot, establishes
permanent class-size reduction

funding for school districts that
establish parent-teacher councils,
and requires testing for teacher
credentialing and pupil suspension for drug possession. This
will cost up to $60 million in
new state programs, offset in
part by existing funds. Annual
costs to school districts are potentially in the high tens of millions of dollars. If the election
were held today, would you vote
yes or no on Proposition 8?

43% yes
38   no
19   don't know

12. Proposition 8 would create a
state office of Chief Inspector of
Public Schools, which would report each year on the quality of
public K-12 schools. Do you
think this would make a big difference, a moderate difference,
or no difference in helping children learn reading, writing, and
arithmetic?

12% big difference
27   moderate difference
55   no difference
6   don't know

13. Proposition 8 attempts to increase parents' involvement in
their children's schools by establishing parent-teacher councils.
Do you think this would make a
big difference, a moderate difference, or no difference in helping
children learn reading, writing,
and arithmetic?

38% big difference
31   moderate difference
27   no difference
4   don't know

14. On another topic: So far, how
closely have you been following
the news stories about the upcoming 1998 California elections?

15% very closely
52   fairly closely
26   not too closely
7   not at all closely

15. And how would you rate the job that news organizations are doing in reporting about the 1998 California elections?

5% excellent
32 good
42 fair
18 poor
3 don't know

16. Next, some questions about the state. Which one issue would you most like to hear the candidates for statewide office, such as governor and U.S. senator, talk about between now and the November 3 election? (*Code, don't read.*)

31% schools, education
8 crime, gangs
6 jobs, the economy
6 taxes
4 state budget, finance
3 poverty, the poor, homeless, welfare
2 immigration, illegal immigration
2 drugs
2 environment, pollution
2 abortion
2 health care, HMOs
1 housing, housing costs, housing availability
1 race relations, ethnic tensions
1 state government, governor, legislature
1 government regulations
1 morality, values
1 traffic and transportation
1 white house scandal, President Clinton, impeachment
1 Indian casino
1 what they would do in office
0 gun control
1 "three strikes"
0 growth, overpopulation
0 urbanization of farmland
0 sprawl

0 campaign finance
0 character
0 death penalty
0 past record in office
0 Social Security
2 other (specify)
20 don't know

17. And do you think things in California are generally going in the right direction or the wrong direction?

62% right direction
30 wrong direction
8 don't know

18. What about the next 12 months? Do you expect economic conditions in California to get better, get worse, or stay the same?

25% better
24 worse
48 same
3 don't know

Next, we are interested in your opinions about the citizens' initiatives that appear on the state ballot as propositions. Do you agree or disagree with these statements? (*Rotate questions 19–21.*)

19. Citizens' initiatives bring up important public policy issues that the governor and state legislature have not adequately addressed. Do you strongly agree, somewhat agree, somewhat disagree, or strongly disagree?

22% strongly agree
51 somewhat agree
16 somewhat disagree
6 strongly disagree
5 don't know

20. The ballot wording for citizens' initiatives is often too complicated and confusing for voters to understand what happens if the initiative passes. Do you strongly agree, somewhat agree, somewhat disagree, or strongly disagree?

44% strongly agree
35   somewhat agree
11   somewhat disagree
6   strongly disagree
4   don't know

21. Citizens' initiatives usually reflect the concerns of organized special interests rather than the concerns of average California residents. Do you strongly agree, somewhat agree, somewhat disagree, or strongly disagree?

34% strongly agree
44   somewhat agree
12   somewhat disagree
6   strongly disagree
4   don't know

22. How do you feel about these proposals for initiative reform: After an initiative has qualified for the ballot, the legislature would have a short time period to hold hearings on the initiative and to adopt technical or clarifying changes. If the proponents of the initiative agree, the measure would be submitted to the voters as revised by the legislature. Do you favor or oppose this initiative reform?

63% favor
29   oppose
8   don't know

23. And do you favor or oppose allowing the legislature, with the governor's approval, to amend initiatives after they have been in effect for six years?

44% favor
49   oppose
7   don't know

24. On another topic, how do you rate the job performance of President Bill Clinton at this time?

26% excellent
34   good
19   fair
21   poor
0   don't know

25. How do you rate the job performance of the U.S. Senate and House of Representatives at this time?

5%   excellent
34   good
40   fair
19   poor
2   don't know

26. On another topic, do you think it is better for California to have a governor who comes from the same political party that controls the California legislature, or do you think it is better to have a governor from one political party and the California legislature controlled by another?

39% better when same party
36   better when different parties
25   don't know, it depends

27. The California legislature has operated under term limits since 1990, meaning that members of the state senate and state assembly are limited in the number of terms they can hold their elected office. Do you think that term limits is a good thing or a bad thing for California, or does it make no difference?

65% good thing
14   bad thing
19   no difference
2   don't know

Now, please tell me how much you agree or disagree with these statements.

28. People like me don't have any say about what the government does. Do you . . .

47% agree
6   neither agree nor disagree
47   disagree
0   don't know

29. Public officials don't care much what people like me think. Do you . . .

54% agree
5 neither agree nor disagree
40 disagree
1 don't know

30. How much do you feel that having elections makes the government pay attention to what the people think—a good deal, some, or not much?
44% good deal
37 some
19 not much
0 don't know

31. And over the years, how much attention do you feel the government pays to what the people think when it decides what to do—a good deal, some, or not much?
15% good deal
54 some
30 not much
1 don't know

32. Now, a few questions about affirmative action programs in hiring, promoting, and college admissions. First, what do you think should happen to affirmative action programs—should they be ended now, should they be phased out over the next few years, or should affirmative action programs be continued for the foreseeable future?
25% ended now
31 phased out
37 continued for future
7 don't know

33. Do you favor or oppose employers and colleges using outreach programs to hire minority workers and find minority students?
59% favor
35 oppose
6 don't know

34. Do you favor or oppose high schools and colleges providing special educational programs to assist minorities in competing for college admissions?
64% favor
33 oppose
3 don't know

35. On another topic, some people are registered to vote and others are not. Are you absolutely certain you are registered to vote in the precinct or election district where you now live, or haven't you been able to register to vote yet? (*If yes:* Are you registered as a Democrat, a Republican, another party or independent?)
37% yes, Democrat
30 yes, Republican
14 yes, independent or other party
19 no, not registered (*skip question 36*)

36. Some people who plan to vote can't always get around to it on election day. With your own personal daily schedule in mind, are you absolutely certain to vote, will you probably vote, are the chances about 50-50, less than 50-50, or don't you think you will vote in the California election on November 3?
78% certain to vote
11 probably vote
8 50-50 chance
1 less than 50-50 chance
1 don't think will vote
1 don't know

37. Generally speaking, how much interest would you say you have in politics?
21% a great deal
49 fair amount
24 only a little
5 none
1 don't know

38. How often do you watch local news on television?
59% every day
24 a few times a week
8 once a week

4   less than once a week
5   never
0   don't know

39. How often do you read the local newspaper?
    45%   every day
    21   a few times a week
    13   once a week
    8   less than once a week
    13   never
    0   don't know

40. How often would you say you vote—always, nearly always, part of the time, seldom, or never?
    50%   always
    25   nearly always
    10   part of the time
    5   seldom
    9   never
    1   other
    0   don't know

41. On another topic: As far as your own situation, would you say you and your family are financially better off or worse off or just about the same as you were a year ago?
    34%   better off
    11   worse off
    54   same
    1   don't know

42. Now, looking ahead, do you think that a year from now you and your family will be financially better off or worse off or just about the same as now?
    44%   better off
    6   worse off
    47   same
    3   don't know

Now, some questions about the region of the state you live in.

43. In the past few years, do you think the racial and ethnic makeup of your region has been changing a lot, somewhat, very little, or not at all?
    36%   a lot
    30   somewhat

20   very little
12   not at all (*skip question 44*)
2   don't know (*skip question 44*)

44. Overall, would you say that the change in the ethnic and racial makeup is good or bad for your region, or does it make no difference?
    22%   good
    20   bad
    55   no difference
    3   don't know

45. Overall, how would you say that the racial and ethnic groups in your region are getting along these days—very well, somewhat well, somewhat badly, or very badly?
    21%   very well
    58   somewhat well
    15   somewhat badly
    4   very badly
    2   don't know

46. Which of these views about racial and ethnic groups in your region today is closest to yours? (*Rotate.*) (a) It is better if different racial and ethnic groups change so that they blend into the larger society as in the idea of a melting pot. (b) It is better if different racial and ethnic groups maintain their distinct cultures.
    61%   better if groups change
    29   better if groups maintain cultures
    6   other answer
    4   don't know

Next, we are interested in how people are spending their time these days. I am going to read a list of types of activities that people get involved in, and for each one I'd like you to tell me whether you feel very involved, somewhat involved, or not really involved in that activity these days. (*If asked:* By involvement, we mean how much time you spend on something compared to other people.)

47. First, how about working on local issues and neighborhood problems? Are you . . .
    7% very involved
    34 somewhat involved
    59 not involved
    0 don't know

48. How about working on public issues or problems at the state or national level? Are you . . .
    3% very involved
    18 somewhat involved
    78 not involved
    1 don't know

49. How about volunteer work and charity work for which you are not paid? Are you . . .
    21% very involved
    40 somewhat involved
    39 not involved
    1 don't know

50. How about political activities related to political parties, candidates, or election campaigns? Are you . . .
    2% very involved
    15 somewhat involved
    83 not involved
    0 don't know

(51–61: demographic questions)

December Survey

Methods

The PPIC Statewide Survey findings are based on a telephone survey of 2,022 California adult residents interviewed from December 4 to December 13, 1998. Interviewing took place on weekend days and weekday nights, using a computer-generated random sample of telephone numbers to ensure that both listed and unlisted telephone numbers were called. All telephone exchanges in California were eligible for calling. Telephone numbers in the survey sample were called up to four times each to increase the likelihood of reaching eligible households. Once a household was reached, an adult respondent (18 or older) was randomly chosen for interviewing using the "last birthday" method to avoid biases in age and gender. Each interview took an average of 20 minutes to complete. Interviewing was conducted in English or Spanish.

We used recent U.S. Census and state figures to compare the demographic characteristics of the survey sample with characteristics of California's adult population. The survey sample was closely comparable with U.S. Census and state figures. The survey data in this report were statistically weighted to account for any demographic differences.

The sampling error for the total sample of 2,022 adults is ±2 percent at the 95 percent confidence level. This means that 95 times out of 100, the results will be within 2 percentage points of what they would be if all adults in California had been interviewed. The sampling error for subgroups is larger. The sampling error for the 1,562 voters is ±2.5 percent and for the 996 likely voters is ±3.5 percent. Sampling error is just one type of error to which surveys are subject. Results may also be affected by factors such as question wording or order and survey timing.

In the PPIC Statewide Survey in December, questions were repeated from the national surveys conducted by *Newsweek* in 1998 (questions 8, 9), by the Pew Research Center in 1998 (questions 36, 37, 38), and by the Gallup Organization in 1998 (questions 42, 43, 44) in order to compare California with the nation. We also adapted questions asked by the Texas Poll in 1995 and 1997 (questions 46, 47, 48), by the University of Michigan's National Election Studies in 1996 (questions 29, 30, 31), and by the Pew Research Center in 1996 (question 45). We also repeated questions that were asked in surveys of California voters conducted during the 1994 election cycle by Mark Baldassare for the California Business Roundtable (questions 15, 16, 17, 18, 19) for time trends.

APPENDIX F DECEMBER SURVEY:
QUESTIONS AND RESPONSES

December 4–13, 1998; 2,022 California Adult Residents; English and Spanish
Margin of Error ±2% at 95% Confidence Level for Total Sample

*(Responses recorded for first thirteen questions are from likely voters only.
All other responses are from all adults.)*

1. First, I have a few questions about elections. In March 2000, California will hold an open presidential primary. That means the voters will be able to vote for anyone they choose, regardless of the candidate's party. If the election were held today, who would you vote for? (*Rotate names, then ask,* "or someone else?")

31%	Al Gore, a Democrat
21	George Bush, Jr., a Republican
9	Elizabeth Dole, a Republican
5	Pete Wilson, a Republican
4	Steve Forbes, a Republican
4	Richard Gephardt, a Democrat
3	Dan Quayle, a Republican
4	someone else (*specify*)
19	don't know

2. If these were the candidates for the presidential election in the year 2000, who would you vote for? (*Rotate.*)

47%	George Bush, Jr., a Republican
45	Al Gore, a Democrat
8	don't know

3. And if these were the candidates for the presidential election in the year 2000, who would you vote for? (*Rotate.*)

37%	Pete Wilson, a Republican
54	Al Gore, a Democrat
9	don't know

4. On another topic, a number of propositions are being considered for the state ballot in the year 2000. One initiative would create a voucher system that would allow the use of public funds for parents to pay to send their children to private or parochial schools. If the election were held today, would you vote yes or no on this initiative?

52%	yes
43	no
5	don't know

5. Which of these two views is closest to yours? (*Rotate.*) (a) The voucher system would make public schools better by making public and private schools compete for students and public funds. (b) The voucher system would make public schools worse because the loss of students would result in less public funds.

50%	make schools better
41	make schools worse
1	other, no difference
8	don't know

6. Which of these two views is closest to yours? (*Rotate.*) (a) A voucher system will subsidize wealthy parents who send their children to private and parochial schools. (b) A voucher system will help lower-income parents send their children to a better private or parochial school instead of their local public school.

32%	subsidize wealthy parents
57	help lower-income parents
3	other, no difference
8	don't know

7. On the 2000 ballot, there will be a "definition of marriage" initiative, which would provide that only a marriage between a man and a woman is valid or recognized in California. If the election were held today, would you vote yes or no on this initiative?

64%   yes
33   no
3   don't know

8. Thinking about what might be done to protect gay rights, do you think there should or should not be special legislation to guarantee equal rights for gays and lesbians?
46%   should
48   should not
6   don't know

9. And do you think there should or should not be health insurance and other benefits for domestic partners of gay and lesbian employees?
58%   should
35   should not
7   don't know

10. On another topic, after the 2000 census, state legislative and congressional district boundaries will be redrawn. This reapportionment is done by the governor and state legislature. An initiative would take reapportionment out of the hands of the governor and the state legislature and give it to an independent commission. If the election were held today, would you vote yes or no on this initiative?
46%   yes
41   no
13   don't know

11. The new California governor is a Democrat, and the state legislature may be controlled by the Democrats after the 2000 election. Do you think the governor and state legislature will provide a reapportionment plan that is fair or one that is unfair, or don't you know enough about it to have an opinion?
25%   fair
23   unfair
52   don't know

12. On another topic, how closely have you been following the news stories about California politics and elections?
19%   very closely
59   fairly closely
19   not too closely
3   not at all closely
0   don't know

13. And how would you rate the job that news organizations are doing in reporting about California politics and elections?
5%   excellent
32   good
43   fair
18   poor
2   don't know

14. Next, some questions about the state. Which one issue facing California today do you think is most important for the governor and the state legislature to work on in 1999? (Code, don't read.)
36%   schools, education
7   crime, gangs
5   immigration, illegal immigration
5   jobs, the economy
5   poverty, the poor, the homeless, welfare
4   taxes
3   health care, HMOs
2   environment, pollution
2   state budget, state and local finance
2   traffic and transportation
1   drugs
1   government regulations
1   growth, overpopulation
1   housing costs, housing availability
1   race relations, ethnic tensions
1   state government, governor, legislature
1   water
4   other (specify)
18   don't know

15. And do you think things in California are generally going in the right direction or the wrong direction?

    63%   right direction
    28   wrong direction
    9   don't know

The state government faces a $1 billion deficit next year. Given the state's limited funds, what priorities should be given to each of these categories of public spending in the state budget, on a scale of 1 to 5, with 1 being a very low priority and 5 being a very high priority? (*Rotate questions 16 to 19.*)

16. What priority should be given to spending for kindergarten through twelfth-grade public education, on a scale of 1 to 5, with 1 being a very low priority and 5 being a very high priority?

    4%   (1) very low priority
    2   (2)
    9   (3)
    18   (4)
    67   (5) very high priority

17. What priority should be given to spending for public health and welfare, on a scale of 1 to 5, with 1 being a very low priority and 5 being a very high priority?

    7%   (1) very low priority
    9   (2)
    28   (3)
    24   (4)
    32   (5) very high priority

18. What priority should be given to spending for public colleges and universities, on a scale of 1 to 5, with 1 being a very low priority and 5 being a very high priority?

    5%   (1) very low priority
    8   (2)
    29   (3)
    28   (4)
    30   (5) very high priority

19. What priority should be given to spending for corrections, such as

prisons, on a scale of 1 to 5, with 1 being a very low priority and 5 being a very high priority?

    17%   (1) very low priority
    22   (2)
    35   (3)
    13   (4)
    13   (5) very high priority

20. On another topic, people have different ideas about what they think is wrong with California's K-12 public schools. What is the one reason you think is most responsible for public schools not performing as well as they could? (*Code, don't read.*)

    22%   teachers
    12   lack of state funds
    11   overcrowded classrooms, school buildings need repairs
    11   parents
    5   local school boards, local school administrators
    4   curriculum, books
    4   lack of local funds, local voters not passing taxes
    4   lack of standards and testing
    3   students
    2   gangs, crime, drugs, alcohol
    2   immigrant students, non-English-speaking students
    2   state officials
    1   unions
    8   other answer (*specify*)
    9   don't know

How do you feel about the following proposals that have been made for improving K-12 public schools in California? (*Rotate questions 21 to 26.*)

21. Do you favor or oppose increasing teachers' pay based on merit, to attract and retain more and better teachers?

    84%   favor
    15   oppose
    1   don't know

22. Do you favor or oppose requiring that teachers be given more training and have tougher credential standards before they teach in the classroom?
    85% favor
    14   oppose
    1   don't know

23. Do you favor or oppose increasing standards for learning and requiring that students pass achievement tests before they are promoted to the next grade?
    88% favor
    10   oppose
    2   don't know

24. Do you favor or oppose reducing class sizes to a maximum of twenty students from kindergarten through the sixth grade?
    83% favor
    15   oppose
    2   don't know

25. Do you favor or oppose requiring remedial after-school programs and summer school for students who are not performing at their grade level?
    91% favor
    8   oppose
    1   don't know

26. Do you favor or oppose making local school-site officials accountable for student performance by requiring the state to take over a local public school when their students have low test scores and have not shown signs of improving?
    56% favor
    39   oppose
    5   don't know

27. On another topic, how do you rate the job performance of President Bill Clinton at this time?
    26% excellent
    33   good
    20   fair
    20   poor
    1   don't know

28. And how do you rate the job performance of the U.S. Senate and House of Representatives at this time?
    4%   excellent
    29   good
    42   fair
    22   poor
    3   don't know

On another topic, people have different ideas about the state government in Sacramento. These ideas don't refer to Democrats or Republicans in particular, but just to government in general. We want to see how you feel about these ideas.

29. How much of the time do you think you can trust the state government in Sacramento to do what is right—just about always, most of the time, or only some of the time?
    4%   just about always
    33   most of the time
    60   some of the time
    2   none of the time (Code, don't read)
    1   don't know

30. Do you think that the people in state government waste a lot of the money we pay in taxes, waste some of it, or don't waste very much of it?
    52% a lot
    41   some
    5   don't waste very much
    2   don't know

31. Would you say the state government is pretty much run by a few big interests looking out for themselves or that it is run for the benefit of all of the people?
    64% a few big interests
    29   benefit of all of the people
    7   don't know

32. What do you think is the best way to address the most important problems facing California today? (*Rotate.*) (a) The governor and state legislature should decide what to do and pass state laws. (b) California voters should decide what to do by bringing citizens' initiatives to the ballot box and passing them.

    21% governor and legislature
    75 citizens' initiatives
    4 don't know

33. And how much confidence do you have in the governor and state legislature when it comes to their ability to solve the state's most important problems? Do you have a great deal, only some, very little, or no confidence?

    11% great deal of confidence
    58 only some
    21 very little
    9 no confidence
    1 don't know

34. On another topic, some people are registered to vote and others are not. Are you absolutely certain you are registered to vote in the precinct or election district where you now live, or haven't you been able to register to vote yet? (*If yes:* Are you registered as a Democrat, a Republican, another party, or independent?)

    37% yes, Democrat
    27 yes, Republican
    3 yes, other party
    12 yes, independent
    21 no, not registered

35. Would you consider yourself to be politically very liberal, somewhat liberal, middle of the road, somewhat conservative, or very conservative?

    8% very liberal
    22 somewhat liberal
    32 middle of the road
    26 somewhat conservative

    11 very conservative
    1 don't know

36. Generally speaking, how much interest would you say you have in politics?

    18% a great deal
    50 fair amount
    28 only a little
    4 none
    0 don't know

37. Would you say you follow what's going on in government and public affairs most of the time, some of the time, only now and then, hardly ever, or never?

    37% most of the time
    42 some of the time
    15 only now and then
    4 hardly ever
    1 never
    1 don't know

38. How often would you say you vote—always, nearly always, part of the time, seldom, or never?

    55% always
    19 nearly always
    10 part of the time
    4 seldom
    11 never
    1 other
    0 don't know

39. California voters elected a new governor on November 3. Could you give me the name of the new governor of the state of California? (*Code, don't read.*)

    53% Gray Davis
    5 other name
    42 don't know

40. On another topic, as far as your own situation, would you say that you and your family are financially better off or worse off or just about the same as you were a year ago?

    31% better off
    14 worse off
    54 same
    1 don't know

41. Now looking ahead, do you think that a year from now you and your family will be financially better off or worse off or just about the same as now?

    43% better off
    7   worse off
    48   same
    2   don't know

42. On another topic, some people think California is divided into economic groups, the haves and have-nots, while others think that it is not divided in that way. Do you think California is divided into haves and have-nots, or do you think California is not divided in that way?

    56% divided into haves and have-nots
    41   not divided that way
    3   don't know

43. If you had to choose, which of these groups are you in—the haves or have-nots?

    57% haves
    35   have-nots
    8   don't know

44. Do you think that in California today: (Rotate) (a) all people have an equal opportunity to get ahead, or (b) the government should do more to make sure that all Californians have an equal opportunity to succeed?

    52% people have equal opportunity
    45   government should do more
    3   don't know

45. On another topic, which of these views about immigration from Mexico is closest to yours? (Rotate.) (a) Mexican immigrants are a benefit to California today because of their hard work and job skills. (b) Mexican immigrants are a burden to California today be-

cause they use public services and schools.

    52% immigrants are a benefit
    36   immigrants are a burden
    7   neither
    5   don't know

I'd like to ask you a few questions about immigrants who are in California illegally.

46. In the past four years, do you think that illegal immigration from Mexico to California has been a big problem, somewhat of a problem, or not a problem?

    44% big problem
    40   somewhat of a problem
    14   no problem
    2   don't know

47. Do you believe that the federal government's increased border patrols and building walls and fences on the California-Mexico border will make a big difference, some difference, or no difference in preventing illegal immigration?

    13% big difference
    51   some difference
    35   no difference
    1   don't know

48. And do you think that children who are illegal immigrants in California today should be prevented from attending public schools or not?

    22% yes
    75   no
    3   don't know

On another topic, California's population is 33 million today and is expected to reach nearly 50 million by 2020. People have different ideas about what the state government should be doing now to plan for the future. (Rotate questions 49 to 51.)

49. How important do you think it is for the state government to be spending public funds to build and expand water storage facilities along the Northern California

rivers that feed into the
Sacramento–San Joaquin delta?

50%   very important
39   somewhat important
8   not important
3   don't know

50. How important do you think it
is for the state government to be
spending public funds to build
more K-12 public schools, public colleges, and universities?

69%   very important
27   somewhat important
3   not important
1   don't know

51. How important do you think it is
for the state government to be
spending public funds to build
more roads and expand the state's
highways and freeway system?

48%   very important
42   somewhat important
9   not important
1   don't know

(Questions 52–63 are demographic
questions. They include the question
below, which appears with the other
tables presented in the survey report.)

Five years from now, do you see
yourself living in your current
county of residence or do you expect to be living somewhere else?
(*If elsewhere:* Is that inside or outside of California?)

63%   living in current county
22   elsewhere in California
11   elsewhere outside of
        California
4   don't know

References

Adams, Charles F. 1992. *California in the Year 2000: A Look into the Future of the Golden State as It Approaches the Millennium.* Palo Alto, CA: Pacific Books.

American Association of Retired Persons. 1996. *The AARP Survey on Civic Involvement.* Washington, DC: AARP.

American Farmland Trust. 1995. *Alternatives for Future Urban Growth in California's Central Valley.* October. Washington, DC: American Farmland Trust.

Associated Press. 1998. "Spending in November Election Sets Ballot Measure Records." December 2.

Baldassare, Mark. 1986. *Trouble in Paradise: The Suburban Transformation in America.* New York: Columbia University Press.

———. 1991. "Is There Room for Regionalism in the Suburbs?" *Journal of Architectural and Planning Research* 8:222–234.

———. 1992. "Suburban Communities." *Annual Review of Sociology* 18:475–494.

———. 1994. *The Los Angeles Riots: Lessons for the Urban Future.* Edited volume. Boulder, CO: Westview Press.

———. 1996. "New Immigrant Communities in a Suburban Region." *Research in Community Sociology* 6:105–122.

———. 1998. *When Government Fails: The Orange County Bankruptcy.* Berkeley: University of California Press and Public Policy Institute of California.

Baldassare, Mark, Joshua Hassol, William Hoffman, and Abby Kanarek. 1996. "Possible Planning Roles for Regional Government: A Survey of City Planning Directors in California." *Journal of the American Planning Association* 62:17–29.

Baldassare, Mark, and Cheryl Katz. 1997. *Orange County Annual Survey: 1997 Report.* Irvine: University of California.

———. 1998. *Orange County Annual Survey: 1998 Report.* Irvine: University of California.

Baldassare, Mark, and Georjeanna Wilson. 1996. "Changing Sources of Suburban Support for Local Growth Controls." *Urban Studies* 33:459–471.

Barabak, Mark. 1998. "Changing Face of the Farm Belt Makes It a Political Plum." *Los Angeles Times,* August 18.

Bok, Derek. 1996. *The State of the Nation: Government and the Quest for a Better Society.* Cambridge, MA: Harvard University Press.

Bouvier, Leon. 1991. *Fifty Million Californians?* Washington, DC: Center for Immigration Studies.

Bowler, Shaun, and Todd Donovan. 1998. *Demanding Choices: Opinion, Voting and Direct Democracy.* Ann Arbor: University of Michigan Press.

Bowler, Shaun, Todd Donovan, and Caroline Tolbert. 1998. *Citizens as Legislators: Direct Democracy in the United States.* Edited volume. Columbus: Ohio State University Press.

Bowman, David, John Elwood, Frank Newhauser, and Eugene Smolensky. 1994. "Structural Deficits and the Long-Term Fiscal Conditions of the State." In John Kirlin and Jeffrey Chapman (eds.), *California Policy Choices,* vol. 9. Los Angeles: University of Southern California School of Public Administration, pp. 25–50.

Cain, Bruce, Sara Ferejohn, Margarita Najar, and Mary Walther. 1995. "Constitutional Change: Is It Too Easy to Amend Our State Constitution?" In Bruce Cain and Roger Noll (eds.), *Constitutional Reform in California.* Berkeley, CA: Institute of Governmental Studies Press, pp. 265–290.

Cain, Bruce, D. Roderick Kiewiet, Michael Chwe, David Ely, Juani Funez-Gonzalez, Amita Shastri, and Carole Uhlaner. 1986. "The Political Impact of California's Minorities." Paper presented at Minorities in California: A Major Public Symposium. Pasadena: California Institute of Technology.

Cain, Bruce, D. Roderick Kiewiet, and Carole Uhlaner. 1991. "The Acquisition of Partisanship by Latinos and Asian Americans." *American Journal of Political Science* 35:390–422.

Cain, Bruce, and Roger Noll. 1995. *Constitutional Reform in California.* Berkeley, CA: Institute of Governmental Studies Press.

California Business Roundtable. 1998. *Building a Legacy for the Next Generation.* Sacramento: California Business Roundtable.

California Commission on Campaign Financing. 1992. *Democracy by Initiative: Shaping California's Fourth Branch of Government.* Los Angeles: Center for Responsive Government.

California Constitution Revision Commission. 1996. *Executive Summary: Final Report and Recommendations to the Governor and the Legislature.* Sacramento: State of California.

California Department of Finance. 1992. *California Statistical Abstract, 1992.* Sacramento: State of California.

California Department of Finance. 1997. *California Demographics: Winter 1997.* Sacramento: State of California.

California Department of Finance. 1998a. "New State Projections Show No Ethnic Majority in Two Years: Total Population Nearly Doubling over 50-Year Period." Press release. Sacramento: State of California.

California Department of Finance. 1998b. *California Demographics. Winter 1998,* Sacramento: State of California.

California Economic Development Corporation. 1990. *Vision California: 2010 Revisited.* August. Sacramento: California Economic Development Corporation.

California Futures Network. 1999. *Smart Growth Summit: Building the California Dream.* January 28. Sacramento: California Futures Network.

California Secretary of State. 1980. *Statement of the Vote, November 1980.* Sacramento: State of California.

California Secretary of State. 1982. *Statement of the Vote, November 1982.* Sacramento: State of California.

California Secretary of State. 1984. *Statement of the Vote, November 1984.* Sacramento: State of California.

California Secretary of State. 1986. *Statement of the Vote, November 1986.* Sacramento: State of California.

California Secretary of State. 1988. *Statement of the Vote, November 1988.* Sacramento: State of California.

California Secretary of State. 1990. *Statement of the Vote, November 1990.* Sacramento: State of California.

California Secretary of State. 1992. *Statement of the Vote, November 1992.* Sacramento: State of California.

California Secretary of State. 1994. *Statement of the Vote, November 1994.* Sacramento: State of California.

California Secretary of State. 1996. *Statement of the Vote, November 1996.* Sacramento: State of California.

California Secretary of State. 1998a. *Statement of the Vote, June 1998.* Sacramento: State of California.

California Secretary of State. 1998b. *Statement of the Vote, November 1998.* Sacramento: State of California.

California State Treasurer. 1999. *Smart Investments: Special Edition of California's Debt Affordability Report.* Sacramento: State of California.

Caliper Corporation. 1997. Maptitude. Newton, MA: Caliper Corporation.

CBS/New York Times. 1997. National survey. December.

Center for Continuing Study of the California Economy. 1998. *Land Use and the California Economy: Principles for Prosperity and Quality of Life.* Palo Alto: Center for Continuing Study of the California Economy.

Center for Continuing Study of the California Economy. 1999. *California Economic Growth: 1999 Edition.* Palo Alto: Center for Continuing Study of the California Economy.

Chao, Julie. 1998. "Voters Will Continue to Be Rich, White, Old." *San Francisco Examiner,* October 31.

Chavez, Lydia. 1998. *The Color Bind: California's Battle to End Affirmative Action.* Berkeley: University of California Press.

Chawkins, Steve. 1999. "Homes Sprouting, Farms Dying: Sunday Report." *Los Angeles Times,* February 7.

Citrin, Jack. 1974. "The Political Relevance of Trust in Government." *American Political Science Review* 68:973–988.

Citrin, Jack. 1979. "Do People Want Something for Nothing? Public Opinion on Taxes and Government Spending." *National Tax Journal* 32:113–129.

Clark, Terry, and Lorna Ferguson. 1983. *City Money*. New York: Columbia University Press.

Clark, Terry, and Vincent Hoffman-Martinot. 1998. *The New Political Culture*. Edited volume. Boulder, CO: Westview Press.

Clark, Terry, and Ronald Inglehart. 1998. "The New Political Culture." In Terry Clark and Vincent Hoffman-Martinot (eds.), *The New Political Culture*. Boulder, CO: Westview Press, pp. 9–72.

Clark, William A.V. 1998. *The California Cauldron: Immigration and the Fortunes of Local Communities*. New York: Guilford Press.

Covarrubias, Amanda. 1998. "Latinos Prove Powerful at Polls." *San Jose Mercury News*, November 8.

Craig, Stephen C. 1996. *Broken Contract: Changing Relationships between Americans and Their Government*. Boulder, CO: Westview Press.

Dardia, Michael. 1995. "The California Economy: Issues and Research Ideas." Staff briefing. June. San Francisco: Public Policy Institute of California.

Dardia, Michael, and Sherman Luk. 1999. *Rethinking the California Business Climate*. San Francisco: Public Policy Institute of California.

Dear, Michael, H. Eris Schockman, and Greg Hise. 1996. *Rethinking Los Angeles*. Edited volume. Thousand Oaks, CA: Sage Publications.

DeBow, Ken, and John C. Syer. 1997. *Power and Politics in California*. Boston: Allyn & Bacon.

De la Garza, Rodolpho. 1987. *Ignored Voices: Public Opinion Polls and the Latino Community*. Austin, TX: Center for Mexican American Studies.

DeSipio, Louis. 1998. *Talking Back to Television*. Austin, TX: Tomas River Center.

Dionne, E.J. 1992. *Why Americans Hate Politics*. New York: Simon & Schuster.

Dowall, David. 1984. *The Suburban Squeeze: Land Conversion and Regulation in the San Francisco Bay Area*. Berkeley: University of California Press.

Egan, Timothy. 1998. "Dream of Fields: The New Politics of Urban Sprawl." *New York Times*, November 14.

Ellwood, John. 1994a. "Alternatives for California's Future." In Jesse D. Shaw and Frank Neuhauser (eds.), *California Fiscal Reform: A Plan for Action*. Sacramento: California Business–Higher Education Forum, pp. 1–8.

Ellwood, John. 1994b. "California's State and Local Public Sector Compared to Other States and the National Average: 1960–1990." In Jesse D. Shaw and Frank Neuhauser (eds.), *California Fiscal Reform: A Plan for Action*. Sacramento: California Business–Higher Education Forum, pp. 64-81.

Employment Development Department. 1996. *California Annual Average Labor Force and Industrial Employment*. Sacramento: State of California.

Employment Development Department. 1998. *Monthly Seasonally Adjusted Civilian Employment*. Sacramento: State of California.

Ferejohn, John. 1995. "Reforming the Initiative Process." In Bruce Cain and Roger Noll (eds.), *Constitutional Reform in California*. Berkeley, CA: Institute of Governmental Studies Press, pp. 313–325.

Fernandez, Kenneth, and Max Neiman. 1997. "Models of Anti-Immigration Sentiment and Other Speculations Regarding the Rise of Contemporary Xenophobia." Paper presented at the 1997 Annual Meeting of the Southwest Political Science Association, New Orleans.

Field, Mona, and Charles P. Sohner. 1999. *California Government and Politics Today.* Reading, MA: Addison Wesley.

Field Institute. 1998. *Proposition 13 Twenty Years Later.* May. San Francisco: Field Institute.

Field Institute. 1999. *Voting in California's 1998 General Election.* January. San Francisco: Field Institute.

Field Poll. 1998. *Primary Election Turnout Estimates.* June 1. San Francisco: Field Institute.

Fischer, Claude S. 1984. *The Urban Experience.* New York: Harcourt Brace Jovanovich.

Fishman, Robert. 1987. *Bourgeois Utopia: The Rise and Fall of Suburbs.* New York: Basic Books.

Fradkin, Philip L. 1995. *The Seven States of California: A Natural and Human History.* New York: Henry Holt.

Fulton, William. 1997. *The Reluctant Metropolis: The Politics of Urban Growth in Los Angeles.* Point Arene, CA: Solano Press.

Gabriel, Stuart. 1996. "Remaking the Los Angeles Economy: Cyclical Fluctuations and Structural Evolution." In Michael J. Dear, H. Eric Schockman, and Greg Hise (eds.), *Rethinking Los Angeles.* Thousand Oaks, CA: Sage Publications, pp. 25–33.

Gallup Organization. 1996. *Giving and Volunteering in the U.S.: 1996 Survey.* Princeton, NJ: Gallup Organization.

Garment, Suzanne. 1991. *Scandal: The Crisis of Mistrust in American Politics.* New York: Times Books.

Garreau, Joel. 1991. *Edge Cities.* New York: Doubleday.

Gerber, Elisabeth. 1995. "Reforming the California Initiative Process: A Proposal to Increase Flexibility and Legislative Accountability." In Bruce Cain and Roger Noll (eds.), *Constitutional Reform in California.* Berkeley, CA: Institute of Governmental Studies Press, pp. 291–311.

Gerber, Elisabeth. 1998. *Interest Group Influence in the California Initiative Process.* San Francisco: Public Policy Institute of California.

Gissinger, Steve. 1998. "Top Gubernatorial Vote-Getters Spend the Least, Records Show." *Orange County Register,* August 4.

Glickfeld, Madelyn, and Ned Levine. 1990. *The New Land Use Regulation "Revolution": Why California's Local Jurisdictions Enact Growth Control and Management Measures.* Los Angeles: University of California.

Governing. 1999. "Who's Doing Well and Who's Doing Badly in Public Management? A State Report Card." *Governing,* 12, February.

Greenberg, Stanley B. 1995. *Middle-Class Dreams: The Politics and Power of the New American Majority.* New York: Times Books.

Guterbock, Thomas, and John Fries. 1997. *Maintaining America's Social Fabric: The A.A.R.P. Survey on Civic Involvement.* Charlottesville: University of Virginia Center for Survey Research.

Hahn, Walter. 1998. *Residential Data Trends. December 1998.* Newport Beach, CA: E & Y Kenneth Leventhal.

Inglehart, Robert. 1998. "The Trend Toward Postmaterialist Values Continues." In Terry N. Clark and Michael Rempel (eds.), *Citizen Politics in Post-Industrial Societies.* Boulder, CO: Westview Press, pp. 57–68.

Jackson, Kenneth. 1985. *Crabgrass Frontier: The Suburbanization of the United States.* New York: Oxford University Press.

Jacobs, John. 1999. "Candidate Lungren: Right Wing, yet Politically Correct?" *Sacramento Bee,* January 26.

Jeffe, Sherry Bebitch. 1998a. "The Elections Will Depend on What Women Voters Want." *Los Angeles Times,* October 4.

Jeffe, Sherry Bebitch. 1998b. "Why Politicians Love to Talk about Reforming Education." *Los Angeles Times,* January 19.

Jeffe, Sherry Bebitch. 1998c. "The Pull of the Center: Voters Shift Sides to Be in the Action." *Los Angeles Times,* June 7.

Johnson, Hans. 1996. *Undocumented Immigration to California: 1980–1993.* San Francisco: Public Policy Institute of California.

Johnson, Hans. 1998. *The Demography of the Great Central Valley.* San Francisco: Public Policy Institute of California.

Joint Venture. 1998. *Joint Venture's 1998 Index of Silicon Valley.* San Jose: Joint Venture Silicon Valley Network.

Keil, Roger. 1998. *Los Angeles: Globalization, Urbanization and Social Struggles.* New York: John Wiley.

Keith, Bruce E., David B. Magleby, Candice J. Nelson, Elizabeth Orr, Mark C. Westlye, and Raymond E. Wolfinger. 1992. *The Myth of the Independent Voter.* Berkeley: University of California Press.

Kimball, Larry J, and Mary Richardson. 1997. "The Long Term Forecast for the California Economy." In Xandra Kayden (ed.), *California Policy Options 1997.* Los Angeles: UCLA School of Public Policy and Social Research, pp. 1–15.

King, Peter. 1999. "Smart Growth Movement Gaining Strength." *Sacramento Bee,* February 10.

Kling, Rob, Spencer Olin, and Mark Poster. 1991. *Postsuburban California: The Transformation of Orange County since World War II.* Berkeley: University of California Press.

Kotkin, Joel. 1998. *Orange County: The Fate of a Post-Suburban Paradise.* Claremont, CA: La Jolla Institute.

Latino Issues Forum. 1998. *The Latino Vote 1998: The New Margin of Victory.* San Francisco: Latino Issues Forum.

Lee, Eugene. 1997. "The Initiative Boom: An Excess of Democracy." In Gerald C. Lubenow and Bruce E. Cain (eds.), *Governing California: Politics, Government and Public Policy in the Golden State.* Berkeley, CA: Institute of Governmental Studies, pp. 113–136.

Legislative Analyst. 1995a. *Cal Guide: A Guide to State Programs.* Sacramento: State of California.

Legislative Analyst. 1995b. *Los Angeles County's Fiscal Problems.* Sacramento: State of California.

Legislative Analyst. 1996a. *Cal Facts: California's Economy and Budget in Perspective.* Sacramento: State of California.

Legislative Analyst. 1996b. *Understanding Proposition 218.* Sacramento: State of California.

Lewis, Paul, 1996. *Shaping Suburbia: How Political Institutions Organize Urban Development.* Pittsburgh: University of Pittsburgh Press.

Lichtblau, Eric. 1998. "A Valley the Upturn Left Behind." *Los Angeles Times,* November 6.

Lieser, Tom K. 1999. "Long-Term Projections for California: Will There Be Enough Housing?" In Daniel Mitchell and Patricia Nomura (eds.), *California Policy Options 1999.* Los Angeles: UCLA School of Public Policy and Social Research, pp. 1–7.

Lipset, Seymour Martin. 1996. *American Exceptionalism: A Double-Edged Sword.* New York: W.W. Norton.

Lipset, Seymour Martin, and William Schneider. 1983. *The Confidence Gap: Business, Labor and Government in the Public Mind.* New York: Free Press.

Lo, Clarence. 1990. *Small Property versus Big Government: Social Origins of the Property Tax Revolt.* Berkeley: University of California Press.

Logan, John, and Harvey Molotch. 1987. *Urban Fortunes: The Political Economy of Place.* Berkeley: University of California Press.

Los Angeles Times Poll. 1990. November election exit poll.

Los Angeles Times Poll. 1992. November election exit poll.

Los Angeles Times Poll. 1993. "California Issues." September.

Los Angeles Times Poll. 1994. November election exit poll.

Los Angeles Times Poll. 1996. November election exit poll.

Los Angeles Times Poll. 1998. November election exit poll.

Los Angeles Times/CNN Poll. 1998. June primary exit poll.

Lubenow, Gerald. 1995. *The 1994 Governor's Race.* Berkeley, CA: Institute of Governmental Studies Press.

Lubenow, Gerald, and Bruce Cain. 1997. *Governing California: Politics, Government and Public Policy in the Golden State.* Berkeley, CA: Institute of Governmental Studies Press.

Lucas, Greg. 1999. "Governor Race Spending Clobbered 1994 Record." *San Francisco Chronicle,* February 6.

Lupia, Arthur. 1998. *The Democratic Dilemma: Can Citizens Learn What They Really Need to Know?* New York: Cambridge University Press.

Maharidge, Dale. 1996. *The Coming White Minority: California's Eruptions and the Nation's Future.* New York: Times Books.

McConnell, Patrick. 1999. "1990s on Track to Set a Record for Immigration." *Los Angeles Times,* January 24.

McCormick, Erin. 1998. "Campaign Spending Breaks Record—Again." *San Francisco Examiner,* November 8.

Miller, Arthur. 1974. "Political Issues and Trust in Government." *American Political Science Review* 68:951–972.

Miller, Warren E., and J. Merrill Shanks. 1996. *The New American Voter.* Cambridge, MA: Harvard University Press.

Moore, Joan, and Harry Pachon. 1985. *Hispanics in the United States.* Englewood Cliffs, NJ: Prentice Hall.

Morain, Dan. 1999a. "Handful of Tribes Broke Initiative Spending Record." *Los Angeles Times,* February 6.

Morain, Dan. 1999b. "Wealth Buys Access to State Politics." *Los Angeles Times,* April 18.

Morrison, Peter, and Ira S. Lowry. 1994. "A Riot of Color: The Demographic Setting." In Mark Baldassare (ed.), *The Los Angeles Riot: Lessons for the Urban Future.* Boulder, CO: Westview Press, pp.19–46.

National Commission on Civic Renewal. 1998. *A Nation of Spectators: How Civic Disengagement Weakens America and What We Can Do about It.* College Park: University of Maryland.

National Election Studies. 1996. *National Election Studies.* Ann Arbor: University of Michigan.

National Election Studies. 1998. *National Election Studies.* Ann Arbor: University of Michigan.

National Opinion Research Center. 1996. *General Social Survey.* Chicago: University of Chicago.

NBC News/Wall Street Journal. 1998. National survey. January.

Neiman, Max. 1997. *Inland Empire Annual Survey: 1997.* Riverside: University of California.

Neiman, Max, and Kenneth Fernandez. 1998. "Dimensions and Models of Anti-Immigrant Sentiments: Causes and Policy Relevance." Paper presented at the Annual Meeting of the American Political Science Association, Boston.

Neiman, Max, and Ronald Loveridge. 1981. "Environmentalism and Local Growth Control: A Probe into the Class Bias Thesis." *Environment and Behavior* 13:759–772.

Nye, Joseph S., Philip D. Zelikow, and David C. King. 1997. *Why People Don't Trust Government.* Cambridge, MA: Harvard University Press.

Ong, Paul, and Evelyn Blumenberg. 1996. "Income and Racial Inequality in the United States." In Allen J. Scott and Edward W. Soja (eds.), *The City: Los Angeles and Urban Theory at the End of the Twentieth Century.* Berkeley: University of California Press, pp. 311–335.

Orren, Gary. 1997. "Fall from Grace: The Public's Loss of Faith in Government." In Joseph S. Nye, Philip D. Zelikow, and David C. King (eds.), *Why People Don't Trust Government.* Cambridge, MA: Harvard University Press, pp. 77–108.

Pachon, Harry. 1998. "Latino Politics in the Golden State: Ready for the 21st Century?" In Michael B. Preston, Bruce E. Cain, and Sandra Bass (eds.), *Racial and Ethnic Politics in California,* vol. 2. Berkeley, CA: Institute of Governmental Studies Press, pp. 411–438.

Pachon, Harry, and Louis DeSipio. 1995. *New Americans by Choice.* Boulder, CO: Westview Press.

Palen, John. 1995. *The Suburbs.* New York: McGraw-Hill.

Pew Research Center. 1996a. *Voter Typology.* October 25. Washington, DC: Pew Research Center for the People and the Press.

Pew Research Center. 1996b. *Diminishing Divide*. June 25. Washington, DC: Pew Research Center for the People and the Press.

Pew Research Center. 1998a. *Pew Values Update*. April 20. Washington, DC: Pew Research Center for the People and the Press.

Pew Research Center. 1998b. *Compared to 1994: Voters Not So Angry, Not So Interested*. June 15. Washington, DC: Pew Research Center for the People and the Press.

Polsby, Nelson W., and Aaron Wildavsky. 1996. *Presidential Election: Strategies and Structures of American Politics*. Chatham, NJ: Chatham House.

Portes, Alejandro, and Ruben G. Rumbaut. 1996. *Immigrant America: A Portrait*. Berkeley: University of California Press.

Preston, Michael, Bruce E. Cain, and Sandra Bass. 1998. *Racial and Ethnic Politics in California*, vol. 2. Edited volume. Berkeley, CA: Institute of Governmental Studies Press.

Purdum, Todd. 1999a. "TV Political News in California Is Shrinking, Study Confirms." *New York Times*, January 13.

Purdum, Todd. 1999b. "Suburban Sprawl Takes Its Place on the Political Landscape." *New York Times*, February 6.

Putnam, Robert D. 1995. "Bowling Alone: America's Declining Social Capital." *Journal of Democracy* 6:65–78.

Quinn, Tony. 1988. "Analysis of the 1988 California Vote." Unpublished report. Sacramento, CA.

Reed, Deborah. 1999. *California's Rising Income Inequality: Causes and Concerns*. San Francisco: Public Policy Institute of California.

Reed, Deborah, Melissa Glenn Haber, and Laura Mameesh. 1996. *The Distribution of Income in California*. San Francisco: Public Policy Institute of California.

Rieff, David. 1991. *Los Angeles: Capital of the Third World*. New York: Touchstone.

Rodriguez, Gregory. 1998. *The Emerging Latino Middle Class*. Malibu, CA: Pepperdine University Institute of Public Policy.

Samuelson, Robert. 1995. *The Good Life and Its Discontents: The American Dream in the Age of Entitlement, 1945–1995*. New York: Times Books.

Sandel, Michael. 1996. *Democracy's Discontent: America in Search of a Public Philosophy*. Cambridge, MA: Harvard University Press.

San Francisco Chronicle. 1999. "José Is the Name on Everyone's Lips." January 8.

Schneider, William. 1991. "Rule Suburbia: America in the 1990s." *National Journal* 39:2335–2336.

Schrag, Peter. 1998. *Paradise Lost: California's Experience, America's Future*. New York: New Press.

Schrag, Peter. 1999. "The Immigrant Issue: Forgotten, but Not Gone." *Sacramento Bee*, February 24.

Scott, Allen J., and Edward Soja. 1998. *The City: Los Angeles and Urban Theory at the End of the Twentieth Century*. Edited volume. Berkeley: University of California Press.

Sears, David O., and Jack Citrin. 1982. *Tax Revolt: Something for Nothing in California*. Cambridge, MA: Harvard University Press.

Skelton, George. 1990. "Need for a Change a Key Issue in Governor Race." *Los Angeles Times,* November 7.

Skelton, George. 1998. "Election Shows GOP Needs Some New Republicans." *Los Angeles Times,* November 19.

Skelton, George. 1999. "Election Autopsy Shows Lungren was DOA." *Los Angeles Times,* January 25.

Sonenshein, Raphael. 1993. *Politics in Black and White: Race and Power in Los Angeles.* Princeton, NJ: Princeton University Press.

Steinberg, James David Lyon, and Mary Vaiana. 1996. *Urban America: Policy Choices for Los Angeles and the Nation.* Santa Monica, CA: RAND.

Stiles, Jon, Jonathan Cohen, Zachary Elkins, and Frederic Gey. 1998. *California Latino Demographic Databook.* Berkeley: California Policy Seminar.

Teaford, Jon C. 1997. *Post-Suburbia: Government and Politics in the Edge Cities.* Baltimore: Johns Hopkins University Press.

Tobar, Hector. 1998. "In Contests Big and Small, Latinos Take Historic Leap." *Los Angeles Times,* November 5.

Tolchin, Susan J. 1996. *The Angry American: How Voter Rage Is Changing the Nation.* Boulder, CO: Westview Press.

Uhlaner, Carole, Bruce Cain, and Roderick Kiewiet. 1989. "Political Participation of Ethnic Minorities in the 1980s." *Political Behavior* 11:195–231.

Uhlaner, Carole, and F. Chris Garcia. 1998. *Foundations of Latino Party Identification: Learning, Ethnicity and Demographic Factors among Mexicans, Puerto Ricans, Cubans and Anglos in the United States.* Irvine, CA: Center for the Study of Democracy.

Umbach, Kenneth. 1998. *A Statistical Tour of California's Great Central Valley—1998.* Sacramento: California Research Bureau.

U.S. Census. 1994. *County and City Data Book: 1994.* Washington, DC: Department of Commerce.

U.S. Census. 1998. *Statistical Abstract of the United States: 1998.* Washington, DC: Department of Commerce.

Vernez, George. 1992. "Needed: A Federal Role in Helping Communities Cope with Immigration." In James B. Steinberg, David W. Lyon, and Mary E. Vaiana (eds.), *Urban America: Policy Choices for Los Angeles and the Nation.* Santa Monica, CA: RAND, pp. 281–296.

Voter News Service. 1990. November election exit poll.

Voter News Service. 1992. November election exit poll.

Voter News Service. 1994. November election exit poll.

Voter News Service. 1996. November election exit poll.

Voter News Service. 1998. November election exit poll.

Walters, Dan. 1992. *The New California: Facing the 21st Century.* 2nd ed. Sacramento: California Journal Press.

Walters, Dan. 1999. "Voters Prefer Open Primary." *Sacramento Bee,* January 26.

Weisberg, Jacob. 1996. *In Defense of Government: The Fall and Rise of Public Trust.* New York: Scribner.

Index

Compositor:	Publication Services, Inc.
Text:	10/13 Sabon
Display:	Sabon
Printer and Binder:	Haddon Craftsmen, Inc.